El Dorado? No! Heathrow Airport

TONY LEVY

ISBN:
ISBN-13: **978-1548319922**

DEDICATION

This book is dedicated to my darling wife Jacinta, without whom it may never have been written.

Without her strength of character and her caring and kindness, I'm not sure I would have survived my recent illness to be able to have written this book.

I also took her good advice as to the title of this book, thank you my darling for your wisdom which as always shows through.

Thank you, you are my life and my soul mate, and I dedicate this book to you.

CONTENTS

Part One

Passengers

Part Two

Security Officers

Part Three

The Management

ACKNOWLEDGMENTS

I would like to thank my editor and publisher for her amazing confidence in my fledging ability to write, without her confidence I would never have contemplated this book. Right from the start she showed belief and always encouraged me, her faith drove me on to complete this book, and her verve and enthusiasm still drives this book forward. I have been amazingly lucky to have met her. I hope we stay friends. Thank you so much, Misti.

Thanks to all the background staff, the editor, and cover designer, who made my raw manuscript into a wonderful professional book.

Thanks to Jacinta my wife, my rock, my love and my biggest supporter (well most of the time). You filled in lots of gaps that my memory failed to grasp. You are much cleverer than you think, or maybe not, as you did marry me, so that must have proven to you how clever you are. You offered advice and encouragement and cracked the whip when I was flagging, and interrupted me often, without realising it. But you are my rock, and I couldn't have written this book without your support.

I would also like to give special thanks to Raminder for her help in answering my often-asked questions to some of the technical details my mind had forgotten. Yes, I still have a bad memory for names. But her help has been invaluable in completing this book.

She tolerated me as a colleague for several years but was never unfriendly or rude and often offered me help and encouragement when I needed it. Thank so much for your help Raminder.

Dan, you know how much I appreciated the constant supply of tea during our rest periods at work, along with the fun we had, and your great sense of humour to my Mr Angry, it made working a pleasurable time. You're not the messiah, but you are a very naughty boy. I don't think I've ever worked with somebody who was so laid back and unflappable as you except on that one occasion!

Special thanks to Amanda and our first patrol together, which was amazing and so informative, and I loved every minute of that day. I hope we became good friends during that patrol.

My thanks go out to a lovely female colleague. On the day I had my migraine attack she was so concerned that she called the medics to attend. I am sorry I've forgotten your name, (you know how bad I was at remembering names) you were always enthusiastic about me writing this book, so please forgive me but here is the book. I hope you enjoy it.

The trainers, RIP Shane, a wonderful man and so kind and considerate towards me in my early days of screen reading. You died much too young.

Tim, even though you are a Chelsea supporter, you were always a great character to be with and to be taught by. Your stories were what legends are made of.

And thanks to all the other trainers, especially my blonde bombshell Tanya, who went on to better things within the organisation. Thanks for your patience and help during my training and your continued support when you became an STL.

I'd like to thank many of the security officers at Heathrow Terminal Five who were always friendly and helpful, not just in my early days but at all times during my work at Heathrow. Thanks to all my past colleagues who often gave me help in my early days and encouragement to Amanda, Susan, Suzanne, Crystal, (who proofread my first book) Dee, Jonathan, Jas (the silver fox), Gav, Aaron, Charlotte, Sian, Eric and Paul. In fact, you are too numerous to mention, so thank you to everybody who I've not mentioned, but you all know who you are.

The STL's who always offered me help and sympathy and to the TDM's who likewise offered me great support especially towards the end, both ex-policeman, you all know who you are.

My thanks to the RA's for the great shoots, and the security officers who gave me such brilliant subject matters to write about.

And finally, thanks to all of you, the travelling public, without whom this book would not have been possible. Maybe next time you travel through an airport, you might consider your behaviour towards the staff who are, after all, only trying to save your lives.

Preface

Do you want to know what goes on at a busy International Airport? Do you want to know how you behave when at the airport?

Do you?

Travel behind the scenes of one of the world's busiest airports, and discover how you and your fellow travellers behave towards the very security that's put in place to ensure your safety. Learn how behaviour can influence the workings of the airport and attitudes of your fellow passengers. See how the staff working there can either make or spoil your journey, both within the airport and to your destination. They can ruin your day just as you can theirs; the difference though can be severe. Ruin your day, make your journey unpleasant, and you feel like you don't want to use that airport again, but ruin their day, and they might lose concentration leading them into making tragic mistakes that could eventually cost lives.

I kid you not; the concentration needed for staff working for your security and particularly those directly dealing with aircraft safety or in this book's case - passenger safety is mentally and physically tiring. Just one mistake could lead to a plane malfunction or a terrorist attack on either the airport or the aircraft.

Your attitude and conduct as passengers can be both pleasant and intolerable. I previously wrote a book about my twenty-five-year career working for Her Majesty's Prison service. Well, I can honestly say that in the few years of working at an airport I suffered more insults and bad behaviour from passengers, management, and sometimes my colleagues than I ever did working with prisoners.

Airport's, you either love them or loathe them, are excited by them or fear them. The airport is the place to meet and greet loved ones, and friends. It's a place to say your goodbyes, adios, farewells. It's a place of excitement or trepidation depending on your views. Happiness and sadness intermingle on the concourse in the waiting areas and the car parks. It's there on the roads leading to the airport. In fact, the whole of life's spectrums on display at an airport in whatever country you may live.

Airports exist to enable us to go from A to B in the quickest and shortest time, and safely. It allows us to visit countries and cultures that our grandparents and parents before them could only dream about. It's there to shorten our journey times, and it is making the world a much smaller place.

It's a place of fun, and frills, the buzz of humans going about their business but it is also a place of great danger especially in our modern world. Airports were not always like this but unfortunately, they reflect the world at large, the ever-present danger of terrorist and terrorism, of extremist, protesters, green issue campaigners and just over excited children and adults and sometimes passengers who due to whatever reasons indulge in the readily available alcohol and are the worse for wear especially if they have already been on a flight and are transferring through the airport.

It's the place where business people go about their lawful (and unlawful) business making the global economy of the world work. Friends visit friends and families visit families; lovers meet up and go on journeys sometimes illicitly together, business visit business to expand the global finances of the world in which we live. To complete deals that could have implications for us all. To complete deals that could have consequences for us all.

It's a place where VIP's pay to be escorted through the airport procedures because they can afford it or first-class passengers still think that due to their (sometimes self-) importance they should be treated differently and have their lounges, so they don't have to mix with the general public.

It's a place where members of Royal families or Heads of state come and go completing their business for the good of their countries, along with diplomats of all nationalities, using the private facilities, so their arrivals or departures are discrete and secure. Of course, these travellers do not come into contact with the general public but have their departure lounges, decorated exclusively and able to accommodate their unique needs.

The airport is a busy vibrant place; the buzz is enough to get you excited even if you are a frequent flyer.

I remember how airports have changed and how they have reflected the change in the society they service. Back in 1967 I took my first ever flight from Luton airport to Spain on a package holiday to Lloret-de-Mar on the Costa Brava. How excited we were, four boys of 16/17 going on our first adult vacation without our mum and dad's, we thought we were so worldly. I remember it like it was yesterday, never thinking that forty-five years later I would work at one of the busiest airports in the world.

In those days - back in the sixties in the area we lived you'd arrive at Luton airport, park in the car park opposite the terminal building, cross the road, and walk into the airport departure lounge. When I say lounge, it's a slight exaggeration a large room about the size of an aircraft hangar. There was a buzz in the air. Excitement intermingled with trepidation, apprehension with a sense of adventure, but overall excitement and anticipation of the adventure ahead, to visit a foreign land by air.

We felt like old time pioneers, going on an adventure that nobody before us had been able to do, and it was fun. There were no terrorist's threats directly aimed at this country. Indeed, acts of terrorism on aircraft were almost never heard of at that time, and we certainly never thought they would happen in our country. How times have changed all that.

But now in our modern world of rush, rush, rush, and terrorist fears, it's altered beyond all recognition. It makes you wonder what the Wright brothers would think of the changes, from their early pioneering days to today's modern world of air travel.

Heathrow International Airport's the biggest and busiest in the United Kingdom, one of the largest in Europe, and the third busiest in the world. Heathrow's also one of the top five hub airports in the world. It's currently the busiest two-runway airport in the world today.

Astonishingly, Heathrow employs around 76,600 people within its boundaries - the same number as the population of Guildford in Surrey, and across the UK as a whole. It supports almost 206,000 jobs and plays a hugely important role in the economies of the United Kingdom. Jobs range from domestic cleaners to airport duty manager, from aircraft cleaners to pilots. From supplying the electricity to selling duty reduced goods in shops in each of the five terminal buildings. Heathrow provides parking spaces for workers and passengers, alike, VIP parking to Exclusive business parking with shuttle service to the terminals. Heathrow is also responsible for having one of the busiest bus terminals in the country.

Over its five current terminals (terminal one was due to close sometime during 2015) it deals with around 250,000 passengers a day, and the total annual number of passengers arriving and departing Heathrow is 73.4 million which is more than the entire population of the United Kingdom, in effect Heathrow is a city. Within this city, you will find all kinds of human nature some good, some bad, some plain stupid, some crazy, and some amazing. An airport is the only place where sane people with hugely responsible jobs can come to and act in the most irrational manner, and nobody seems to care.

Just a little background on airport security and the reasons behind the current screening we are all subject to: Airport security refers to the techniques and methods used in protecting passengers, staff and aircraft from accidental/malicious harm, crime and other threats. People pass through airports every day presenting as possible targets for terrorism and other forms of crime, ideal because of their vast number at a particular location. Similarly, a considerable amount of travellers on airliners, the conceivable high death rate from attacks on aircraft, and the potential to use a hijacked aeroplane as a lethal weapon may provide an alluring target for terrorism. Whether or not they succeed with their high-profile nature following the various attacks and attempts around the globe in recent years is a matter of conjecture.

Airport security aims to deter threats or potentially harmful situations from happening or coming entering countries. If successful then the chances of any dangerous conditions, illegal items, or threats entering aircraft, country and airport are significantly reduced. As such, security serves several purposes: To safeguard airport and nations against a threat, to reassuring the public of their safety and protecting the country and its people.

Monte R. Belger of the U.S. Federal Aviation Administration notes "The goal of aviation security is to prevent harm to aircraft, passengers, and crew, as well as to support national security and counter-terrorism policy."

People screened through airport security emerge into areas where exit gates to the aircraft are. Passengers discharge from airliners into the sterile area; they will not typically need to be re-screened if alighting from a domestic flight; however, they are subject to search at any time.

The world's first acknowledged terrorist attack intending to indiscriminately kill civilians while in flight was back in 1976 when Cubana Flight 455 from Barbados to Jamaica was brought down on October 6, 1976, killing 73 passengers. Evidence incriminated several Central Intelligence Agency-linked anti-Castro Cuban exiles and members of the Venezuelan secret police DISIP, including Luis Posada Carriles. Another onboard bomb slipped through airport security in 1988, on Pan Am Flight 103, killing 270 people; 259 aboard the plane, and 11 residents of Lockerbie, Scotland.

During 1968 to 1972, hijackers took over a commercial aircraft every other week, on average. Yes, seriously. Not surprisingly, this was known as the golden age of hijacking, and it coincided with some rather lax airport security. Gosh, things sure have sure changed, huh?

Just look at how far we've come.

In 1970 even with soaring skyjacking rates (40 attempts on US planes in 1969 alone), most airlines rebuked the idea of individual passenger screening. No ID was required. Ticket agents gave each traveller a once-over, looking for behaviour would-be hijackers might display (lack of eye contact, deficient concern about their luggage). If a person demonstrates these traits, they face scanning with an electronic magnetometer before boarding. (Only 0.5 percent of passengers were screened.) Just suspicious travellers who set off the detector could be searched.

Since the Lockerbie bomb, all European airport staff have to go through checks every time they cross into the secure area of the airport. However, often they leave and re-enter, in the same way that passengers are screened. But surprisingly enough there isn't the same system in place in the US and many other countries, yet subsequent world events have proven this to be an apparent weakness in aviation security. Here in the UK, all staff at airports have to undergo criminal records checks (and of course be given clearance by the Home Office) before they can even enter the security areas of the airport and become accepted for employment.

There have been several high-profile attempts to sabotage aircraft and airports with some success in some countries. Including the well-publicised shoe bomber Richard Colvin Reid who tried to blow up an American Airlines jet on 22 December 2001. And Umar Farouk Abdulmutallab, known as the 'underpants' bomber who planned to blow up an aircraft on Christmas day 2009. They are amongst many terrorists who have influenced the changes in security screening at all our airports. And the threats continue to this day. Security at our airports is a sad reflection of the daily threat to society.

Throughout the world, a few dozen airports have instituted a version of a "trusted traveller program". Proponents contend that security screening can be made more efficient by detecting the people that are threats and searching them. They reason that searching trusted, verified individuals shouldn't take up the amount of time that it does. Critics claim that such programs decrease security by providing an easier path to carry contraband through. Passengers still complain daily that the level of security is entirely unnecessary. This attitude seems endemic with the more frequent flyers, strange to think then that the terrorist who flew the planes into the 'twin towers' in New York back in 2001 were frequent flyers who were known to the airport security staff as they travelled so often.

The September 11th attacks in New York rendered the United Kingdom high-risk due to its support of the United States, and its invasion of Afghanistan and Iraq. The Department for Transport (DfT) is the authority for airport security in the United Kingdom. All security measures implemented at all UK airports, seaports, etc, come directly from instruction from the DfT which is reviewed on a regular basis. Individual airports do not set their security standards in the United Kingdom, however, in many passenger opinions they still seem to think that airport security is down to the security staff just being 'jobsworths' rather than professionally trained security staff implementing the DfT's laid down legal requirements.

Moreover, the 2006 transatlantic aircraft plot was a terrorist plot to detonate liquid explosives transported onboard seven airliners. They travelled from the UK to the United States and Canada. The plot was discovered and foiled by British police before it could be carried out and, as a result, unprecedented security measures were instantly put in place causing chaos at all airports.

The restrictions relaxed in the following weeks, but the ability of passengers to carry liquids onto commercial aircraft is still limited. But yet again every day at Heathrow we have passengers coming through the security screening system and complaining that they did not know about the liquid rule and how ridiculous the limitation of carrying liquids in your hand luggage is.

Many travellers throughout the world consider airport security a waste of time especially if it involves themselves after all 'do I look like a terrorist' is a monotonously regular comment. Oh, if only we knew what a terrorist looked like then the world would be a much safer place, but we don't, and the world is not a safer place, so we have to undergo security screening at any airport in the world we travel to whether we like it or not.

Having worked at Heathrow my view would be - search everybody, time is not as important as safety, and I would prefer to spend one extra hour getting through security screening than being dead or having members of my family die in an aircraft. There is also the constant fear that the 'Landside' part of any airport has no security screening, so anybody can walk into these public areas without fear of being stopped, or searched regardless of what may be contained in their bags, or hidden upon them. I always thought this was a vulnerable area but what can you do? Search everybody who enters the departure lounge to meet or greet family, or friends or colleagues. It would be an almost impossible job, needing to be carried out in all public areas where many people gathered, impossible to implement.

I enclose this information so you can at least have a reminder as to why security and its staff is omnipresent at all airports throughout the world whether we like it or not it is now an integral part of the process of flying to any destination in the world.

Terrorists will always be that one step ahead. They have all the time in the world to look at our weak spots and utilise them to their means. Security will always respond to the threat, although the sad thing is that our response is always behind the actual events. (Brussels International Airport has shown weakness in our security and the public's safety) That I am afraid is a sad truth; however, the world needs to join forces and cooperate with one another, exchange information in an attempt to close the gap. Your behaviour towards your security must also change, whether liked or not security is there for your protection.

This book's written in three parts; the first is how I got to work at the airport and the behaviour of you the travelling public. The second part is about my colleagues and their attitude, working practices, and some of the favouritism and nepotism of the working environment. And the third part is about management; their attitude to security versus profit, and the final experience of how management deal with its staff. And in particular how they dealt with me during my period of poor health which finally led me to leave work at Heathrow and return to my dream of living in Spain and my own El Dorado.

Chapter by chapter I'll tell you the story of our idiosyncrasy's and irrational behaviour when travelling through an airport. I will describe real circumstances that I have encountered while working here. Reactions from passengers and staff and the attitude, behaviour and comments that come with these situations. You will read them and say, 'that couldn't possibly be true or couldn't happen'. But all these stories in the ensuing chapters are real bar one and all stories have happened specifically to me, or my excellent working team, who incidentally were all blessed with much more patience than I ever possessed, and helped make our team one of the best working teams at Terminal 5. Thanks, guys!

As I said, the stories within this book are events that happened during my time at the airport. Some of you might recognise yourselves, I sincerely hope you do, and you may be embarrassed by your behaviour, I make no apologies for this. I didn't set out to upset anybody but wanted to show you, the public, that you can sometimes be unusual and irrational. I don't know why it happens, but it does. I hope that it will make you stop and think next time you either work here or come as a passenger.

Incidentally, there's a fantastic comedy program starring David Walliams and Matt Lucas (Little Britain) called 'Come Fly With Me' filmed at London Stanstead Airport. Many of the characters in their comedy show exist and during my time working at Heathrow Airport I met many of them. David and Mat must have keenly studied both the travelling public and the airport workers. I also actually met David Walliams when he was travelling as a passenger through Terminal 5 with his wife one day.

So, read on, see if you can identify yourself or a friend because we are all here within the following pages.

This book is not fiction, but I have used a Literary licence on some of my stories, as my memories of exact conversations are not perfect, but you will get the gist of what I'm putting across to you the reader easily enough.

But first where to start?

My starting point begins where my previous one ends. I wrote my first book 'A Turnkey or Not?' as an autobiography of my 25-year career working for Her Majesty's Prison Service, originally as a one-off. But many people have asked me what happened next. After my retirement did my dreams all come true? Did I find my El Dorado? Was there a 'happy ever after' story?

The answer is yes, but many things happened in the ensuing months and years, which led me to work at one of the world's busiest International Hub airports and then subsequent final retirement and back to our dream of living the life of El Dorado in a country we had come to love - Spain.

This book's dedicated to all those people who use and make Heathrow airport one of the best and safest in the world. Thank you all.

PART ONE - PASSENGERS

1 THE RETURN

This story begins where my previous one ended. My first book, an autobiography of my 25-year career working for 'Her Majesty's Prison Service', was written as a one-off. But many people asked me what happened next, after my retirement, did my dreams all come true? Was there a 'happy ever after' story? Did I find my El Dorado?

The simple answer is yes, but many things happened in the ensuing months and years and needs to be told.

At the peak of the world economic recession, back in 2010, we realised our financial situation was starting to unravel. Like many ex-pat Brits living the life of El Dorado in Spain, our world began to come crashing down. Several coincidental factors led to us making the reluctant decision to return to the UK, and back to work. Having retired early, we had planned that if things didn't work out, then we were young enough to do so (providing we could obtain jobs). At least until the world's financial crisis improved along with our finances.

A life of bliss in Spain lasted until the world economic climate strangled many people's dreams of living in healthy retirement in a warmer climate. The Spanish authorities moved the goalposts for all under retirement age ex-pats. They started charging for health cover if we wished to remain in Spain without working and contributing to their health service, despite EEC rules to the contrary. I believe the argument between Spain and the European Commission regarding free health care continues today.

The world economy meant our pounds when converted to euros were worth much less than anybody could ever have imagined. So little that poverty was almost upon us, rendering many financial plans in turmoil. Unemployment was incredible; buildings even today remain incomplete. Cranes still stand there idle and awaiting a return to the boom days. The Spanish banking system was also in dire straits, banks going under and savings disappearing. The Spanish economy and many other European economies were sick and on their feet.

Dwindling savings were disappearing too fast for comfort with no prospect of getting work in Spain. My wife now needed regular medicines that we had to buy. And with a small private pension which was due to start paying her going into liquidation (as did many people's private pensions), we were forced to return. Although informed that the UK government would subsequently take it over, there was no prospect of it happening in the foreseeable future. And with no way of telling how much the UK government would pay the former pension clients of the company, it was the final straw.

And this we did. I obtained work, and we lived with a relative until we could afford a place of our own. Due to the Spanish property crash, there was no prospect of selling our home there. In fact, at the time of writing this book, the Spanish banking system estimates that there are nearly a million properties for sale at less than 50% of the value they once were. Banks took ownership of many properties as the original owners just left the keys with them and returned to their parent countries.

I returned to work as an Operational Support Grade at Feltham prison working permanent nights. I'm not suited to those shifts; I find it difficult to sleep during the day and relied on only four hours sleep - not enough to stay healthy. My philosophy had always been that if God had meant us to work at night, he would have made it light so we could see what we were doing, and dark in the mornings so we could go to bed and sleep, but I gave it my best shot.

After some time, the night working proved not good for either my health or my wife's. And when a job opportunity arose at Heathrow Airport as a Security Officer, I jumped at it. Fortunately, while working at HMYOI Feltham on nights, I did manage to write my first book 'A Turnkey or Not? It's the autobiography of my 25-year career working for Her Majesty's Prison Service. And subsequently, it was published by Apex publishers and is still available to buy.

I'd often thought of working in an airport, and now opportunity presented itself, enabling me to work as an officer. It was an environment that I was hopefully familiar with, albeit of a different type of security compared to working in prisons. I completed my application for the job with great enthusiasm.

Weeks later I received a letter with details of a telephone interview. I hate phones! Do what you have to do, say what you have to say, and end the call. I'm not particularly social on a telephone and find it difficult to make small talk, so this type of interview was not amongst my best attributes. However, the time came, and during it, I learned that I'd need to take a computer-based competency test - over the telephone. Ouch!

Fortunately, it worked out, I passed the test, and now had to await a formal invitation to attend an assessment day at Heathrow Airport. Christmas came and went, so did New Year (2011) before it arrived, my assessment was at the Compass Centre Heathrow.

Of course, nothing runs smoothly, and as the day approached, so too did our typical British winter weather just to make things difficult. Heavy snowfalls blocked many of the roads where I now lived. Saturday was assessment day, and thankfully most of the main roads were clear of snow. My journey was not too difficult, but the Compass Centre was now devoid of heating. It was freezing and most of us attendees had to keep our coats on, which is not the best way to conduct an assessment assignment, thankfully I passed the test. Out of around 70 candidates' we were whittled down to just seven. Now, all we needed was a formal interview (which apparently nobody ever failed), and then we'd be given a date to come to the airport for a medical before being offered a position on a training course to become an airport security officer.

All of a sudden one of the assessor's called my name and asked if I could come to an office with them. Oh shit, I thought, surely, I couldn't have failed, they'd said nobody fails at this point. Like Richard Gere in An Officer and a Gentleman, I had nowhere else to go but couldn't understand how I could have failed at this stage; I'd spent six hours doing the test, simulated role plays and answered questions, what the hell could I have done so wrong.

As it turned out I'd done nothing wrong, the assessors had reviewed my performance and looked again at my CV, and with my previous prison service experience, they wondered if I'd be interested in going straight into the job as an STL (Service Team Leader). I needed to think about it but initially felt that to be a supervisor of staff I'd need to fully understand the workings of the Security Officers role before taking on a position of authority over them. And to do that I would need to experience the actual job of a Security officer first. I had been of the same opinion when working in the prison service and I think that's what made me a good manager of people and a popular one too, so I was not about to change my philosophy. But I would think about it.

I did, after long consideration, turn them down. And as things turned out, I'm so glad I made that decision. An STL's role was one of a manager with no authority. The STL's were there for management to kick ass and relay that down the line, they seem to have little respect for either higher management or the officers on the ground floor. I was gob-smacked at the way some officers spoke to and reacted to STL's. It was a reaction to authority that I wasn't used to from the disciplined way of the Prison Service. Here officers told STL's to 'piss off' 'fuck off' 'take a hike' and such, and then in the next breath be inviting the STL out for a drink as they were 'mates' outside of work. Not a healthy situation, yet it was rife throughout Heathrow.

As STL's, theirs was a thankless task and I'm glad I never took the opportunity to become one. It's a shame because some of them were conscientious workers who only ever wanted to do what was best for the company, the passengers, and their staff. But it was like spitting in the wind, however retrospectively some of them were just vindictive bullies, who had no man management skills whatsoever, you know who you are!

Like everything else at Heathrow, the STL role has now changed, yet it's still not in their role to have any disciplinary power. Needless to say, nepotism runs rife throughout all the terminals and offices', but more of that later in the book.

Formal interview completed and now I had to await the date for my medical and then hopefully be accepted onto a training course.

A letter arrived inviting me to attend a medical at D'Albiac House Heathrow. Situated between Terminal one and Terminal three, they tested my eyesight, then my hearing - by getting me to stand in a corner and then whispering and asking me to repeat what they'd said, hey a real cutting edge medical examination. A few other tests and questions about my general health and hey presto I'd passed. Now to await a formal offer of employment and a date to start the training course.

My start date came 24 February 2011 I was to report to the Compass Centre to start my initial training, where I would get my officers uniform, and discover what terminal I was to be assigned to work.

There was a group of around 20-25 new officers ranging from a member of the local council to ex check-out operators at Tesco and Sainsbury, and we also had one lad whose family ran a pizza delivery shop. We were a very diverse group, the majority being from the Indian culture (these are the predominant ethnic groups who are living in the local surrounding catchment areas of Heathrow) and a mix between male and female. I was the only one in the group from a previous security environment and also the oldest member of the group.

As I didn't live locally in London and as a non-London resident, it had to be explained to me during one training session what an 'oyster' card was. It's a pre-paid card for travelling around London by either bus or underground. It was new to me, the last time I'd used public transport in London must have been back before most if not all of my fellow new recruits, including Instructors, were even born, so an 'oyster' card was like a foreign language. Having said that I think English was a foreign language to many of the group as they spoke a London lingo, I didn't understand much of the time. Oh, how the city I was born in had changed over the years.

A lot of the training was giving the background to why security was needed; we watched some awful videos about how little explosive material was required to cause significant damage to either an aircraft or airport. Some quite scary stuff. We learned the parts of a firearm, and about explosives including the ease of which they are constructed. In fact, most of the instructions are readily available on Google. Now that is bloody frightening.

We watched videos of the events leading up to the 'shoe bomber' Richard Reid and the 'underpants' bomber Umar Farouk Abdulmutallab, and of course in graphic details of the 9/11 bombings, using aeroplanes to fly into the twin towers in New York in 2001. All seem relevant to our job as security officers at a major International airport, which beggars belief that I was the only recruit that had come from a security background and the rest of the group came mainly from customer service areas. But once working at the Terminals, I realised that the job was more about customer service than actual security, yet that in itself is quite a conundrum. But more about that later!

We were taught how to conduct a search on a passenger, whether able-bodied, in a wheelchair, or with limbs missing. How to search children, all to the standard laid down by the Department for Transport (DfT). We faced testing before being allowed to move on to the next phase of training. The DFT set it, and you were only allowed one failure. We also had to pass a test on how to search a bag and a 'passenger'. The passenger search was strange because we had to carry out the search on a person posing as a passenger wearing a jacket, strange because we didn't allow passengers to wear jackets or coats when coming through security screening at any of the terminals at Heathrow. However, it was a DfT regulation for training to be carried out this way.

The searching of passengers was hard to grasp. You might think that strange given my experience as a prison officer, but in the prison service, you are taught to search prisoners while never offering yourself as a target for them to either grab, kick, or hit you. So standing face to face with a passenger and searching them within kicking distance, was at first difficult for me to grasp. However, once I got the hang of it, there was no problem for me to carry out the search to the level required. Many of my fellow trainee's, struggled with being able to place their hands on another human being, touching them over their bodies. I can understand this as it

16

seems alien to touch another person albeit not in an intimate situation but purely for searching purposes. And to make sure when searching that you apply the correct pressure to enable a compliant search, without being too aggressive or touching the other person in an inappropriate place. However, the tutors are excellent at monitoring trainees during this part of the training. We practised on each other (women on women, and men on men, as over here a man is not allowed to search women and vice versa). By doing this, you get to know how much pressure you need to apply to be carrying out your search correctly. As I said when I'd overcome the initial defensive search as opposed to this new (to me) type of searching I was ok and able to help some of my colleagues when they were practising on me.

Our education continued with the history of Heathrow, the hopes of a third runway, and how the five terminals were coping with the sheer amount of passenger movements per day. It is after all still the busiest two-runway airport in the world, and it's amazing that it runs smoothly every day. We were instructed on - who were the groups that were of most concern, to the safety of the aircraft and airport and passengers and staff alike? These groups are not just the obvious terrorists, but environmental groups caused significant concerns, or a passenger the worse for the freely available alcohol (on BA flights of course), and children who out of sheer excitement and enthusiasm could be the cause of security breaches.

On the second or third day, I was selected to work at Terminal 5, on the late shifts. Thank goodness for that, T5 easy to get to and from the staff car park and easy access for me to the M25 for my journey to and from work. For the training at the Compass Centre, I had to leave home at around 6.45 to ensure I would get to work for our 9 am starts. The M25 could take two hours in the mornings, and even when working at the terminal on the late shifts I once spent four hours trying to get to work due to accidents on the M25, very frustrating, so you can imagine how passengers felt after these sorts of journeys. I was relieved that I was not on the early shift (5.45 starts) or the extra early (4.45 starts). As my journey was around 38 miles each way and most of it on the M25, I had to allow at least 1.5 hours per trip, so you can imagine what time I'd have to get up to make it in for early shifts. No, late starts suited me at the time.

Any new starters wanting to work part-time went to Terminal 4, at the time the arrival and departures of flights were either early in the morning (4.30am) or later at night, so security officers were at a minimal during the working day. It was a choice between Terminal 1, 3. or 5. Terminal 2 was under reconstruction so didn't need new staff. Terminal 5 was the newest and exclusively used by British Airways. It changed in 2012 when it was in use for BA and its partner airlines; it was considered by many to be the best terminal for new officers, as the old guards (as they were still called by many at Heathrow) did not have as much respect for management as T5 did. Wow if T5 had respect (as I found out to the contrary) I would have hated to have worked at any of the other terminals, although occasionally I did.

I remember one training session on Diversity. Not only were the staff at Heathrow from many and varied ethnic backgrounds but in fact just looking around at the team, we all came from several different ethnic groups. There was also many age difference, me being the eldest amongst us. The tutor was carrying out a classroom exercise involving us standing in a group and taking a step back or forward depending on the answer to his question, "take a step forward if you know somebody from a different ethnic background to yourself", we all stepped forward.
"Step forward if you know someone whose mother language is not English." we all stepped forward. "Step forward if you know somebody who is 20 years older than you." everybody stepped forward except me. "Tony," the tutor said, "don't you know anybody 20 years older than you?"

"You're joking." I replied and continued, "Everybody who is 20 years older than me is dead." Well, that was it, a new nickname for me now - 'Grandpa'.

Not everybody coming through the airport would be able to speak English. So how we approached people was critical, especially hand gestures, voice levels, and tones could be crucial. However once working at the terminal, I realised that most staff must have missed this part of the training, as I saw some appalling behaviour from my colleagues when dealing with non-English speaking passengers. I, too, found it difficult in some situations and at certain times to remain calm and professional when dealing with these passengers especially given the pressure of the numbers we faced every day. I always tried to use good hand signals and keep my voice tone at an acceptable level. Just to note that during my four years working at T5 there was only one complaint made against me by a passenger. It was regarding my behaviour towards him and his family, and subsequent video evidence completely vindicated me and proved that he was questionable, to say the least, but that's what we had to tolerate on an hourly basis some days.

The training came to an end shortly after we all sat the National Security Screening Exam, to enable us to be licensed to sit at the security screens at the airport. It's an annual National exam set by the regulating authorities. You only had two chances, and if you failed both, you could not qualify to be Security Staff. The pass mark was high, but thankfully we passed, I made it by three points. Bloody hell I thought I need to get to grips with this screen reading lark or else I'm going to be up shit creek without a paddle and out of a job. I felt concerned and spoke to one of my trainers who assured me that once I'd completed my full training, my screen reading would become automatically as good as everybody else's.

I was off to Terminal 5 to complete my 'on the job' training. A few more weeks, learning exactly how to search bags, staff, passengers, and how to operate all the equipment to the standard set by the Department of Transport or DfT who were the regulating authority throughout airport security in the UK.

----

2 HEATHROW TERMINAL 5

Heathrow Terminal 5 opened in 2008. Its main building is the largest freestanding structure in the United Kingdom. It's used exclusively as one of the three global hubs of International Airlines Group, served by British Airways and Iberia; before 2012 it was solely BA who used the terminal.

It was designed to handle 35 million passengers a year. In 2012 it handled 29.8 million on 199,627 flights. That's 41% of the airport's passengers on 43% of its flights with an average of 149 travellers per flight. It's the busiest terminal at the airport, measured both by passenger numbers and flight movements.

The terminal's leading architects were from the Richard Rogers Partnership and aviation architects Pascall & Watson completed production design. Its engineers were Arup and Mott MacDonald. The building cost 4 billion and took almost 20 years from conception to completion, including the longest public inquiry in British history.

The hardest things to overcome for architects of airport terminals anywhere in the world is the logistical side of the building. Remember the terminal has to be split into two parts, 'landside' - where ordinary members of the public will come and go, either to the departures area or the public area. Here they get to meet and greet loved ones, families, or business meeters and greeters, and this area is referred to as the 'dirty' area, as nobody has gone through the security process. Then we have the 'Airside' of the terminal or 'clean' area, this is the area that's restricted, and nobody can gain access unless they have gone through some security screening, and this includes everybody and everything that comes to the airport for any reason. All staff must have and display their 'airside' passes at all time, and they would denote what areas of the airport you could have access to.

But as Heathrow's an International 'Hub' airport, many passengers fly in from other airports within the UK as well as from other countries to connect to flights to other places in the world, hence the word Hub.

It leads to a logistical conundrum, how to move passengers freely through an airport without breaching its security. All Hub airports have this same problem, and it's resolved similarly. 'Clean' passengers must never mix with 'dirty' ones otherwise the security of the terminal becomes breached. Thankfully cleverer people than me work all this out in the design of the buildings inner structure. But suffice to say that if you fly in from another country and need to connect onto a flight from the airport you've arrived at, you will need to go through that airport's security screening system. It's not unique to the UK; all International airports have the same rules and similar logistical problems to solve.

Please remember this, as at Heathrow this was often an area that caused unnecessary confrontations. America was one of the worst areas passengers would fly in from, to get their connecting flight to their final destination, yet would not understand the need to go through our security as in their opinion they'd undergone it at their departing airport. I used to say to anybody who wanted to complain "Sorry, but we don't just trust your countries security, so you get processed again." Or "I'm terribly sorry but it's an International agreement, and the same happens if we fly into your country from here to get a connecting flight." But some passengers never seemed to understand this process.

I do think that booking agents or the airlines themselves could ease this problem by just communicating with customers and explaining the process that's likely to be encountered at the 'Hub' airport.

T5 is now working at nearly full capacity and its busiest working day was Friday 4 April 2014. Nearly 52,000 passengers made their way through Heathrow Terminal 5. I know because I was on duty that day working a 1230 to 2100 shift.

One of the strangest things about the terminal was that in all the years I worked there the air-conditioning units were never adequate to cover the security screening areas. It was pleasant and cool as you entered this area, but once in a queue on a busy day, it soon became inadequate. As for the areas we worked in with the volume of passenger standing and milling about in front of us, we never got to feel any benefit from them, and often on hot days, we would be searching passengers with perspiration dripping from every orifice of our bodies. Not a pleasant experience.

The other phenomenon of T5 was the lighting, due to very high arch ceilings some 40 metres (130 feet) tall, nobody ever considered how the maintenance department could get up to change the light bulbs. Eventually, they employed trained high-wire walkers to come into the terminal at night to renew the bulbs. Much needed as many complaints were heard about the poor lighting especially during the long winter months.

My first working day started at 6 am, we'd report to the training room in T5B, but have to take the shuttle train over to T5B from T5, travelling with passengers due to fly from T5 around that time of the morning, a relatively busy period. I dreaded being asked questions from the passengers in case I didn't know the answers.

I'd hide behind a post and stand deliberately near some British Airways cabin staff and pilots, thinking that if anybody had questions, they would ask a pilot rather than a security officer. Our uniforms at that time were rather weak, in my opinion, they offered us no sort of image of authority unless we wore our uniform jackets, something I never did. Probably due to having to wear one when I started in the prison service all those years ago. If I saw a group of passengers approaching, I made sure I stood near the pilot, and sure enough, they immediately started asking him questions. I had inadvertently learned a valuable lesson and used this ploy whenever I could. I also discovered that passengers asked ridiculous questions, like is this shuttle going to T5B? It was the only way to get to that terminal, and there were signs around three feet high!

Also, why do people ask what gate their flight is going from? I understand they want to know this vital information, but it's displayed on so many screens I couldn't count them, so why ask the cleaners pushing their carts? Come on! Or they would ask, "Is our flight on time?" yet they don't tell you what flight they're on or where they are going but expect us (staff) to know the answers. Weird or what?

I arrived at my T5B classroom to learn exactly how to become a Security Officer and carry out security screening duties; we also had to pass an exam to get classified as live qualified staff and then we were assigned a team.

We had a great bunch of tutors; our main one was a young, vivacious blonde, Linda, who we all secretly lusted after. I think she was already in a relationship, but I must admit it was sometimes a nice distraction for us during some of the more boring information we had to listen to. The other guys in the tutor team all had great personalities, even the taxi driving Chelsea supports, (sorry mate I liked you honestly).

There were seven of us starting together; again, I was by far the eldest. To be honest, I struggled where it came to the screen reading, I'm not sure if in scraping through the National Exam at the Compass Centre I'd created a psychological problem, but these youngsters were spotting things that I just could not see on the screen.

Our trainers would put an image of a passenger bag on a large screen on the wall, and we'd identify what threat items we saw within it. I remember Linda saying to me on one occasion "Come on Tony surely you can see that knife on the screen?" But honestly, I bloody well couldn't, even when she pointed it out right in front of me.

One of the lads would say what he saw almost as the image went on the screen and I would just sit there saying "I can't see that." or "How the hell did you see that so bloody quickly?" He was that good that I think he added to my apprehension.

But the training continued, and we learnt new skills to enable us to become airport security officers. After about a week we were taken to the main airport security area, and under strict supervision, we were allowed to practice the skills we had learnt on real passengers.

It was daunting at first, however, thanks to the trainers we soon got into the rhythm of running a security lane. Passengers were informed that they were in a training lane, and it might take them a little longer to get through than if they'd approached another, but to their credit, we never had any complaints that we were taking longer than any other security lane.

I had no problem talking to the passengers at the 'loading' point of the rotation system of running a security lane. I had a natural skill of being able to get my message across to them and gain a professional rapport, however from the 'loading' position I then moved on to the screen reading area, my nemesis!

Not only was I now viewing real passengers hand luggage but other trainers were placing bags at the loading point that had threat item contained within them, and I had to spot them and carry out the correct procedure. Also, all airport x-ray machines are very similar; ours had a computerised system that superimposed real threat items into the viewing bag (TIP or Threat Image Projection). The screen reader is allowed 15 secs to decide whether the bag is a threat or not, and what action should be taken if it is deemed a threat. Not a lot of time to make those decisions, but the equipment used is very technical, and it allows operators certain options which we can utilise to help us identify the differences between innocent items and possible threat items. We were only allowed 15 minutes for each position in the security process and believe me those 15 minutes were extremely stressful for me. You could be on the machine for several hours at a time so you can imagine how often you rotated around the equipment and how mentally tired you'd become during a session. The concentration needed to do this work is in the extreme but is necessary to ensure your safety, the airports, and the aircraft. Security officers do this day in and day out for up to an eight hour working period.

Our trainers were very helpful and always reassured us. One used to say "Right, what do you see in the bag?" and I'd say, "A hair dryer, phone, lots of cables, etc." and he'd say, "Yup a load of crap, now move on and let's see the next bag."

He was so casual and reassuring that I soon started to overcome my fears of screen reading and reached a good standard. Sadly, he passed away all too early in his life, and my condolences go out to his family. He was sadly missed.

I remember on one occasion, while still under supervision, I was at the back of the process 'bag searching'. The screen reader had rejected a bag for a 'hand search' and told me that there was a sharp object within the bag. I asked the passenger who was a youngish man probably in his early thirties, "Sir, may I search your bag?"

"Blimey," he said, "you're very polite of course you can."

"Do you have any sharp items in your bag, as I don't want to catch my fingers on anything?" I questioned.

"Naw, although I might have some pens in there, nothing sharp no scissors or anything like that." he replied.

"That's great, so could you just open all the compartments in your bag for me please?" I asked.

He opened all the compartments of his bag, and I started my systematic search while continuing to make small talk with him.

"Are you going anywhere nice?" I asked.

"Yes," he said, "a group of us are off to Ireland for the rugby, England versus Ireland."

"Should be a good match." I said as I continued my search. By this time his travelling companions had gathered around the search table area, which can be a bit intimidating but again this is something that has become an occupational hazard which most officers learned to ignore. Having worked in a prison environment it certainly wasn't a problem for me to tolerate, however as his mates continued to egg him on, he stopped watching me and turned around to face them. At this point, I stopped the search and asked if he would please look at me as it was his property I was searching, and he needed to observe my actions. The fact that there are around six cameras also watching me is irrelevant; the passengers must witness us searching as if they didn't, and we did find a banned item, they could claim we 'planted' it. So, I would never search if the passenger was not watching what I was doing.

He said, "That's ok, I trust you."

"That's as maybe, but I can't continue the search until you are witnessing me."

I then asked his friends to step back to allow the search to continue.

He turned around to face me, and I continued my search following the correct procedures. I realised that there was indeed a knife located near the bottom of the bag. I produced the item, which was a 'lock knife' and a banned item, and said to the passenger "Sir! Is this your knife?"

He went red in the face and said: "How did that get there?"

Good question I thought, but as it was this passenger's bag and had been identified by him as his, I think I might have been the wrong person to ask. I called an STL (Service Team Leader) and stopped the search, as per the laid down procedure.

The passenger continued to speak saying that he could not understand how the knife got in his bag etc. The supervisor joined us and questioned the passenger, but as was the law at the time, he called for the Airport duty police to attend, which they did, and they too questioned the passenger, before arresting him. At this point, I had to complete the search. Finding no other banned items, I asked the passenger if he would like me to repack his bag, to which he said: "Get stuffed I'll pack it myself." And he mumbled something like 'wanker', but I couldn't be certain of what he said.

'Charming' I thought, he appeared to believe I'd done something wrong in finding his illegal weapon. How strange people behave when they are the guilty party.

The police told the passenger to collect his personal items and taking him and the knife, escorted him out of airport security, and I assumed to their police station located somewhere within the airport. The STL walked away without another word to the trainer or me to continue with his duties.

Wow, I thought, and I hadn't even completed my training and gone 'live' yet! My trainer told me I'd carried out an excellent job, keeping calm and professionally dealing with the passenger, however, he could not say the same of the supervisor I had called.

Another early lesson learnt about our STL's and their attitude to their staff. Oh well!

We reached the day designated for us to be tested and signed off as competent at all parts of the security process. We had already passed the National Exam for screen reading. However, we had to prove that we could spot the bags placed on the loading area by our trainers, which contained real threat items. We had to identify all of the items the first time. Although I can't remember, I think we were also processing live passengers at the same time, so the pressure was on. We all passed, though I must admit I scraped through and after my 15 minutes of screen reading, stood up with a blinding headache, the first of many I would suffer from this procedure. Not sure if it was my age or I took the job very seriously, or the younger staff were just much more confident than me, but they always seemed so relaxed when screen reading and yet I felt under pressure throughout my time working there, although I learned how to cope with it.

Thankfully I passed and then it was my turn to be testing on a bag search. It was to be held in front of the head of the training department to assess me, and the role played by Linda as the passenger. I carried out the search in the same manner as I'd been trained to and again I tried to form a rapport with Linda; she had a book in her bag which I searched correctly. I said, "I don't think this book is appropriate reading to take through an airport, do you?"

I believe she was shocked by this, but still in role play, she said, "Why is that officer?"

"Well, it's about an IRA plot to make a bomb and blow up a building in London." I think I embarrassed her, as I'd read the book and it was an excellent story thwarted by MI5 and special branch.

But after getting my feedback and being told how good my searching technique was, both the Head of Training and Linda asked if the book really was about a plot to make a bomb? I explained that I'd read, and indeed it was.

"Linda, from now on we'll not use that book on our assessments."

"Definitely not, thanks for telling us Tony, we had no idea, just picked the book at random."

Then onto the final test at the loaders position and again dealing with the public in a professional, polite manner. With the correct amount of humour and rapport, I passed this test with my tutor saying that I should be a trainer as the way I carried out the loading duties was exemplary. Blimey, praise indeed.

----

3 FIRST DAY LIVE

I'm driving down the M25 on my way to work. It's my first day live as a security officer; I was introduced to my new team last week, ha! New team, that's a joke. The team should have consisted of five colleagues but was in fact just one. He had worked at T5 from its opening day so knew the ropes well, but gradually over time his team mates had moved on to different shifts and different teams, And, in fact, he was waiting to move to a new team too. I was to be in a team consisting of just me. Oh well, at least I'd get the chance to 'fill in' with other teams and get to know lots of people on the same shift as me. A good way to meet lots of new colleagues. It was an advantage, though at the time I didn't realise.

But here I am on the M25. I'd allowed 90 minutes to make the 25-minute journey, but as Chris Rea had sung back in 1989, the M25 really was the 'Road to Hell.' Notoriously busy and unpredictable with accidents that could and usually did occur on this nightmare road. I thought allowing 90 minutes at this time of day (my shift started at 1230 and I was leaving at 1100) would be sensible. Having said that during the summer of 2014 it took me over four hours to get to work due to two separate accidents along a three-mile stretch of the road, so it was indeed a 'Road to Hell'.

But today my luck was in, traffic flowed smoothly, so I got to work in plenty of time, parking my car in the designated secure area for Security staff working at T5. I then boarded the terminal's staff courtesy bus, packed with British Airways and BAA staff of all ethnicities, ranging from British Airways ground employees to engineering staff, office workers, security officers, and the whole spectrum of staff who worked at T5. Each terminal had its car parks and courtesy buses, taking staff to and from their place of work.

Dropped at the terminal, I made my way up to the security screening area for staff. All staff, irrespective of position, had to go through a search which was as rigorous as the passengers. In fact, when working in 'staff search,' I always treated them as a bigger threat than the general public as my philosophy was always beware the enemy within. Maybe this was just my previous prison paranoia kicking in, but there have been many attempts to infiltrate via staff connection into the core of airports. Indeed, many well know terrorist attempts have come directly from employees.

Being searched never bothered me I was well used to it from my days in the prison service, but others resented the search, and I will relate some incidents involving staff later in the book. But today through the search and onto the area which was called the 'Tick in area'. Staff had to report to this area and be 'ticked in' for work and told what part of the terminal that they would be working. The tick in area was located in the South Concourse. This was changed to the North Concourse some months after I started work at T5. Its location was in the same office as the RA's (Resource Allocators) who were the ones who allocated you and your teams to where you should be working. The tick-in staff were known collectively as Manpower; it was their jobs to make sure the shifts were covered with the correct amount of staff and gender mix Not always easy to achieve.

Not sure if it was true, but I was told the reason for the 'tick in' was that from its early days the 'tick in area' had moved to airside from landside because in the past staff would get ticked in and then disappear for the day. Nobody knew that they were missing from their place of work. Poor communication and organisation led to staff getting away with this on regular occasions.

I ticked-in and was told to report to South concourse at my start time. I headed there as I knew that there was a staff restroom and I could relax, await the start of my shift, and get a cup of tea out of the free machines. I subsequently found out that this free facility only seemed to work on Monday afternoons until Friday mornings, as Heathrow did not employ the contracted company to maintain the machines over the weekend. Simple, make sure the vending machines are filled on a Friday afternoon. But in all my time working there, this never happened, although some STL's did hold keys to the machine to refill them over the weekends, I never witnessed this.

After my third cup of tea in the South concourse restroom, it was time to report to the Resource Allocator or 'RA'. The RA was a Security Officer who had taken on this important role. The stress of getting the correct staff onto the correct lanes to coincide with the needs of the terminal, and making sure staff got their allocated meal breaks, along with having to provide extra staff whenever required, made their jobs extremely stressful. And despite some of them being openly prejudiced towards their 'mates' or 'Bruvs' and often making sure their 'mates' got the cushy jobs, I would never have taken their roles on, as I felt they were on a hiding to nothing. So, I have nothing but admiration for them despite blatant favouritism from some towards their mates.

We reported to the RA along with all other staff starting at this time. Names were called, and machines or work area's designated. I looked around the South concourse and thought to myself, bloody hell this is busy. I'd never worked the machines in training when they were this busy. I realised my name had been called, and the rest of the team were making their way to our designated security lane.

I was detailed to work with a team I had previously met while training. They were a good team to work with, so my nerves were a little settled, but I was still very apprehensive.

However, we were placed by the 'RA' on a machine in a separate little annex to the main South Concourse. It had low ceilings, was small, and echoed, which for me felt claustrophobic although over the coming months I realised that there were some good plus points for working in this area. One of which was that although you were always busy, it was not a security lane that was monitored for its flow rates so we could take a bit longer to load passengers and search them on the archway.

In those days regular teams teamed up with their regular partners. You would have people on the walk-through metal detector who always worked together. No such luck for me of course but I was teamed up with a lovely lady, who was the mainstay of the team and over the years I always got on well with her. She had worked at T5 since its opening as had most of this team, so I was fortunate to be with them. She, like me, loved a similar part of Spain and we often talked about living over there.

Loading wasn't too bad but the low ceiling echoes really didn't help me. I suffered from tinnitus and sometimes found it hard to hear or concentrate on what I was doing due to the surrounding acoustics, but it all seemed to be going well until I sat on the screen reading position for the first time. Bloody hell, this wasn't like the training. The bloody bags came onto the screen at a ridiculous rate, I barely looked at one before the next one came along and as for the 'tips' shit, I was missing virtually every one of them. A Tip was a false image of a threat item that was computer-enhanced onto the screen to make sure its readers concentrated and knew what they were looking for. Most staff in T5 had a Tip score of 95% and over, and I was missing them all. How can you look at a real passenger's bag and miss a superimposed AK47 rifle bang in the middle of the bloody screen? Well I was, yet I watched my colleagues, and they were all so blasé about screen reading. 15 minutes later with sweat running down my face, my time was up, and I moved on to the next area of the security screening process but had already worked it out that in another 90 minutes I would have to sit at the screen again and go through this whole process. Bloody hell I'm never going to get to the high standards of everybody else.

The team were great offering me lots of encouragement "You'll get the hang of it after a while." and "We were all like you when we started honestly." And they were right, but it did take time to realise what the technique was to control the flow of the bags appearing on your screen and still give enough time to look for real threat items. After several weeks my TIP score had gone up to 96% where it remained for the rest of my time working there, but it was a stressful start.

At one stage I asked for extra training. I was concerned that my screen reading was not up to the required standard, even though I'd passed the annual screen reading examination conducted by the DfT and failure meant the sack.

I received the said training and spent over an hour there to only miss one threat item. I accepted it wasn't that I was missing the items; I just wasn't reacting quick enough to carry out the correct procedures. Once I understood this, whenever I saw anything suspicious I stopped the screen allowing me extra seconds to examine the item and decide whether to reject, stop, or allow it through.

Because of my initial experience, whenever I worked with new staff I went out of my way offering them encouragement or helping them overcome the nerves of screen reading. And I would like to think they appreciated my help and understanding.

My first day consisted of working the archway, bag searching, swabbing, screen reading, loading, and back to the archway. It was the day's routine until we went on our first break and then it continued until our main meal break and then until it was time to go home. It would be the same most days. The north concourse always seemed more manic to me, but that was where all the International Transfer passengers arrived to go through the security screening process again as we had a diverse range of duties, one day on machines another on patrols, then T5C and then machines again, and after four days two days off. Yes, I have to say I did enjoy those early months, but all things come to an end, and the shift patterns changed, which wouldn't be the only time during my time there, and our range of working areas changed too.

But this was my first day, and around 8 pm the airport starts to slow down, and the passenger flow starts to ease off until we are all just hanging around for a few late passengers. Two machines were to be left open and taken over by the night shift. So as our machines were closed down the rest of us start to gather or 'mingle' on one or two machines until 15 minutes before our finish time when the Night Orderly Officer ('NOO') tells us we can go home.

A mad rush ensues to get out of the terminal and down to the stop to await the bus to the staff car park. Then the drive out of the airport perimeter and onto the lovely M25, my drive home. Thirty to forty-five minutes later I am home with a glass of wine in my hand, absolutely shattered but this would be my routine for the next four years.

----

4 SECURITY SCREENING ROTATION SYSTEMS

When I started work at Heathrow airport, the security screening procedure was designated by the DfT (Department for Transport) who make all the rules and regulations regarding the airport security screening systems throughout the UK, along of course with their international counterparts from both the EEC and the USA aviation authorities.

At the time here in the UK there was a strict laid down procedure for the rotation of staff moving around the security equipment. 15-minute screen reading, 15 minutes at the front of the system bag loading, 30 minutes searching passengers on the walk-through metal detector (WTMD or archway) and then 15 minutes searching and 15 minutes of random bag tracing (we used special swabs to check for explosive material trace randomly). Finally, 15 minutes of screen reading, although of course, you could start in any position of the rotation. You were often on this rotation for up to four hours before getting a break. We got two breaks during our shifts, one for 20 minutes and then one for around 45 to 50 minutes depending on how busy the airport was. But because of the amount of passengers and the shift rotas being completely wrong for the volume of traffic through the terminal you would often come on duty and be sent on a break virtually immediately then be on machines for nearly five hours without a break, bloody tiring and stressful and not good for your health.

The system has changed several times since then. However, none of the changes has ever taken into account staff health regarding getting regular breaks. For instance, do you want to start an eight and half hours shift at 2 pm and be sent on a break at 2.30pm then be given your long break at around 8.30pm and come back to work until 10.30pm, certainly not good for your digestive system?

There was an expectation amongst staff to get 'shoots'. I will explain this in a dedicated chapter in part two of the book. But suffice to say, there was one. Indeed, it was custom and practice that towards the end of a shift if the airport was quiet, and the overall plan meant you were surplus to requirement's, then you'd be released to go home or get a 'shoot' as it was referred to by the staff. This was usually around 15 minutes, which gave you time to leave the airport terminal building, get a bus to the staff car park and be on your way home by the actual end time of your shift. Sometimes this shoot would involve up to 20 members of staff being allowed to leave early. As I said the shift rotas were completely inappropriate for the requirements of the terminal, but it seemed at that time to be an accepted part of working at Heathrow. It appears that all other terminals worked similarly, so the shoot was part of the fabric of working at Heathrow as a security officer.

Many staff that had worked at T5 since its opening expected the 'shoot' and complained when they got less than a 30-minute 'shoot'. Amazing I know, but as I was to learn many things seemed to happen at Heathrow that amazed and astonished me, compared to working in the public sector.

The 15 minutes of screen reading could be stressful, but most of the staff seemed to be very casual about it, and I suppose over time I too developed that approach. But it is an important part of the job and one that is probably the most stressful to carry out as you are looking at the inside via x-rays of passenger's bags. You have only seconds to decide if the bag is safe or needs to be searched as it has banned items contained within. And you also are looking for real threat items, like firearms, devices, knives, etc., and you only have these seconds to use the enhancements on the equipment to aid you to identify threat items. In the early days, I used to have a bad headache by the time I had finished a shift.

I used to find it a relief when my fifteen minutes were up (in my latter days this time had increased to twenty minutes but with less staff in the rotation), to then move to the next piece of equipment. The most important part of the screen readers role was that this person controlled the movement of staff around the six-operational position of each team, it was the screen reader completing their allotted time at that post that controls every other member of the team moving around the equipment. The pace of reading the operators screen would dictate the speed the loader could load passenger's baggage and the number of bags the bag searcher would have to search.

Some screen readers would 'pull' bags off just because they didn't like the look of the passenger and not because of any suspicious item inside the bag. I know of one officer who would deliberately pull a bag off for searching just because the passenger was an attractive woman and his mate was on the bag searching position and it gave them the opportunity to chat them up. Unprofessional but it did happen. I remember approaching this officer once about why he was rejecting particular passenger's luggage, and he said, "My mate wanted to chat to her, well she was good looking don't you think?"

I said, "But it's unprofessional and childish."

To which he replied, "For fuck sakes, what's your problem, Tony? Get a life."

Oh well, this was Heathrow T5.

From screen reading you would swap with your female partner, she would move to the reading position, and you would take over her role at the loading position. Most staff seemed to treat this as a rest area, but in truth, the loader's job was vital as was displayed to me during our training. If the loader does not load a bag correctly but allows a passenger to put their bag on the designated tray, it would be easy for them if they were attempting to conceal items in their bag to place the bag in a position that would not easily if at all reveal what was contained within it. The bag loaders responsibility was to ensure they placed the bag on the conveyor belt. I used to turn the bag upside down then the correct way around before placing it on the belt. I will reveal in a later chapter what happens if this fundamental approach to loading is ignored and the consequences of bad loading.

As we often had the DfT and a private company called Red Line coming to the airport and bringing with them real threat items to test us to see if the security screening system was up to the required standard, and on many occasions this simple act of changing how the bag is placed on the belt can be the difference between a threat item getting through or the screen reader seeing the item on their screen. So I always thought the loaders position was one of the most important of the whole procedure, strange then that later in my career here, the management removed the loader's job in the name of efficiency. Never did I understand that idea it was never more efficient but probably saved Heathrow millions per year so perhaps that was one of the earliest examples of profit versus security.

A strange thing for me to understand and I don't think I ever really did, was that if you missed a DfT or a Red Line test you were immediately removed from being able to work on a security lane until you had undertaken a retraining session. Yet, if you found the item you were rewarded with a fifty-pound airport gift voucher. A fifty-pound reward for just doing your job was just unbelievable to me.

For now, we had bag loaders with this important function for the whole of the process. As it was here that we asked for metal objects, to be removed to help our colleagues on the Archway to only have to search passengers when necessary and not because they left their mobile phone in their pockets, but of course as passengers, many thought these ground rules did not apply to them.

The same applies for the bag searcher, trying to ensure that all liquids, pastes and gel were removed from passenger bags and were placed in their trays in clear plastic bags, to help the bag searcher at the other end of the process to only have to search passenger belongings when necessary. Many passengers didn't comply, thinking these rules were irrelevant to them and unnecessary. If you were loading correctly, you could make life easier for all of your colleagues, but many just didn't bother.

There was also the added issue that if your security lane were randomly picked out to test the 'flow rate', the STL's, who had been informed surreptitiously, would come along to try and ensure we made the strict schedule by 'helping' the loader. I remember one particular STL coming up to me while I was loading and taking over, he stopped me doing my job, and he was allowing passengers to put their bags on the belt irrespective of asking them to remove liquids, etc. At one point I just stopped loading and said, "If you want to do this then go ahead." and I stepped back and allowed him to carry on. Afterwards, he approached me and said, "You know why I came to help you don't you Tony?"

"Of course, but you weren't helping. All you've done is made my screen readers job harder, and the bag searcher is inspecting more bags than necessary, and the two on the archway are now packed solid with passengers to search, just because you were helping me, Well thanks a bundle."

"You know your lane was being timed, and we cannot afford another breech, so I made sure we didn't."

"Yes, but if you'd just told me that instead of coming over and taking over, I could have achieved the same result but without all the extra work you've caused us."

"We cannot afford another breach this month." he said.

"You can't afford staff going off sick either, and in truth, you slowed down the flow as you started confusing the passenger. So, in future just tell us what's going on and trust us to do our jobs because you obviously can't do yours, and we have now got disgruntled passengers being searched at the archway because the loader - who was you - didn't tell them to take their phones out of their pockets. And we have a queue of passengers waiting for their bags to be searched because you didn't tell them to take their liquids out of their hand luggage, and you call that help, brilliant."

He stormed off, and to be honest; this wasn't the last time I came into conflict with this particular STL and his 'help'.

Whereas, and although the biggest area of potential conflict, I enjoyed my time working on the archways (WTMD). Albeit physically demanding after all in a 30-minute session you would search maybe 30 people, which would mean doing 30 squats in 30 minutes every 90 minutes, so a lot of exercises. But it was an opportunity to be able to chat and establish a rapport with the passengers which might help any potential conflict for the bag searcher if their bags were required to be searched after they had completed the process of the WTMD.

However, it was very tiring, and at the end of a busy day, you felt you had completed a good workout, by just being on the WTMD.

The same can be said of bag searching. Physically moving bags from the end of the conveyor belt onto the bag search area in readiness for conducting a search. This position in the process on reflection is probably the biggest area of conflict, after all, do you want some complete stranger rummaging through all your personal property, I think not.

I used to try and develop a rapport with the passenger who's bag I was searching, but some passengers who initially would be okay would suddenly change character as soon as you said to them that they had an item that was banned. Boy, was that the magic switch for them. I suppose apart from the WTMD this area is where I had more conflict than any other part of my job as a security officer. But read on, and I will reveal more about conflicts at the WTMD in the next chapter.

----

5 THE WALKTHROUGH METAL DETECTOR

He was smartly dressed. It looked like he was wearing an Armani suit. He was a trim man of around 45 to 50 years old. Perfect Windsor knotted tie along with a pristine white shirt, buttoned down at the sleeves. The Walkthrough Metal Detector

His hair was cut very precisely, and he seemed the archetypal businessman used to being in a position of authority.

As he walked through the archway metal detector, there was an audible buzz; indicating that this passenger had metal on him. Pretty obvious really, it wouldn't have done so unless of course it was a randomly selected passenger and then the audio tone would have been different. The machine revealed that he had metal in at least two of the four body zones. The metal items were from approximately his arms to his knees.

He stopped, stung to the spot as if he'd been shot. He spun around and looked at the machine accusingly.

 "Sir," I said, as he continued to stare at the machine. "Sir, you've indicated that you have metal objects on your person and I need to search you." He continued to ignore me and went to walk back through again.

"Sir," I called again only a little more loudly. It seemed to work as he stopped and turned back to me. "Sir, I need to search you, please step over here." I was trying to move him away from the exit of the archway to a more convenient spot to allow our other passengers (only the women through as I needed to search this gentleman and we cannot permit men through unless there is a man that can search them should they indicate too).

"Sir, may I search you please?" I asked, we always ask it's much more polite than just being frisked by some airport security guard.

"What choice do I have?" he said in perfect American mid-west English.

"Sir, of course, you have the choice, but the consequences of refusal are that you will not be allowed to fly with us today." I said, and quickly added, "Not much of a choice, but at least you'll get a free massage with the search, unfortunately by me and not my female colleague."

I was trying to add a bit of humour. It can, after all, be very stressful travelling through a modern airport with all the new security measures in place. But at the end of the day, these security measures are there to protect the traveller and ensure the safety of everybody in the airport and our aeroplanes are safe. But it was evident that on this occasion the passenger's sense of humour was missing.

"Sir, do you have any metal object in your pockets?" I asked.

"No, only my mobile phone." he said.

"Your mobile phone? Sir is that not made out of metal; we did ask you to remove all metal object from your pockets before you came through the archway?"

"No.," he said "It's only a mobile phone, no metal in there." he added

"Sir," I said, amazed that I was so calm "what sort of phone doesn't have metal in them then?"

"The plastic one's of course." he said, taking his mobile phone out of his pocket to show me.

"Sir," I said "I can assure you that there's not been a mobile phone invented so far that doesn't have metal in them. What about all the wired connections and electronic gismos inside, they have to be made of metal don't they, and I have never come across a plastic battery in a model yet."

"Well of course they do." he said, "I'm not stupid, I'm the CEO of my own electronics company back in the states."

Without answering, I placed a tray in front of him and asked, "Would you put it in there sir. I'll just put it back through the x-ray machine, and you can collect it at the other end once I've finished searching you." I added, "Do you have anything else in your pockets made of metal or any sharp objects; you know anything I might catch my hand or fingers on when I search you?"

"No," he replied, "but the mobile phone is plastic, not metal." he said.

At this point, I grabbed for the 'hand held metal detector' these are used throughout the world and are very sensitive metal detectors, even used in the UK's prisons.

I switched the detector on and ran it over the passenger's mobile phone; it gave out a high-pitched audible beep,

"And there you go, sir, full of metal. As I said there's no phone invented that doesn't have metal in them."

"Huh," he said, "you don't have to be so patronising, and I suppose the few coins I have in my pocket are made of metal too?"

"Sir," I said with my patience starting to wear thin, "Of course they are made of metal and will also go off when you walk through a metal detector. I know our currency is doing pretty poorly at the moment, but we haven't started making our coinage out of plastic." Again, trying to keep the conversation light.

"Could you please place your coins in the tray as well?" I asked.

He placed them in the tray provided and said, "This is all a load of crap anyway. We don't have this sort of security back in the states it's not needed, and it's over the top." He went on, "And really, do I look like a terrorist?"

"Sir," I said trying to keep calm. "What does a terrorist look like then?" I added "I'm surprised you say you don't have this security back in the states. We're just doing our job in the hope we can keep everybody flying safe, and going through the metal detector is part of that procedure, now I just need to search you."

"This is crap," he said, "You've got everything out of my pockets so why search me?"

"Because it's my job sir, not always a pleasant job but one that's very necessary in our modern world." I replied.

"Well," he said, "I think it's a complete waste of time, especially mine. You should be looking for the real terrorist and not just us travellers going about our lawful businesses." he said and then continued "Anyway, maybe you should be looking closer to home for your terrorist." He inclined his head towards my female colleague who was standing adjacent to me and allowing only women through the archway. My colleague was from an Indian ethnic background, had worked at the airport for many years and like all staff had been vetted to a very high level of security to obtain the job in the first place.

"Sir, I'm not sure what you're inferring. But if you mean what I think you do, then I would advise that if you're not happy with the professionalism of my security colleague, that you speak to a supervisor. Would you like me to call one for you?"

"For Christ sake, all I am saying is, how many of these Indians are Muslims?" he said, spreading his arms to encompass all around.

I felt my blood pressure starting to rise, and given that we had a queue of male passengers still waiting patiently to come through the Archway, I began to search this passenger in the correct laid down procedure. But said, "Sir, I would be careful what you say about my colleagues. We all pass strict security vetting to get the job in the first place. And for your information, most Indian people are not Muslims but are Sikhs or Hindu's, and it's very insulting for them to be referred to as any other religion especially by somebody like you who doesn't even know them." I continued "And what gives you the right to make such disgusting accusations, who do you think you are?" I was trying not to get angry, but some people's ignorance goes beyond belief.

"I'm American, and we know all about terrorists. For Christ sake don't you remember the twin towers and 9/11?" he said as he continued to moan and grumble about Muslims and terrorists.

"Of course, I do Sir. We also had our attack on a bus and three underground tube stations on 7/7, and attempts at both Glasgow Airport and here at Terminal 4, and that's why we have all these security measures in place so that people like you with your racist views can travel safely through our countries airports. And if your security had been up to a decent standard then 9/11 may not have happened." I said realising that I had gone a little over the top, but sometimes people need to know the truth, and this gentleman was one of them.

I was by now getting pretty exacerbated, why do people always want to complain about a process they have to go through every time they travel through an airport, and then get agitated because they cannot accept that the measures are there for their safety or worse still, think security did not apply to them. Then make it worse by making stupid accusations about other ethnic groups believing they are entitled to state their views publicly.

As I was finishing my search of this passenger, and he was obviously not happy with the way I had spoken to him, he said, "You people make me sick, I'm an American, why would I be a terrorist?"

I shook my head in amazement and said, "You have clearly never heard of Timothy McVeigh. He was a white man who killed over 160 Americans including 19 children at the Oklahoma City bombing's in 1995, long before 9/11. Anyway, thank you for your cooperation today sir, have a safe journey and good day." and I proceeded to call forward the next male passenger.

I know ignorance is bliss, but this incident is not an isolated one. Coming through airport security screening and particularly the walk-through metal detectors can be stressful, but at the end of the day, it's there to enable you, the passenger, to come from the landside of the airport into the secure departure area. Most people do so with little regard or notice of the security officers stationed there, and that is how it should be, but please remember we are not doing this for fun. I did my job and assumed that every passenger I dealt with could be a member of my family and I wanted them to get on their aircraft, go about their business, and know they would be safe.

We are taught to try and de-escalate a situation if it seems to be getting out of hand. But when you have this sort of confrontation at least two or three times during a 30-minute session on a very busy archway, it's hard not to respond by 'hitting 'back. But to exacerbate the situation you have just had 15 mins searching passengers bags getting the same sort of discussions. And spent 15 minutes at the loading position, also having the same discussions while trying to get the passengers to understand and comply with the regulations of which personal belongings need to be placed in the provided trays. So, you can see that our stress levels are at the limit. And you also have to include that fact that you have spent 15 minutes of pure concentration looking at the x-ray machine and trying to analyse whether that mobile phone and all the wiring on top of a bottle of water is just that, or something more sinister. And you only have 15 seconds to decide on whether to let the bag go, hold it and investigate or reject it for a hand search. A lot of stress can build up very quickly, and one awkward passenger who wants to argue and harangue you after three hours working on the machines without breaks (more of this later) can get your stress to extreme levels very quickly.

But it's not always so bad because thankfully the majority of passengers just want to get from the security area into the departure lounge with as little fuss as possible. After all, it's the start of their journeys, and they want it to go smoothly.

It's also often the case that immediately after having to deal with an argumentative passenger, the next passenger will say something that completely restores your faith in the human race. Often, I've had passengers come through an archway and say, "How on earth do you put up with people like that?" as they point to the passenger we have just processed, who had been rude or had argued with us. I usually shrug my shoulders and say. "It's people like you that allow us to put up with people like that, thank you."

----

6 MY TEAM

One of the most important aspects of working as a Security officer at Heathrow was the make-up of the team you were assigned to. From all different cultural, ethical and ethnic backgrounds it took all of the members to make it a good team but only one bad one to make it terrible.

I had been lucky that at the start of my working at Heathrow I was in a very exclusive team of one, me! Yes to start with there had been two of us. But my colleague who was Spanish, (and very useful, as I had a home in Spain he taught me a lot of Spanish) had already had his name down to move to another team which he did shortly after I joined him, so I found myself in a team of one.

This was great as I couldn't really fall out with myself (even though my wife often said I could) but it meant that I was often put with other teams on the same shift as me to fill in for their vacancies. It meant I quickly got to know many staff on similar shifts to myself.

However, this could not last, and I soon had two new male members

joining the team. Both were from the local area, and both of similar ethnic backgrounds namely of the Indian culture. I got on with both of them immediately. We all shared a sense of humour and were great colleagues. They were quickly followed by another young lad from a similar background, whose attitude at times I found to be unprofessional and childish but we are all different, and sometimes age differences in this sort of team working environment do not always work.

I remember thinking back to my prison service career, where we were always conscious of keeping the ethnic and age mix of our wing staff on an even footing but at Heathrow, no apparent thought process went into making up of working teams. Given the stress of the working environment, I found this an alien concept. But as I was only a grunt and not part of management my job was to accept the decisions from on high, which I did. I can honestly say I never liked this latest member of the team and he led me to request a change of teams some months later. I went off on holiday and returned to find we now had three more members of the team, all females. Two, once again from a similar Indian ethnic background to the three men in the group, and one from an Asian background. Mad as a hatter but one of the nicest girls I have ever worked with, she immediately called me gramps in deference to my age.

However, the team never really gelled. The girls often and repeatedly fell out with the young Indian lad in the team, and he did have a way of winding everybody up from time to time.

I remember on one occasion; he wound me up so much after putting his hand palm in my face during an argument that he'd started. It wasn't unusual for him. It was while we were working Lane 15 on the South concourse, I was on the archway, and it was lucky it was during a quiet period. But when he made this gesture I had started to pull my arm back to hit him, when my female colleague said, "Tony he's not worth it." She placed her arm on mine, and I withdrew my fist and agreed with her.

But I knew it couldn't continue as he'd already and systematically made each of the girls in the team burst into tears at different times.

I made a formal request to move teams just at the time when all the teams were changing onto a new shift system, and the unique teams from North Zone 1, and South Zone 2 concourses were joining with Zone 3 teams. We would now all become one team carrying out all the functions that had been separated previously. It meant a more diverse work schedule, and I would now be working in area's I had never worked previously. I think this was a better idea, we all got to do our fair share of the less desirable jobs as well as the good ones. It seemed a more equitable way to utilise the terminal security resources. Also, the three men on my team were all going onto the early shift as was one my favourite females. Of the other two, one resigned, and one went part-time to continue her further education towards obtaining a law degree.

The new team was so different from my first. For a start we all seemed to hit it off, (well I would like to think so) there was Alan, an officer similar in age to me, although he left the team sometime after, we always got on with each other. Then there was a very tall Indian lad who had come from a similar background to me; he'd worked for a private prison company. He became an STL, and I believe he became one of the better STL's at Heathrow. Then there was a young lad called Stan; he was great, so laid back I think he was comatose most of the day, the most unflustered person I have ever met. When faced with angry passengers Stan would just sail on oblivious to what insults passenger would throw at him. I immediately took to him, and I would like to think we had a great relationship during our three years working together.

Stan and I both loved Monty Python and especially the film 'The Life of Brian'. Our party piece was to say to each other "He's not the messiah he's a very naughty boy." in a similar high pitched voice to the film character. We'd do this to each other whenever a passenger got agitated and aggressive towards one of us. The other would say to the passenger in the same style of voice as in the film, "He's not the messiah

he's a very naughty boy." hoping to de-escalate the situation, not always successfully it has to be said. But we had great fun doing it.

Then we had 'Rami', I think she was the rock of our team. She was from an Indian background and knew many staff and management as neighbours and friends from home. She was the foundation that kept our team together. Rami should have been a manager, her ability, in my opinion, was without question brilliant and why she was not an STL was a mystery to me but great for our team. She kept me sane on many occasions, but I am sure I must have exacerbated her on many occasions too. I like to think that as we still communicate with each other via 'WhatsApp', we were and still are good friends.

Then we had our Polish lady, Elsa, (well she did remind me of the character from Frozen). She could be very abrupt and moody with us as well as impatient, and she was the same with passengers, often to my embarrassment. Yes, I could be rude and belligerent towards passengers but only if they had provoked me, but she didn't seem to need the passengers to upset her first. I think to be fair that this was just her manner and I met many girls from Poland while working at Heathrow with similar attitudes.

There was another lad who changed teams shortly after I joined them.

His interests were Sport and mainly football (and horse racing which was not an interest of mine for personal reasons), as was mine and we often had friendly but heated discussions about a sport, it helped to pass the time.

Juicy was a real tough cookie. I'd hate to encounter her late at night after being out on the town. She frightened everybody, but boy was she great to work with, another one like me who took no messing from anybody. She was a real asset to the team, and it was a real shame when she appeared to have left the company with no explanation.

Then there was our wonderful young girl 'Simi'. I believe her family came from Singapore, and although she had long jet-black hair, she was an archetypal blonde. Mad as a box of frogs but I loved working with her. An amazing person who never got upset with travellers and used to be the butt of many wind ups by the rest of the team. I don't think she ever had a wrong word to say about anybody, staff, managers or passengers. I was bereft when she moved over to the early shifts along with Elsa and my sports crazy mate.

But to replace them we got the steady Di who I'd worked with while in Zone 2 South concourse. Another officer who'd fallen foul of the bad sick management system and who'd been treated unfairly for some time.

Along with Di, we welcomed Alex to the team (his brother worked at T5 as a security officer, so he knew the score). Another mad keen Spurs supporter, just like me, but so much so that he went to many home matches, which we mainly lost. Not blaming you though mate, at all, honest.

Last, we had a lovely young Afro mixed race girl, Bubbles. She had a bubbly personality, a great match to her brilliant curly black hair. She was full of life. A perfect replacement for Simi, only she was from a well-educated background, and it was a waste of her talents being used in this capacity at Heathrow. I suppose it's the same now; there's not always the vacancies to suit the skills. Bubbles was a fabulous asset to the makeup of our team. I loved working with her when we were on patrols, fantastic fun to be with which made my days easy ones. I hope her feet have recovered.

This was my team, and I hope I played my part in making it one of the acknowledged better teams at T5.

We'd had some memorable times together and a lot of fun. We frequently spent our breaks in the rest rooms together, so our team bonding was superb right from the start.

And when working in the quieter zones of T5, like T5C and T5B, or down in the dungeons of the good inwards area, and staff search areas, we had some great laughs. We shared happy experiences and nasty ones too, with passengers insulting us. We managed to laugh about them afterwards.

----

7 T5C

Heathrow's T5C opened for business in June 2011. It reduced the number of passengers bussed to their aircraft from the main terminal from around 20 percent to five percent.

On Wednesday 1 June 2011, British Airways inaugural San Diego flight, was the excuse for the official opening. Although travellers had been using T5C for several weeks, as BA trialled the new satellite terminal.

The T5C satellite is linked to Terminal 5 via the existing underground transit system. It has twelve boarding gates, of which eight are triple bridges designed to cater for the new twelve strong fleet of Airbus A380 aircraft that joined British Airways around the early part of 2013.

It was considered one of the best places to work. And although exclusive to those of us who were detailed to work in Zone 2, when the reviewed shift rotas came into being all staff gained the opportunity in their new teams.

At first, as I was in my exclusive team of one, whenever they needed an extra body at T5C due to annual leave or sickness I was often detailed to work there. In its early days, it was boring; you might have as many as a dozen passengers come through the security lane in an eight and half hour shift. We'd have to self-break, and although eight members of staff were detailed to work there to cover our meal breaks, there would only be six on duty. Our finish time was 2100, yet T5C closed at 2030. It gave staff time to catch the transit train back to the main T5 terminal building and then out to the station for the bus to our car park. We'd get there around 2050, so still be driving home before our official finish time.

There were occasions, throughout my time working there, that there was a late flight coming through T5C. If this were the case a night shift team would relieve us around 2030; sometimes they would arrive at 2010, so we would get a great shoot.

T5C in its early days left us with nothing to do for long periods. But hey

I wasn't management, and so I didn't have to justify the waste of staff resources to anybody.

I remember on one such occasion, during a week of four days I'd been detailed to work at T5C on three consecutive days. On my fourth and final day, the RA informed me that I was to go to T5C again. I said, "Please, I've spent three days over there, it's doing my head in, can I swap and work on the machines as the time goes so slow over there, and I need a break from doing nothing." She agreed, and I was placed with a team on the concourse. Yes, it was busy but my eight and a half hours shift sped by.

I remember coming back after my two rest days only to be detailed over to T5C yet again; do you think they were trying to tell me something?

It was whilst working over in T5C on one occasion I received an e-mail informing me that a publisher was interested in publishing my first book 'A Turnkey or Not? And what was strange was that one of the girls in the team 'diamond' who I was working with on that day had asked if I wanted her to proof read my book. She was doing this at the very moment I received the e-mail with the contract offer. Strange world! And diamond lived up to her name, some months later due to health reasons she moved onto permanent nights. Their gain was our loss, she was lovely, kind, honest and a fantastic security officer, who was always helpful and supportive.

Over the ensuing months, T5C did become busier and just as stressful as working on the main concourse. Again, we had the omnipresent prospect of a confrontation, and never an STL available when needed.

An STL had to come to T5C each night at the end of the shift to close the security doors. On one occasion a particular STL, who disliked coming over asked via the secure radio network if we could close them for him, as he couldn't make it in time for us to finish at 2030 and if we couldn't we'd be late off shift. He'd tried this several times earlier, and oddly enough none of our security passes had the required access codes to allow us to close these doors. Even if they had, we'd have called his bluff, as it was his job and not ours.

By chance, he made it by 2015 and closed the doors early, so we got a good shoot that day. It led to repercussions because BA staff who checked passenger tickets before they came through security, also had to leave when we did to enable us to close the security lane. Heathrow was contracted to BA to keep it open until 2100. It meant that from then on, the Night orderly officer had to send one of their teams over each night to make sure we got off at 2030. They kept T5C open until 2100.

On another occasion, a group of American travellers were coming through T5C. They'd transferred from one flight, I seem to recall from somewhere in India and connecting to another back to the USA. They were elderly, and almost all had to be searched or have their hand luggage searched because they'd been given water bottles on their earlier flight. They'd kept their water bottles with them not realising they had to come through security screening again at Heathrow, requiring a search as the bottles were over the allowed size. As was often the case with transfer passengers in either the main concourse or any of the satellites (T5B or T5C).

This lady who must have been in her late 80's took umbrage at not being allowed her water bottle. She also had loads of liquids and creams over the allowable sizes. It was my job to carry out the search. I started off as I always did "Madam may I search your bag?"

"Yes," she said, "but I don't understand what's wrong."

"I think you may have liquids in your hand luggage that aren't allowed."

"Young man, what do you mean not allowed?"

"Well they're over the size the regulations allow us to accept."

"Why? Do you know I am American and in America, we make allowances for older people?"

"That's as maybe madam and noble, but in the UK, we make none, regardless of age or nationality. Where it comes to the security of aircraft and passengers, the rules are clear over 100ml, and it's not allowed." The actual rule is anything in a container that is larger than 100mls isn't allowed, and not the amount of liquid within the container."

"But young man do I look like a terrorist?"

"Madam, I cannot say as I don't know what a terrorist looks like, do you?"

"Well they don't look like me I can assure you of that."

"Really?' I said, "Well I bow down to your knowledge, not sure how you would know, but even if you are not one, the bottle of water is still over the allowable size. Therefore, you cannot take it through security."

The point of reason had now been breached as she turned on me and said, "My husband fought a war to rid the world of Nazis like you! You fucking wanker how dare you take my water off me, I'm an old woman, and I've never been treated like this anywhere in the world. You people think you can treat all American's in this manner, well I'm not having it you Nazi bastard."

Shit, I was so taken aback at her outburst. But more important than that, I'm Jewish, and I lost family members during the war. For her to call me a Nazi bastard upset and angered me, "Madam," I said "I'm Jewish, and many of my family were murdered by the Nazis in concentration camps in Poland. And my father fought the Germans during the second world war from 1939 until 1945, with the British Army. You lot only came into the war in 1942, and only after Pearl Harbour was attacked. So please, do not refer to me as a Nazi bastard. I'm only doing my job, keeping the likes of you safe from modern day Nazis. Now, you cannot have the water so tough luck." and I picked up the bottle and threw it in the bin. I didn't offer to repack her bag but just walked away from the search area.

I was so livid at her attitude over a bottle of water given to her free from an airline. For her to complain in this manner was uncalled for. You could have cut the tension with a knife as all my colleagues had gone quiet when this passenger referred to me as Nazi Bastard.

Stan came over and said to the passenger, "He's not the messiah, but he's a very naughty boy." and with that, the tension was broken as we all laughed. Well done Stan.

There were many incidents like this while working in T5C, but passengers were mostly understanding and helpful. It's a shame that some feel they have to belittle the staff that are there to ensure their safety.

I recall on another occasion; Stan and I believe Bubbles were on the archway when we had a large influx of passengers that had to be processed. An older woman approached the archway and said to Stan "I'm an old age pensioner, do I have to remove my shoes?"

He looked at her shoes, "Based on my experience I would suggest you do. Those shoes tend to activate the Archway, and if you take them off it will save you having to be searched by my colleague." and he pointed to bubbles.

"Well in America if you're over 70 you don't have to take your shoes off."

"Well in the UK whatever your age there are no exceptions to the shoe rules I'm afraid!" said Stan "So they need to be removed." As she took her shoes off, she said, "This is silly, do you think I would be a terrorist at my age?"

"Well," he answered "to be honest as I've never met one I'm not experienced enough to know whether they have a retirement age or if they continue to be terrorists. Most of them blow themselves up before they get old, but we cannot be certain, can we?"

He was so laid back he was horizontal. How could anybody get annoyed when he always said everything with a smile and sailed through whatever onslaught was thrown at him? I'd have bitten back with the same attitude as the other person, but Stan didn't change, you never knew if he was upset or not.

Anyway, the passenger sailed through the WTMD without activation. She collected her shoes and was putting them back on. I was at the search table next to her, and I said in our now familiar Monty Python voice, "You know he's not the Messiah," as I pointed to Stan "but he's a very naughty boy."

I think she walked away to her departure gate believing Heathrow security staff were mad and to be honest she wouldn't have been far from the truth.

----

8 SO OUR COINS CONTAIN NO METAL?

We often got strange answers from passengers when they walked through the archway metal detector and activated the alarm by having metal on their person.

A common reaction, when the archway gave its audible activation signal, was to swing around and look at it accusingly. Surprising when they know they're walking through a sophisticated detector that activates if they have metal on their person.

Often the passenger would go into defensive pose 'why did it go off' or into an aggressive pose 'who set that off?'

Many passengers seemed to believe the security officers at the archway had control over the activation of the system. Some thought we had a hidden switch that if we fancied, we pressed, and 'voila' the archway activated and the passenger had to be searched by us.

Do you think my colleagues and I enjoy having to place our hands all over somebody's body? Having to feel around their sweaty necks and under their sweaty armpits, down the front and back of their bodies, around the crutch area and down the legs for fun! Maybe that's why so many wore the supplied gloves in the security screening process. I didn't wear them because they inhibited me from being able to feel small hidden items on a passenger. A detonator for an explosive device is tiny and hard to detect. And the gloves themselves caused your hands to sweat, and I had an allergic reaction to the make-up of them.

Another reason I didn't wear gloves stems from my days working in the prison service when on one occasion a colleague and I were searching a prisoner's cell. He was wearing gloves; I wasn't. As he removed his gloved hand after he finished feeling along the table surface, I noticed he had some brown objects on the tip of his fingers. And as he went to scratch his face, I realised that the brown objects were human excrement. I was too late with my warning. I'd never wear them after that. I'm sure that had my prison colleague not been wearing gloves he'd have noticed what was on his fingers before scratching himself. Anyway, I digress.

Suffice to say, working the Archway was a demanding job. It was made difficult by passengers who either did not think or did not care, or even maybe got enjoyment from being searched by security officers. For whatever reason, many passengers walked through knowing they had metal objects on them but didn't care, or were too arrogant to believe the rules applied to them.

Here I was on yet another busy, hot day at T5 and it was my female colleague and my time for another stint on the WTMD 'Archway'.

"Sir, do you have metal in your pockets?" I asked as a smartly dressed middle-aged male passenger walked through and caused an activation alarm. He reacted in the usual manner by spinning around, not listening, but looking at the archway accusingly "Who did that?" he said.

"Sir, you've activated it as you came through the archway, may I search you?"

"I suppose so, but what set that thing off?" he said pointing at it.

"You did, sir."

"Yes, but how?"

"Do you have anything metal in your pockets, sir, anything sharp on you?

"No, the only sharp thing I have is my wit." (Oh, how many times did I hear that during my time at T5), and he continued "I emptied my pockets before coming through the machine, I put it all in one of those grey trays."

"And you have nothing else in your pockets, sir?"

"No." he said as he patted himself down checking his pockets.

"Ok, but I have to search you anyway as you've activated the archway."

"I didn't; you must have pressed your hidden button somehow."

"Sir, we don't possess a hidden button. Do you really think we do?"

"Well, you must have as I've not got anything that would activate a metal detector."

"Sir, I can assure you we don't, but I do legally have to search you as you activated, so may I search you, sir?"

"Well I suppose so, but I didn't set the damn thing off I can assure you." and he adopted the pose to allow me to start my search. As I started to search him, I said, "Maybe it was an act of God that it activated. But sir I believe you may have something in this right-hand trouser pocket." As I searched down his lower body.

"No," he said, and he placed his hand in his pocket and pulled out several coins, "these are just coins they don't have metal in them."

"Sir, coins contain metal, unless you know differently."

"As it happens I do know differently; you see I'm a metallurgist."

"A metal what?"

"A metallurgist. I study metal for a living and can assure you these coins contain none."

"Ok." I said as I put my hand out to take them. I then walked to the archway and held the coins underneath, and the machine gave its audible alarm for identifying metal. "There you go sir, these coins do contain metal and they are actually our UK coins so I know they contain metal."

"Are you questioning my skills as a metallurgist?"

"No sir, but these coins contain metal whether you like to admit it or not. And as they were in your pocket when you walked through the archway, the machine activated as it identified the metal."

"Well your machine is wrong, and so are you."

I'd had enough. I turned, asked my colleague for the hand-held detector and waved it over the coins. It gave out a high-pitched alarm. "There you go, even the device identified these coins contained metal. And as we've not yet changed our coins to plastic, please don't stand here arguing. Why would you come out with all that rubbish? Now I need to complete my search sir."

He continued to inform anybody who listened that the coins contained no metal and the equipment here was calibrated incorrectly. I'd switched off by now. But come on why would anybody argue with two metal detectors and also try to tell me that coins didn't contain metal. All because he'd either forgotten he had them in his pocket, or he thought he was more special than anybody else and the rules didn't apply to him, was beyond me.

On another occasion, a family of four, mum and dad, and two boys, one about eight the other around six, walked through the archway one after the other. And as the youngest boy walked through the alarm sounded. The boy looked petrified, so I tried to calm him down "It's ok." I said as I turned around to draw his parents' attention to us. I said to the father "Sir, I'm sorry but you son activated the detector and I have to search him. But as he is under age, I need either you or your wife to witness my search."

"Why do you need to search him?" asked the woman.

"As he walked through the archway, it activated, and I now have to search him."

"Why? He is only six, you know."

"I understand that, but the law makes no exceptions for searching irrespective of age I'm afraid, so I have to carry out the search."

"I'm not happy about this." said his father, as the boy got agitated.

"We can go into a private room if you prefer privacy, sir?" I offered.

"No that's ok, but we're just not happy about our little boy being searched."

"I can understand that sir." I said as I turned back to the boy and squatted down on my hunches to the boy's height and said to him "Can you pretend you're a statue and hold your hands out like this." showing him how I needed him to stand with his arm outstretched. He wouldn't do it and cried. His mum was saying in a cooing voice "Come on junior please do what the horrible security man wants you to do." Yup really helpful Mum thanks a million.

"Sir," I said to the father, "could you hold your son's arms out so I can get the search completed as soon as possible and get you on your way?" The boy was getting stressed by now and crying. I knew we would have problems getting the search completed.

"Do you know if he has any metal items in his pockets?"

"No." said the father.

"Maybe it's his lucky coin," said his Mum.

"Lucky coin, lucky coin. Is it metal, please tell me it's not metal madam?" I said.

"Of course, it is." said his Mum "Why do you think we have plastic coins?"

"Sir, madam, you were asked to remove all metal items from your persons before walking through the archway. Why did you leave the coin in your boy's pocket?"

"Because he will throw a tantrum if we take it off him." said Mum.

"But he is throwing a tantrum now, and we haven't even got the coin off him."

"Can't you leave it in his pocket?"

"No. Sorry, we have to put it through the x-ray machine now as it has activated at the archway. Could you please remove it from his pocket?"

Things were getting a little out of hand now as other passengers were getting agitated at the delay. I could hear passengers saying, "For Christ sake search the kid and get on with it." or "Are his parents that bloody inconsiderate." and "I've got a plane to catch."

"Madam, please remove the coin from your son's pocket and give it to my colleague. And sir, please hold your son steady so that I can search him." and all the while this boy was throwing a tantrum and screaming at the top of his voice.

I said to the boy "Junior, mummy will take your coin out of your pocket and put it through the special machine that will make it magic ok." He seemed to accept this, especially at the word magic. He allowed his mum to remove the coin, while his dad held his arms out. And I completed my search, explaining that I would get my magic wand and wave it over him as a present. Because he had activated after a search, we always had to use the hand-held metal detector and re-scan the passenger. And I thought working on the magic idea he would allow me to do this, which he did.

Search completed, and the coin restored to the boy. He'd calmed down and was behaving and almost enjoying himself. But good old Mum had to spoil it, as they walked away much to the relief of myself and the other passengers who'd been waiting patiently, by saying "Well I don't see what the fuss was about. It was only a small metal coin."

----

9 DO I LOOK LIKE A TERRORIST?

"Do I look like a terrorist?" How many times a day that was said to airport security officers, is anybody's guess. But at T5 it was a frequent question. Why? Why would anybody ask if they looked like a terrorist? For a start, if they did, would we say, "Oh yes, you do. Please wait there a minute while I alert the police and special branch of your appearance." Or "Yes you do. Do you have any devices on you, or can you show me your Kalashnikov?"

Strangely enough, it seemed to be predominantly Americans that would say "Do I look like a terrorist?" Why they so obsessed with being able to identify a terrorist just by looking at them is beyond me. It's not going to happen. Shame really, because it would make the anti-terrorist services job so easy. But it will not happen; therefore, our job at the airport is an important fight against the possibility of a terrorist attack at Heathrow.

In the USA Since 9/11, white right-wing terrorists killed almost twice as many Americans in home-grown attacks than radical Islamists, according to research by the New America Foundation. So, what does a terrorist look like?

We are not the only people trying to avert any attempts to terrorise at our public buildings. The police, special branch MI5 etc. all play their parts. But have you ever considered your part in the fight against terrorism?

You play an important part. Thanks to passengers being alert we have stopped potential incidents of not just terror but of a criminal kind too. On one occasion a passenger mentioned to a member of staff that the person in their queue was behaving strangely and the child with them did not seem to be right. It was investigated, and the passenger was abducting the child. It turned out to be an International child trafficking ring.

One passenger, that's all it took to smash a very sophisticated child trafficking ring, well done whoever you were.

What about that unattended bag you walked past and ignored? What was in it? Was it an innocent mistake by a fellow traveller? Or is it something more sinister? If you ignore it, how can security staff deal with it if we don't know it's there?

I was travelling through JFK airport in New York on holiday shortly after 9/11. I noticed a bag left by a supporting concrete pillar in the departure lounge. I called the nearest policeman of which there were plenty and said, 'I have seen this unattended bag left by that supporting pillar.' as I pointed to it.

"Yea bud don't worry 'bout it."

"Ok, but in the UK, we'd investigate that."

"Yea, we will too, but this is New York bud, who's gonna attack us?"

"Yes, you're correct who indeed?" and I walked away thinking to myself, well that explains why 9/11 happened, doesn't it. It goes to show how complacent we all are.

How about that passenger in your security queue? You know the one that looks nervous, that one who's sweating and keeps looking around furtively. What are they hiding or are they just very nervous flyers, who knows, certainly not us if we've not been alerted to the potential? And yes, most of the time there's a good explanation. But what if it was that one time it was not innocent and you didn't inform the authorities, how would you feel?

Israel has one of the most sophisticated security screening systems in the world. Their airline screening system relies on behavioural observation by trained agents. Many countries now use trained profilers to observe passenger's behaviour to spot a problem before it happens. How effective it is remains an unknown factor, but anything that can help is worth trying. We at Heathrow have trained profilers working as security staff too.

This brings me back to the original question. 'Do I look like a terrorist?' A later chapter mentions a well-known celebrity who said that very thing to me during a search of his bag. You'd think he would have known better, but alas no.

I've been asked that question, from smart business travellers going through the Fast track system to passengers who looked like they'd been pulled through a hedge backwards after several flight delays and bad turbulence during an International flight to connect to yet another flight. They all asked that question.

There's no perfect profile of a terrorist. It's one of the main findings in the growing body of literature around terrorism. Terrorists and those who are radicalised towards extremist ideologies come in all shapes and sizes. One of the key features that distinguish terrorists from mass murderers is they are motivated more by ideology than by personal motivations. This line is becoming harder to draw. Two cases to afflict Europe were the massacres in Nice and more recently in Munich. They highlighted this difficulty with both cases appearing to have elements of both within them. How about Anders Behring Breivik who around five years ago murdered 77 people in Oslo, in anger at the government's immigration policies rather than committing the crimes for any terrorist organisation? We have become fixated with terrorists being from the Middle East and in particular from a Muslim dominated background.

In August 2014, a young man, Brutschom Ziamani who'd fallen into the orbit of violent extremists after he'd been thrown out of his family home, was arrested on his way to carry out an attack emulating the Woolwich murder of a soldier. In January 2015, Zack Davies hacked at a South Asian man he saw in Tesco's shouting "white power". He stated he was undertaking the attack in revenge for Lee Rigby (who was murdered while in his army uniform just outside Woolwich barracks). Later investigation showed he was an isolated and paranoid young man, obsessed with the far Right. He'd drawn inspiration from the Jihadi John videos. (Courtesy of the Telegraph Newspaper).

I give this information to add perspective to the world in which we now live; I lived in London through the days of the IRA bombings. That was terrorism too but under a different guise and a different cause. The world has always been subjected to terrorism in its many guises. I remember during the IRA bombing campaign we unfairly looked upon Irish people as potential terrorists.

And so today with the knowledge of terrorism and terrorist attacks immediately relayed to us from news programs, are we looking at Muslim people and anybody wearing a Burka and saying they are all potential terrorist? I hope not; it would be a sad world if that were the case.

Here's another example of what we are up against: Daallo Airlines Flight 159 was an international passenger flight operated by Somali-owned Daallo Airlines. On 2 February 2016, an explosion happened on-board the plane, 20 minutes after it took off from Mogadishu. The plane returned to the airport, with one fatality (the bomber) reported. A subsequent investigation showed that the explosion was caused by a bomb, detonated in a suicide attack. Islamist militant group, Al-Shabaab, claimed responsibility for the bombing. The flight had been delayed before departure. At the time of the explosion, the aircraft was not yet at cruising altitude, and the cabin was not yet fully pressurized. It was thought that a laptop had been rigged with a timer device to explode the bomb mid-flight.

To put a perspective on it, you're more likely to die from brain-eating parasites, alcoholism, obesity, medical errors, risky sexual behaviour or just about anything other than terrorism.

But maybe you could help yourselves, check the latest security rules at your airport, and instead of leaving stuff in your personal effects that might cause a security issue at the airport, why not just be more careful and considerate? Comply with all the rules and regulations that are there to enhance your safety, and not make your journey intolerable, and then it might be easier for the authorities to see what a terrorist looks like. When asked to remove your laptop and electrical devices, do it instead of thinking it's only a laptop, or games console, or tablet, you might know that, but we don't. So they will be seen by the screen reader, and your hand luggage will be searched, delaying you and delaying other passengers. Please, just think security when you're at security.

Here I am searching a passenger bag; I know that despite being asked to remove her laptop from her hand baggage she did not comply and therefore the item must be scanned separately, and the passenger's bag has to be fully searched, "Madam is this bag yours?"

"Yes."

"May I search your bag?"

"Yes, why?"

"You seem to have an unauthorised item in your bag madam."

"I don't think so."

"Well, let's take a quick look and see what my screen reader saw shall we?"

"Yes, but there's nothing in there."

"Of course not."

"After all, do I look like a terrorist?"

Now I'm going to have to search a passenger on the International transfer lanes after they have walked through the Archway and activated. "Sir, may I search you?" He had been on a long haul transatlantic flight; he looked dishevelled and stank of curry, so probably been on a flight from India or somewhere in that area.

"What happened?"

"Well you activated the metal detector as you walked through the archway, so I have to search you."

"For fuck sake again, I've been searched in the US I've been searched in Islamabad and now here."

"Sorry about that sir, have you had a bad flight?"

"Bad flight, fucking bad flight. Delayed in the US delayed in India and now more fucking security. I'm sorry, but I've had enough today and just want to get home."

"Where are you off too now then?"

"Leeds, I live in Hunslett."

Do I know where that is, well apart from somewhere in Yorkshire I've no idea where it is?

"Oh well sir, at least this is the last leg of your journey, and you're going to get a free massage. Sorry, it's me and not my female colleague who's going to search you."

"Yea, but why all this security, after all, do I look like a fucking terrorist?"

And here we go again!

----

10 BUT IT'S ONLY WATER FOR THE BABY

It was a late Saturday evening, and my team and I were working the South concourse. I was spare in the team when I noticed that the bag searcher was having a tough time with one passenger. A little smartly dressed, dapper man, who was wearing a 'Kippah' (Jewish skull cap). I approached my colleague and asked if she was ok and she said, "Well I'm concerned because this man is telling me that the water is kosher water for his baby, and I have never come across this before, so was going to call an STL."

"Don't call an STL they won't know. But as I am Jewish do you want me to chat to the passenger and see if I can sort it out?"

"Oh please, that'll be great."

"Ok, is the bottle of water over sized?"

"Yes, it's a 300ml bottle, but with no label on it."

"Well it's oversized anyway, and as far as I know if it is kosher, there should be a label on it saying that. But as we don't know what the liquid is, we will take it off him and test it, anyway. Let's see if we can work something out with the passenger. I've never heard of kosher water." I said as I quickly and surreptitiously checked my mobile phone for information via Google, oh what would we do without Google?

"What's kosher mean?"

"It's any food sold, cooked, or eaten, satisfying the requirements of Jewish law. With meat, it's the way it's slaughtered, similar to the Muslims Halal meat. Basically, it has to be blessed by the chief rabbi."

I approached the passenger "Sir, can I help?" I asked.

"Yes." he said "Your assistant (He apparently believed I was a supervisor, so I didn't bother to correct him) knows nothing about Jewish law. This water is kosher water, and it's the only water my baby can drink. So, we need to take it with us."

"Where are you flying to today, sir?"

"We're going back to Israel after visiting family in New York. We stopped off in London for a few days first."

"Very nice sir, hope you've had a good time. Unfortunately, the container holding the liquid is over the allowable size sir, so either way, you cannot take its contents with you. We will have to test the liquid to find out what it is."

"It's water, can't you see that?"

"Sir, it looks like water, but so do many other clear liquids, Gin, Vodka, Sulphuric acid. We have to check its contents."

"Do I look like I would give Gin to my baby?"

"No sir, but as nobody has seen you give anything to your baby, we have to establish what the contents of the bottle are. It's normal routine, and if you regularly fly from Israel, you will know how tough security has to be."

"Believe me your security isn't a patch on Jerusalem, but compared to the USA it's ten times better. But yes, if you need to test it, test it and let me have it back for my baby."

"Ok, sir. I said and took the bottle of water to the testing machine. My colleague came up and said, 'Thanks Tony, he was kicking up a fuss."

"Well he still will when I tell him he cannot have the contents of the bottle. But I'll empty it out, and he can keep the empty bottle and fill it up with tap water if he wants. There's no such thing as Kosher water. Only the bottle can come under that title hence let him keep the empty bottle.

"How did you know, you don't follow the Jewish religion do you?"

"Naw, I looked it up on Google, but I'll handle the passenger and tell him what I told you."

I completed the test on the liquid which was just plain water (you'd be surprised how many times water turned out to be Vodka or Gin when tested, the almighty does indeed move in mysterious ways). I walked back to the passenger with the bottle of water, and said, "Sir the liquid is water, but you still cannot take it with you as it's over the regulation 100ml and the container is 300ml, I am sorry, but that is the rules."

"This is incredible. You are trying to deny my family and me our religious rights. It's not acceptable, and I want to speak to a manager. That water is for my baby, and it is kosher do you know what that means? Probably not, have you ever seen anything kosher?"

"Strangely enough sir I happen to be Jewish too, my surname is 'Levy' very Jewish, and I can tell you there's no such thing as kosher water, all water is kosher for drinking purposes."

"That is not the case in Israel."

"Well, we are not in Israel, sir. We're in London, and we follow the Rabbinic rules of our chief rabbi. The reason bottled water may carry a "hechsher" (Kashrut Rabbinic Supervision) relates to the bottle itself, the plant (including machinery), and workers not bringing in other foods into the food processing areas. However, one may drink bottled water internationally without such a "hechsher", as the Halachic concerns here are negligible." I said.

"So the bottle would need to be kosher but not the water. However, I'm willing to empty the bottle of water, and you can take the bottle with you and fill it up at the nearest drinking fountain."

He was dumbfounded. I don't believe he expected to receive such a comprehensive answer. Often passengers think they are dealing with dumb idiots (Security staff) who at the mere mention of religious rules will quake with fear. And not understanding will let them (the passenger) get away with whatever they want. It's a very similar attitude to those with money and status; they believe this gives them the right to run roughshod over everybody else. Strange phenomenon don't you think?

"Sir, would you like me to empty the bottle of its contents? There's a rest room with a drinking fountain just outside of it and you can fill your bottle up there knowing the contents are safe for you baby."

"I'm not happy but don't have a choice, do I?"

"No, sir you don't, but I'm not sure what you're not happy about, I've explained the Rabbinic law to you, so don't understand your dissatisfaction. Do you still want to call a manager, who will tell you the same thing as I've just done? He will refer to me as he knows I'm Jewish and will know what I've told you is correct."

"No! You think you're clever, don't you?"

"Sir, at this moment I've proven I am cleverer than you. I know my religion, which maybe you don't. In future when travelling through Heathrow, please don't try to deceive security staff in this manner as it could result in you being banned from flying. Your action could be deemed a security threat." I secretly thanked Google at this point.

I emptied the bottle of its contents and returned it to the passenger. "Sir, I should point out, as this bottle has no label, are you sure it's kosher?" and I handed it back.

"Would you like me to repack your bag, sir?"

"No." he said as he snatched the bottle out of my hand.

It was good to see another satisfied passenger completing the security screening process and be safely on his way with his family back to his home in Israel.

My colleague came up and said "Thanks, Tony. I don't know how you kept so calm and polite with him."

"It's part of the job when you know you have right on your side. These people try it on because they think we're ignorant, and if they make a fuss or shout about it, we will just let them get what they want. So, it's easy to stay calm dealing with people like that, and it's them that look stupid."

We had many similar incidents almost every day, but this was one occasion that remained in my memory.

----

11 THE YOGHURTS FOR THE BABY

I was bag searching when a tray full of baby foods was rejected for testing. I asked the screen readers "Are these for testing?"

"No mate, they're oversized but have to be tested before being disposed of. You'll have to tell the family, and they seem agitated, so over to you and your diplomacy mate."

I'd already concluded that the parents of the baby had encountered a stressful journey through security so far. The father, with the residue of what looked like baby sick on his left shoulder, seemed fed up with the whole travelling procedure. He appeared to be itching for an argument with authority. Guess what! Yup, that was going to be me. Here we go again, I thought to myself.

"What's the problem now?" he asked.

"Sir, I have to test the yoghurts as per the laid down security requirements."

"Well, who laid down your security requirements? I want to see them now. In fact, I demand to see them now!" he almost shouted this into my face.

Yes, here we were again I thought, yet another stressed passenger who would take it out on me. It was proving to be a bad day, every time I was at the search position I encountered yet another irate passenger. What's going on today I thought, is it a full moon or something?

Just before my first break, we were working on my favourite lane 15, when a large woman wearing a 'Chanel' twin set and fashionable Jimmy Choo shoes, and bedecked out in lots of jewellery had been in a heated discussion with the loader about taking off her jewellery. She then had to be searched by a female at the archway for not taking off all her jewels. She'd been told that she would set off the metal detector and then have to be searched. Which later she did. The search had not gone well. The female working the archway was tiny and the passenger large. My poor colleague had a difficult time searching this passenger due to her bulk. And lucky me, her bag had to be searched, and I was the one that would be subject to all her frustration and her anger.

"You," she said, and pointed a well-manicured finger at me "you, why are you searching my bag?"

"Well madam, it appears you may have left an unauthorised item in your bag. So may I search your bag?"

"No, I refuse."

"That's your right madam. I have to point out that refusal could lead to you being refused to fly with us today."

"I'm not taking any more nonsense from you people, you idiot! Who's going to stop me from flying?"

"Me, madam, if you're refusing to allow your bag to be searched. Would you like me to search it in a private room?"

"No, you will not put your grubby little hands into my bag."

"Madam, if your bag needs to be searched then it will be. There's no use in arguing. I will call a supervisor to advise you of your legal rights, ok?"

"You can call who you like I am not having my bag searched by you, you idiot!"

"Madam, there's no need to insult me."

"Insult you, insult you! I haven't started yet. What is it with you people? Do you all have difficulties comprehending basic English? Although by the look of some of you that's probably the case. I had an argument with that moron over there." she said pointing towards the loader. "Then that stupid girl on the archway thingy searched me so thoroughly that she must have been getting some sexual pleasure out of it. It was disgusting to be touched in such a manner and by her! She's not even English, and now you! No! I'm not having it!

"Ok! Madam, nor am I having it, I shall call a supervisor." and with that, I asked a colleague to get an STL for me. I stood there with the passenger who was re attaching all her jewellery to herself. Bloody hell, she had enough of it. Rings on almost every finger, bracelets adorned both arms, and an expensive-looking wristwatch and pendant. She was either rich or loved to wear cheap imitation tack.

"What seems to be the problem madam?" asked the STL as he arrived at the search desk; it was one of the 'good' ones, an ex-Police Inspector, who I got on well with.

"I will not have this thing searching me." Pointing at me, thing! Thing! Who the hell does she think she is? Does she think her shit doesn't smell because believe me her attitude did so I am sure her shit would too?

"Madam, your bag will have to be searched by my officer if you wish to fly today."

"The attitude of your staff leaves a lot to be desired, that one there!" she pointed again toward the loader "That one was downright rude, telling me to take my jewellery off and my shoes and stuff. And that little thing, that Indian child, got some kind of sexual pleasure from putting her grubby hands all over my body. Does she get off on it, or does she like to touch expensive clothes that are way beyond her wildest dreams?"

Who the hell this woman thought she was, was beyond me.

"Madam if you have any complaint about the quality of your search I will instruct our managers to review the cameras. All security areas are covered by cameras, and we can review my officers conduct of her search."

Nice one, we've got an STL that won't stand for any nonsense, fantastic I thought.

"And I have to say, madam, I find your tone and attitude to my staff insulting and bordering on racist."

"Oh, that's it," she said "throw the racist card at me because I complained. All you people are the same."

"It's not your complaining madam, even though I believe it is unjustified, it's the tone of your language and your use of the English vocabulary. Please resist from making those sorts of ethnical references. My staff are trained security officers that have attained the highest level of competence. Now if you're not satisfied you are within your rights to make a formal complaint. But your bag will still be searched. Unless you would like me to escort you out of the airport, as you'll not by flying today because of your refusal to comply with the safety regulations set down by the Department for Transport. It's your choice, madam."

"It appears that I have no choice, but you people are all the same petty little Hitler's who think we are all criminal or something. And you can treat us with disrespect." "Madam, I can assure you we are not all the same. But your behaviour is bordering on unacceptable. Now are you going to allow my officer to conduct his search or are you refusing? It's your choice, madam."

"Well, I suppose I'll have to allow it (she pointed at me) to search my bag. Otherwise, you'll not allow me to fly. So, yes ok."

"Officer Levy." He said, "Are you ok with conducting this search, after the reference to Hitler from the passenger?"

"Even though I'm Jewish and my father fought for this country against Hitler during the war, I don't hold grudges. So, I will carry out my duties. I am, after all, a consummate professional despite any provocation and insults directed at me." At this point, the women went a shade darker than purple. I'm not sure if she was getting angry or just embarrassed, as we now had a large audience of other passengers waiting for their bags to be searched.

The STL stood there as I conducted my search "Madam is this bag yours?"

"You know it is. But before you search, I want you to wear gloves; I don't want your grubby hands touching the personal effects in my bag."

"Well, madam, the problem is I'm allergic to the coating on the inside of the gloves."

"Well, I insist on you wearing the gloves."

"You know what, madam?" I said, as I reached into the box and took out a pair of the latex gloves "You're quite right. Why would I want to spoil my clean, germ-free fingers to go into your bag and rummage around your dirty germ ridden underwear, and makeup, and catch something from them? So, despite the potential of getting irritation on my hands due to wearing the gloves, I will follow your helpful advice and wear them."

And with that, I continued to search her bag and found a bottle of water. Without the usual courtesy, I held up the offending item for all to see. "You seem to have left a bottle of ordinary water in your bag. You can't take that with you. I'll have to test it and then discard it." I said which I did. On completion of my search, I said, "Madam, would you like me to repack your bag? Or in your case, I can understand that you would prefer to touch your grubby collection of personal effect. I'll leave you to repack it. And I can continue to search the passengers that have patiently waited for you to complete your temper tantrum, in awe of your wonderful personality. Thank you and have a lovely day."

I continued with my job of searching the next passenger bag. Great start to the day, thankfully the team and I were sent on a break shortly after this incident.

But here I was faced with a similar irate passenger. So I said, "Well sir, as it's the Department of Transport (DFT) who's responsible for the security of UK airports, and their policies are implemented at each airport by airport security staff, I'd suggest you contact them to register your complaint. After all, airports, airlines and travel companies do not set these rules.

As it turned out, the yoghurts were ok. They just had to be tested for security reasons. So why this passenger was aggressive for no reason was beyond my understanding. It goes to show what the stress of modern day travel can do to normal human beings.

Had the passenger read the information available, not just at the airport but on the individual airlines travel documents, he'd have known the yoghurts were ok, but just had to be tested. There had been no need for his tantrum or looking for an argument due to his stress of his travel arrangements.

Strangely enough, to get to the start of the security lanes from entering the terminal public areas, there were sixteen different signs, and notice's informing passengers of what they could and couldn't bring through the security screening process. I know because one day I was bored and counted them just to see how many notices there was with this information. Oh well!

----

12 SATURDAY NIGHT SHUTDOWN

"Get an STL." I demanded to a colleague, as I stopped running the screen reading equipment. It was the standard signal that the screen reader has seen something on the screen they were not happy with and wanted to escalate their findings.

It was Saturday evening and a busy time for the airport, so stopping the machine unless absolutely necessary was frowned upon. But after using the equipment's enhancements, I still felt what I'd seen on my screen needed escalating. I was convinced there was a security risk involved.

My loader informed the 'Clio' about our situation so that other passengers could be diverted to other security lanes and try to avoid as much disruption to the passenger flow as possible. Obviously, there'd be passengers in my security lane who couldn't move to another machine as their belongings were already on the security machines conveyor belt. They had to wait, this leads to tension between them and the staff on the security lane, but it couldn't be avoided.

"Ok what do you see on your screen?" asked the STL on his arrival.

"There's a bottle that could contain liquid, and using my enhancements, you can see wires running down both sides of the bottle. There's a battery inside a mobile phone at the bottom of the bottle, and the wires end there. And on the top, it looks like a wrist watch, which could be a timing device. Also, I don't like the way coins have been placed neatly surrounding the whole package." as I showed him on the screen.

"Bloody Hell! This looks serious."

"That's why I stopped the machine and called you."

Of course, by this time my colleagues know what's going on as they also looked at the screen offering advice. But at the end of the day, as the screen reader, it's my call.

"I think you could be right." he said "I'm gonna escalate it." at that point another STL came along and looked at my screen and said "Naw, nothing wrong here. It's just a bottle of water, pull the bag, and we'll have it searched."

"Sorry, I disagree! Yes, it's a bottle, and it probably is water, but the way it's placed in the bag is suspicious. If you look at the passenger, why is he standing there so casually on his mobile phone? And he's wearing a wristwatch. Why does he have both items in his bag arranged in this manner? No, sorry, I'm not happy I want it escalated."

"Be it on your head, but in my opinion, you're wrong." and with that, he walked off from the machine and disappeared.

"Ok." says the first STL "I have escalated it and the TDM's (Terminal Duty Manager) on his way."

He approached the passenger asking him questions I couldn't hear. Usually, the passenger would be asked if he could inform us what items he had in his bag, or where he was going, and other basic questions. He'd never be asked such a direct question as what was in his bag. And they'd certainly never be asked, "Do you have a mobile phone in your bag?"

"Right, well the passenger is from Leicester, and he's travelling to Saudi Arabia. He doesn't recall leaving any unauthorised items in his bag, so I have my suspicions too. This is a good call Tony, well done."

The security lane is evacuated, and so are several of the nearest security lanes. Leaving me sitting at the x-ray machine with the STL, and the passenger still apparently on his mobile phone.

"I've had several looks at this bag again." I said, "I don't think it's a real device as I cannot find any sort of 'det' (Detonator). I think it's a 'dry run' attempt."

"You could be right but still a good call."

The TDM arrived and said, "Ok what you got?" The Terminal Duty

Manager (TDM) was responsible for 50,000 customers, 600 security officers and 30 front-line managers a day. And that was just the T5 TDM. Each terminal had its own team of TDM's, so his arrival at an incident meant it was being treated seriously.

I explained it again, and this time I reiterated what I thought it was. He said, "You could well be right, but I'll escalate it upwards to the police. I'll also take a photo of your screen for training purposes, because, if it isn't a real device it's a bloody good tester. Well done, Tony."

Wow praise indeed, and he knew my name, I was surprised. "Anyway, I'll be over there chatting to the passenger." he said.

As it was my call, I had to stay at the screen. My colleagues and several other security lanes had been evacuated and closed down, with passengers dispersed to other security lanes. The STL and I sat together, occasionally looking at the x-ray screen. I casually said to the him "If it is a real device, how much protection does this equipment give me from getting injured? I read that it's lead-lined and all that but how secure is it for retaining an explosion?"

"Well Tony I'm not sure, but you're on your own." He said and got up and walked away from the machine. Charming, oh well I've had a good life; I hope they tell my wife what a hero I was until the end I thought.

The armed police arrived with a 'sniffer dog', "Ok mate, what you got on your screen?"

I explained what I saw and what I thought the image was.

"Yes," he said "looks bloody dodgy to me, given the passengers travel history from Leicester going to Saudi. He fits the profile, has a mobile phone on him, and then one in his bag, and he's wearing a watch with another in the bag. Pretty suspicious to us, good call mate."

"Thanks, but I hope I haven't wasted everybody's time."

"Don't talk daft; I'd prefer this to be called rather than ignored if it's a dry run who knows what might happen next time."

"Thanks."

"No, thank you for being brave to call it. Do me a favour, let it out of the tunnel and I'll let the dog have a sniff. Then we'll search it along with the passenger."

I allowed the x-ray machine belt to start. The passenger's bag came out of the x-ray tunnel to be taken by the dog handler and placed on the floor for the dog to examine. He found nothing, and then the passengers' bag was also searched. It contained a bottle of water, which he could not have as it was oversized, a mobile phone, a wristwatch, several lengths of wire cable for a laptop, a mobile charger, coins and various bit of paper. The strangest thing of all was when we returned the bag to the passenger he said to the STL "Well how could I avoid having my bag searched next time, even if I have left stuff in it?"

"Easy," said the STL "don't mix organic items with non-organic items."

"Oh okay." said the passenger.

I said to the dog handler, "Did you hear that? How many other passengers would react that way? If somebody said don't mix organic items with non-organic, I'd say what the hell is that then? Not just accept that. This was definitely a dry run attempt."

"I think you're right." said the policeman and added, "Special branch are now questioning the chap, so they're on to it."

"Great, but bloody hell my arse was twitching when I saw the screen and called my STL."

"Yup understandable, I don't know how you guys do what you do, I couldn't."

"Ha that works both ways. Well, thanks for your help."

With that, he walked off the machine, and I went back to the RA's office to find out that my team had been sent on a break. And as I was sitting at the machine all that time all I had left of my break was what the rest of my team had, in this case about ten minutes. This was yet another example of staff care and stress counselling for staff, post incident.

I went to the team's usual rest room to be greeted with "Oh here come the bloke that closed down T5 on a busy Saturday night so that he could watch the football highlights." and "Well done hero, got the concourse shut down because of a bottle of water and a mobile phone. And we got a nice long break, thanks, Tony."

There's no postscript to this incident. We never received feedback or any de-brief, unlike the prison service. Here it was, just get back to work and keep those security lanes running. Oh well, that's what I signed up for.

----

13 SO YOU'RE ONLY GOING TO

NEWCASTLE?

I was working overtime before my actual shift. I started at 0530 doing seven hours until 1230, with my actual shift starting at 1230 until 2100. The good thing about doing overtime shifts was that you got at least one break and then was given at least half an hour between you ending the overtime shift and starting your actual one. Working a seven-hour shift meant you only worked 6 hours, and we had 'Spanish' practices in the prison service that the government got rid of. Hey, outside industry doesn't know how easy they've got it.

I'd been detailed to work a position called 'Clio'. It entailed around four officers placed strategically in front of the queues of passengers waiting to get to the 'loading' position. They then take a tray and put their personal effects, any metal objects, laptops etc. on it, along with their hand luggage being placed on the conveyor belt before walking through the Archway metal detector.

We had eighteen security lanes. I was patrolling between lanes 1 and 6. Lanes 1 and 2 were for 'Fast-Track' passengers who were usually either business passengers or just passengers that paid the extra to get the 'Fast-Track'. Fast-track made no difference to the 'queue time' agreement between Heathrow, British Airways and the DFT. This agreement meant we had to process passengers within a time scale. If we failed, we paid huge fines to BA. This seemed perverse given that most of our delays were caused by the amount of hand luggage passengers could take with them, contrary to BA's own rules. However, it was BA staff that allowed these passengers to take so much, large hand luggage containers on board their aircraft, and not us.

Around lanes 18 back to lanes 5 or 6, depending on the volume of passengers at the time, were the International Transfer passengers. These were in transit; they had flown into the UK to take their flight with BA to their next destination. It made Heathrow the unique busy place it was.

'Transfer' passenger numbers were increasing at a level never predicted and beyond what was controllable, given the current configuration of the terminal.

So the number of available lanes for transfer passengers was controlled centrally, by our terminal controllers. They monitor the passenger flow from their control room by viewing cameras available throughout the terminal. They'd radio us 'Clio's' and instruct us how many lanes we were to use for transfer passengers and how many for everybody else. This could lead and frequently did, to conflict.

Our job was to make sure we got the passengers into the shortest queues to avoid falling foul of the timescale of the queue time agreement.

I was directing fast-track passengers into other queues as at this time of the morning (our busiest) the fast track lanes become slower than the usual lanes. This is partly due to the number of business travellers who used the airport for early flights to their destinations to other European cities in time for short business meetings. This smart, attractive young woman came along the fast track lane, and I lifted the tension barrier and said, "Jump in Lane four, it's quicker than fast-track at the moment."

She looked at me with sheer disdain, like I was a piece of shit needing to be wiped off her elegant designer shoes and said, "I'm fucking fast-track and will go in the fast-track lane ok?"

"Sure! I was only trying to get you into a quicker queue but if your fast track status is more important than getting through quicker, be my guest." and I stepped aside to let her through to the two fast track lanes behind me. All thought of her being attractive had vanished. It's amazing how one minute you can look at a beautiful woman and the next, through their mouths they lose all their attractiveness.

A few minutes later the same passenger came back along the fast-track lanes and said, "I'm going in that lane." pointing to a lane for transfer passengers.

I said, "I'm sorry madam, those lanes are for transfer passengers and it might seem a shorter queue, but due to the type of traveller it could be longer. We're not allowed to let non-transfer passengers into those lanes. Hence I showed you the shortest queue."

"Well, fuck that." she said, "I'm going to Newcastle and am running late so let me into that queue NOW!"

"Sorry madam, I can't. But I'll put you in the shortest queue possible. What time's your flight?"

"It's at 0730, and I need to get through now." she shouted.

"Ok but it's only 0545, and as it's a domestic flight, you have plenty of time. They won't be boarding that flight for at least another hour, so you have plenty of time." I said.

"I'm fast-track." she shouted, spelling out the words "F A S T Fucking Track and paid not to queue up" This was strange behaviour as there were several signs showing arrows to fast track, so I'm certain I knew how to spell the word fast.

I had left my home at 0430 this morning and got up at 0345 to make sure I was at work on time. Only to be abused by a self-important, stuck up business woman who probably didn't even pay for her ticket as most likely her company had. Hence her being a fast track passenger. And she has the audacity to shout at me after I tried to get her through quicker than she now deserved, with loads of time before her flight anyway. What a jumped up self-important bitch she was, but she is a passenger, and we must be polite to them at all times.

"Madam, I'm doing the best I can." I said.

"Well, it's not good enough, is it? Why are the fast-track queues so long, anyway?"

"It's because so many passengers are business people at this time of day. They all seem to be allowed to purchase fast track tickets, you need to take this up with British Airways as it's their ticketing system. We only deal with the consequences. Now lane 3 is a shorter queue than 1, 2 and 4 so go in there, please." I explained.

"Are you deaf?" she shouted. To be honest, at that time of morning it's very noisy, and sometimes I wished I was deaf. Unfortunately, I wasn't and could hear her shouting at me and swearing easily.

"I am F A S T track, and need to get to the front of the queue N O W!" she shouted spelling out 'fast' and 'now'.

Really weird, as I'm certain that if I knew how to spell the word 'fast', I certainly I knew how to spell 'now'. But never mind.

"Madam, again I'm trying to help you. You refuse my help, so just get in any lane you think is up to your special needs. Except you're not going into the transfer lanes ok." I said, then added, "Maybe if you think you're running late you should have got up a bit earlier, don't you think?"

Unbelievably, she went purple and said "I got up early, but there was a lot of traffic on the M25. And who do you think you're talking to? You fucking bastard you're just staff!"

"Madam," I said "do you know I got up at 0345 to get on the M25 by 0430, so I could be here at work for my start time of 0530 so that you can come here and abuse me? Do you think that's fair? I think you're out of order and unless you get in a queue now, I will call the police and have you evicted from this airport. That's who I am. Now, who do you think you are? Oh, and I can assure you I'm not a bastard, my Mum and Dad were definitely married. I suggest you check your facts before throwing insults around. Have you never heard of slander laws?"

I then turned and walked away from her before I lost my temper. I watched her get into the queue for fast track and go through the system, only to have her bag rejected for a search. I found out later she had left loads of makeup and liquids in her bag that had to be voluntarily discarded. Her rush was to meet her boss and her colleagues in a bar to socialise and kiss arse with him. Talk about full of your own self-importance.

Overall, I found dealing with business travellers to be the best. Many of my colleagues would disagree, but because the vast majority of them were frequent flyers. They knew the system. And although many of them were full of their own self-importance, at least we didn't have to keep telling them what to take out of their bags and pockets. And most, although exacerbated every time they had to be searched, accepted that we were only doing a job.

I found I always obtained a good rapport with the business travellers and I got more official praise from this category than anybody else. I must have been doing something right.

I developed a good professional working friendship with one of our frequent flyer passengers. A very distinguished gentleman who knew me by my first name, and used to say 'hello' whenever our paths crossed within the departure zone. However often he travelled through the airport on his journey to Scandinavia, he went out of his way to do so. He never complained about any aspect of the security screening process, no matter how often he was searched or had his hand luggage searched. Except, he like many other passengers, did not like having to be vetted in the 'body scanners'. He was a pleasure to be associated with. I'd like this opportunity to thank him for his politeness whenever we met. He often (without realising it) helped to restore my faith in his fellow travellers.

On one occasion, I was walking through the baggage hall, and this passenger approached me.

"Hello Tony, haven't seen you for a while."

"Oh, hello sir, no we've changed the way we are deployed. I'm not always around the south concourse like before."

"No, more's the pity. I don't like the attitude of some of the staff that work there now."

"No comment but I won't disagree."

"Well, good to see you my boy, hope to see you again."

With that, he went back to talking to a senior BA manager about his missing bags. It goes to show how wide the spectrum of human behaviour at the airport could be.

14 MARMATE GEORGE

"Whose bag is this?" I asked while I stood at the back of the security screening machine. I awaited a response from a passenger whose bag had been rejected by the screen reader. It contained an item identified as being not allowed through the security area. And so, I started the laid down process we had to follow when searching passengers' personal property at the airport security area.

"Is this anybody's bag?" I repeated, and a mousy blonde woman replied "Mine."

"Okay," I said, "When you've collected your belongings, please come around to the front of the desk (I pointed to where she needed to be) I have to carry out a security search of your bag." She was a sassy looking woman and looked to be used to men glancing in her direction. She had a sexy body and beautiful legs.

"Sure," she replied in an American accent, "just need my boots. Where the hell are my boots?"

"They'll come along the rollers any second so don't worry. When you have everything, come around here." I said, again pointing to the place I required her to be to carry out the search.

She walked to the required position and stood bootless in front of me "My boots haven't come out of your machine." she said.

"Are these your boots?" I asked. My colleague handed a grey tray containing a pair of long black boots to my passenger.
"You need these first, after all, you don't want to walk around the airport without them." I said in an attempt to be humorous.

"I was once left with one shoe after searching a passenger's bag. How anybody can forget their shoe and walk around the airport without it, is beyond me."

"Maybe he only had one leg."

"Naw, I'm sure when I searched his bag he had both legs and feet, but hey you never know."

Passengers can become tense, nervous, angry, resentful and downright rude when their property is rejected for a security search. I always tried to inject humour and personality into the situation to reduce any frictions between the passenger and myself to develop a rapport between us. I know I would be pissed off if all my personal effects were going to be searched by some uniformed job's worth. But, after all, it was our duty to ensure the safety of passengers while on their journey through the airport and beyond. We had to ensure that no unauthorised items got into the secure areas of the airport, for the safety of everybody. It was always a surprise how rude and objectionable some passengers could be during this process. It's a necessary part of modern day air travel to enable passengers to arrive safely at their destinations. This passenger fell into the downright rude group, so any humour went over her head. Maybe she was a nervous traveller or just full of her own self-importance, or maybe she was under pressure from her celebrity boss, as I subsequently found out.

She located her boots and put them on, gathered the rest of her personal effects and came around to the front of the machine, where I was waiting with her hand luggage to search it. She was a nice-looking woman, with an attractive body and I thought, "Well, at least she will be nice to look at and chat to." I asked, "Is this bag yours?" An obvious question but part of the procedure.

"Yes," she replied "I can't think what I left in there that is wrong."

"Well, never mind we'll just have to have a look. May I search your bag, please?"

"Wow, you're so polite here, not like at Gatwick, but sure go ahead." she replied.

"Do you have any sharp objects inside your bag? Anything I could catch my fingers on or cut myself with when I search it?" I always try to add a more personal explanation, again to ease any tension and prove that we are human.

"No, I might have a fingernail file in there, but that's about it, although I packed in a hurry today." she answered.

"Ok not a problem, if I could just ask you to open your bag for me, please?" I said.

She unzipped her bag along with the extra pockets that are part of modern day hand luggage bags. I then carried out my search in the correct laid down method; I talk to my passengers to keep things on a calm level and to gain a rapport with them. It works in 90% of travellers, and it's a nice way to carry out a thankless task. After all, who wants their personal effects being touched, taken out of their bags, and placed in a tray for all to see?

We are taught to be discreet with people's clothing. If it's underwear, then try to place something over the top, so when you remove the items, they're not shown to the waiting public. Also, we try to be very discreet with the more personal property that passengers for whatever reason place in their hand luggage. You'd be surprised what some of you put in your bags!

You have to remember that at Heathrow's busy terminals, it might seem to the untrained eye that at the search areas its utter chaos, (sometimes to us, as members of staff, it seems that way too), yet there's some order. Other passengers will be waiting to have their property searched. This area can be bustling and crowded at times.

Our Japanese and Chinese visitors think that when one of their party has to have a bag searched, they can all crowd around the search table, chat incessantly, and try to take pictures. It's illegal to do so while around the security search areas for obvious reasons. But hey, tourists with cameras know no boundaries. You have to be firm and ask them to move away and allow the owner of the bag to be present at the table only.

But anyway, I digress, as I removed the items in her bag, I continued to make conversation "Are you flying anywhere nice today?" I asked.

"Naw, only over to Germany. Got to meet up with the rest of the crew, you know?" she replied.

"Oh interesting, are you aircrew or ground crew?" I asked, assuming she worked for an airline.

"Oh, no," she said "the film crew."

"Ok. It must be fascinating working with a film crew. I see you've a lot of fitness DVDs in your bag. Is that what your films are about?" I asked curiously.

"No," she said "I'm George's personal assistant, and it gets boring when filming. So I like videos that keep me fit and healthy during my free time because the boys and George keep me busy and it can by strenuous." she said, as she ran her hands down her curvaceous body.

"What's the film about then?" thinking to myself, this one loves herself and her body.

"Err, I don't take much interest. Err, I think it's some war film about getting old relics back from the Germans'," she said.

"Wow, that's interesting." I said, "Anybody famous in it?"

"Of course," she said, "George is the main character."

"George! George who?"

"George who! George who? Have you never heard of George Clooney I'm his PA didn't I say that?"

"Well actually, you didn't." I said, "But it must be fantastic working for George Clooney."

At this point, I discovered the items that had caused the screen reader to reject her bag for the hand search.

"I'm afraid I've found the guilty culprits in your bag." I said as I drew out a large bottle of marmite.

"Oh, it's for the crew, they love it." she said.

"Well, I'm afraid they will miss it on this occasion, as this one's not allowed. The container's over the 100ml size and it comes under the restrictions of either a cream, liquid or paste and therefore cannot be taken in your hand luggage."

It was the switch point; you know the one where you go from being an average if not quirky person to an irrational, rude, aggressive and antagonistic person. Boy did this woman's switch kick in; she launched a tirade at me.

"What the fucking hell's wrong with fucking Marmite, you imbecile, it's just fucking marmite, and it's for the crew." she shouted.

"Madam! It's over the allowable limit and cannot be taken on-board in your hand luggage."

I noticed a mother and her young teenage daughter were waiting for their hand luggage to be searched too.

"Please calm down and remember there are other passengers that can hear you."

My passenger went into melt down.

"You fucking moron! Do you think I give a shit about other passengers? What's your problem? What the fuck do I tell George when he finds out?"

I think all reason had left her by now and although I was trying to deescalate the situation, she was not listening at all.

"Madam, please calm down, why not buy Marmite in Germany when you get there?" I suggested.

"Calm down, calm down you, idiot! You cannot buy the stuff in Germany that's why I'm bringing it through here. What the fuck am I gonna tell George?"

"Well, you could tell George that maybe he should try jam for a change. (I was trying to de-escalate the situation, but apparently failing) But please could you curb your language as it's being heard by other passengers?"

"Other fucking passengers can go to fucking hell. I don't believe this fucking place, Heathrow airport. What's your problem, you idiot? I've taken Marmite through Luton, and through Gatwick with no problem. What's your fucking beef with it here?" she shouted causing many passengers to focus on my search area.

Throughout her tirade, I continued the search and discovered more containers of Marmite. Of course, we don't know what the substance was. It said Marmite on the container, but what was really in there we don't know, hence the International rules of liquid, pastes, or creams being restricted items.

I said, "But anyway, thank you madam." in a calm voice.

"What the fuck are you thanking me for you idiot?"

"Well, for a start I'm thanking you for recommending me not to fly through Gatwick or Luton airports. They clearly don't care about passenger safety by allowing items through that are restricted by International Law. Maybe I should contact the authorities and ask them to come and gain further information from you, and we can get the guilty people arrested. As you have four more containers of oversized Marmite, I would suggest that we could get these items checked in as hold luggage. But as you've continued to be rude and upset many other passengers I am not going to offer this option to you now. So maybe you could allow me to repack your bag. And you can continue on your journey in a happier frame of mind knowing Heathrow Airport Security staff know how to make sure their passengers are safe by doing their jobs properly."

The mother and her daughter turned away embarrassed at my passenger and her unacceptable outbursts. I have to admit seeing this woman become more and more agitated over Marmite, and her boss George Clooney was amusing. But my job is what it is, and I have to be as professional as possible at all times.

I took the offending items away and completed my search

"Would you like me to repack your bag Madam?"

"You fucking people! Just wait until George hears about this." and with that, she grabbed her belongings and stuffed them back into her bag.

"Maybe you could tell George that I took his marmite off him. And I'm a famous author Tony Levy, who wrote an autobiography of my 25 years working in the UK prison service. You never know he might want to make a film of that too." I naughtily said still in my calm voice.

At this point she took her bag and moved away, still mumbling and ranting about Security staff at Heathrow, and doing this to an American. The usual comments we hear on a regular basis
"Well, in America.........."

What are you supposed to do when people fly into a rage? As I told her I would have offered for her to go to the British Airways desk and put her items into the hold luggage. It was something that at the time we could provide for passengers (I believe this has now changed but I left before it came into force). Because of her unreasonable behaviour, she made that option impossible. Had she stayed calm and allowed me to do my job, there would have been no conflict, and no issue and she would have gone away thinking how good Heathrow Security staff were. Instead, she'd gone off and will in all probabilities give the opposite opinion about Heathrow because of her bad attitude.

The mother and daughter stepped forward for their bag to be searched. I apologised for the previous passenger's behaviour, and this lovely lady said, "I don't know how you stayed so calm. I said to my daughter that if I'd been you, I would have hit her right on her nose and told her to f off. Such a rude person how do you cope with it? I'm terribly sorry, but I left some water in my bag."

"Thank you." I said, "But dealing with people like that is an everyday occurrence and its only passengers such as yourself that make the job worthwhile."

The postscript to this story is that George Clooney did not read my book, contact me, and want to make it into a film. It would have been great, but it didn't happen. No, one of the STL's came over and said she had been monitoring me (we got monitored on every position of the security screening process to make sure we keep to the DFT standard of operations) during my search of that passenger.
"Oh shit! Am I in trouble?"

"No. I've marked your search down as exemplary under extreme pressure and fully compliant. An example to all staff on how to stay calm."

My goodness, a compliment "Thanks very much." I stammered.

"Personally, I would have probably lost it with her and told her to Fuck off. Incidentally, the next passenger you searched came and gave you a recommendation on how you handled the passenger and I will put that on your record too, thanks, Tony."

So you see we had to learn to take the rough with the smooth. The recommendation was an excellent complement as was the report from the STL. At the end of the day; it's part of the job we do, and if you cannot take that then it's time to change careers. Passengers will always react differently in different circumstances but some for whatever reason are already stressed when they get to the airport, and it doesn't take much to send them over the top.

That's part of what we got paid for. However, more support from management as to how much abuse staff should take before action is taken against the passenger should be much more forthcoming.

Incidentally, I've never liked marmite. It's one of those things you either love or hate; I'm in the latter camp.

---

15 IT'S ONLY WHEELS FOR MY LORRY?

I was at the loading position on a late evening, and we were expecting the usual last-minute rush for the dreaded flight of the day. Both BA staff and the security staff disliked this flight. It was one of the last to leave the airport daily, and we always had problems with passengers and the amount of luggage they brought with them. Abuja! Never heard of it? No, neither had I until I worked at Heathrow. Abuja is the capital city of Nigeria; it replaced Lagos back in 1991. It's still relatively unheard of by the rest of the world. I wish I could say that too after some of my experiences with this flight.

I think many of the passengers thought that as it was one of the last flights, each evening, to leave London, it would be easy to take more hand luggage than even British Airways allowed. Which in itself is some task as it was rare for BA to stop passengers from taking more hand luggage than was allowed. These passengers commonly arrived at the airport running late. They hoped they would be rushed through without having too much security checking them (this was never the case, if you're running late then you run the risk of missing your flight rather than any security procedures being honed down. It never happens). However, on this occasion, I noticed this youngish couple with two young children aged around four to nine approaching my security lane. They each struggled to pull along their hand luggage and had two bags in a pushchair which looked like it was struggling under the weight of the bags.

Both parents were around five foot four. The father struggled to lift his hand luggage onto the grey tray. Once he got it there, he moved the tray from its running slot. I leaned over and went to move it back into position. Otherwise, the loading system would not run.

"Bloody hell. What have you got in here? It weighs a ton."

"It only wheels for my lorry. You know lorry wheel assemblies." he said in his broken English.

"What?"

"Lorry wheel assemblies. I'm building lorry back in Nigeria."

"But this bag is just too heavy to be hand luggage, you know." I said incredulously.

"British Airways say it ok."

"No! No way not even BA would allow your hand luggage being this heavy."

"Well, dey did." said the woman in an aggressive manner.

"Madam, I can assure you that this bag is way over the allowable weight limit. Your husband couldn't even lift it easily onto the tray here." I said pointing to the tray still sitting akimbo to the assembly lane.

"Well, dey did, and we take em as hand luggage."

"Them! Them! How many have you got?"

"Four." he said pointing to the other three bags "You no expect my lorry to have only one wheel, do you?"

"Four! Four!" Bloody hell I kept repeating myself I've gotta stop, I thought. "There's no way you can take four lorry wheels onto a flight as hand luggage; they're just too heavy."

"British Airways said it ok, dey say we could. British Airways said it ok." the woman repeated.

OMG now she was repeating herself, I've started a trend now I thought to myself. "Look you are finding it difficult to get them up here, (as I pointed to the assembly line) how are you going to get them onto the aircraft?"

"British Airways said dey would help as we ave two small children."

"Yes, and the hand luggage also has your lorry wheels inside them correct? No, I'm sorry there's no way you can take them as hand luggage."

"Why not?"

"Why not! What do you mean why not?" Oh, here I go again repeating myself, stop it, stop it.

"We don't see what problem is."

"The problem sir is this, even if I allowed you to take these wheels as hand luggage, how are you going to get them into the aircraft and the luggage racks? For a start, you're not tall enough to reach the overhead racks, for a second they're too heavy to go in them. Just think about it, supposing during your flight you hit an air pocket and the luggage above your head moved. It's so heavy it could slice through the outer skin of the plane. And it'll kill everybody on board."

"No! No! No!" Now he was at this repeating yourself lark; it's getting very catchy "That couldn't happen."

"What do you mean it couldn't happen why?"

"British Airways say so."

"British Airways seem to say a lot of things they probably know nothing about. I cannot believe BA said those things; I really can't. And how would you get them into the overhead storage cupboards?"

"British Airways said cabin crew help."

"No way will BA cabin crew lift this weight and allow it in the overhead storage cupboards, I I can assure you of that. They're just too heavy."

"British airways said we could." Oh, here we go again. Now I've had enough of it. Over my shoulder, I asked a colleague to call an STL, and I would escalate this situation over to him.

I said to the passengers, "Look, I will call my supervisor as I cannot allow these bags into the departure lounge as hand luggage. There's a serious safety issue here. Whether BA likes it or not, these bags are not travelling with you as hand luggage.

"No! British Airways say we can we can."

"Which BA member of staff said it, please?"

"That one out there." he said pointing back out through the security lanes and towards the general area of the booking in desks in the landside concourse.

At that point, I heard the stomping of the recognisable Night STL.

"What's up Tone?" he always called me Tone. Still, it was better than the other STL's who despite me informing them not to, always called me Anthony. That was my official name on my ID badge. It led to confusion as often STL's would call out 'Anthony', and as I was known as Tony, I'd ignore them. To be honest, I didn't hear them as I wasn't tuned in to responding to someone calling 'Anthony'. But this STL had always called me Tone.

"This gentleman wants to bring these (as I pointed to the four bags) as hand luggage. They contain lorry wheels. They are the lorry wheel assemblies and are cast iron; they weigh a ton each. They're too heavy for them to even lift onto here."

"They've got what?"

"Lorry wheels, four of them."

"Lorry wheels, lorry wheels are you mad?" OMG, now he's started repeating! What's going on tonight?

The STL attempted to move the offending bag. He struggled to move it. You could see a tear forming on one side of the canvas surface as the weight of the wheel was too heavy for the material of the case.

"Look," I said "this bag cannot support the weight of the contents. They will never last even to the aircraft; there's no way they can take them as hand luggage."

"British Airways said we could." said the woman yet again.

"Madam, I don't care if the Prime Minister said you could take them. I will not allow anything of this weight to be put on an aircraft as hand luggage, and that is the bottom line."

The STL said, "What we will do is take them to the BA desk downstairs and get them booked into the hold as excess baggage, ok?"

"But that cost money."

'Yes, but it's the only way you can take them with you.'

"But it's going cost money."

"Yes, it's your choice, either pay or you cannot take them."

"You're trying to rip us off for money. This not fair, you English all thieves and bandits."

It would have been funny if it was not such a ridiculous situation to be in. I thought, no, it was funny, and I had to turn away in case I laughed, as we had by now attracted an audience of staff and passengers. It was, after all, a quiet period by now. But the woman had seen me smirk.

"Look they all laughing at us. They bandits, all of them."

"Madam, I can assure you we're not bandits. Now, if you'll allow me, I'll get your bags moved to the BA desk, and we can get them booked in as excess baggage."

"You bandit, you bandits all you!"

"Ok mister, you do that now, but we not pay."

With that, the STL went around to the passenger's side of the security lane and said "Tone we'll have to get them up onto the lane and run them through the machine to check inside, anyway. But we'll have to get them through without going into the trays first." he went to lift the first bag onto the machine and said, "Bloody hell, bloody hell they are bloody heavy." We're all doing this repeating lark. I've started a trend, I thought, as I burst out laughing.

"Tone you Wally, it's not funny."

"It is, it really is. I always thought you were strong but not so sure now." This STL was built like a Rugby lock forward his width made two of me. He was a big powerful man, but even he was struggling with these bags.

"How much do ya reckon these bags weigh?"

"I seem to recall from somewhere, that a small wheel weighs around 25Kg, so this one I reckon up to 75Kg." I said. I had no idea really; I made the figures up out of my mind.

"I reckon you could be right."

We got the bags onto the machine, and the screen reader started the security screening line. At which point we all gathered around the x-ray machine just to see what was inside the bags. Sure enough, they were the full assembly for a small lorry wheel. I think the screen reader thought the image he was seeing was a new TIP. As that's what they looked like, but alas, no, they really were wheel assemblies.

The STL arranged for a trolley to be brought, and loaded the bags onto it. And the family completed their journey through the security lane. When loaded, the STL was going to take the passengers and their 'hand luggage' down to the BA desk. He'd get the bags booked in as hold luggage. I said to the family "Please don't bring heavy items like this through as hand luggage in future. There's a real security implication to doing that."

"Well, you allow us to take gear box through last time."

"Yea right and I suppose you brought the engine through before that?"

"Don't be silly, how would we get an engine through as hand luggage? A lorry engine much too big; I got one cheap over Nigeria."

Just before the end of my shift, the STL stomped up, you know I'm sure the whole concourse floor used to vibrate when he walked anywhere.

"Tone! Tone! You'll never guess what that little black guy said."

"He said, last time he brought the gearbox through."

"How the bloody hell did you know?"

"He told me too." and I laughed.

"Anyway, guess how much excess baggage was?"

"Go on? I really don't know."

"120kg they were going to charge him something around £400. But as the flight was almost boarded, and he only had £200 on him, they charged him £150 and left him with fifty quid."

I laughed out loud "He conned the lot of you."

"How do you mean?"

"Dave, on the archway, told me that when he came through there, the passenger had over two grand in his pocket."

"The crafty little beggar."

And with that, we both laughed.

----

16 THE FRENCH BOY IN A SHOEBOX

It's always difficult when another culture or language comes through the airport. It never ceases to amaze that despite living in an age where air travel is a normal everyday function, there appears, well at least at Heathrow, to be a number of passengers that have never flown on an aircraft before.

If this is possible, then as a traveller you would check out what the security arrangements are at your airport of departure. Although, each country and it appears each airport interprets the internationally agreed security routines in their own way. The basics are the same almost throughout the modern air travelling world.

So why would you come to Heathrow and say, "I didn't know that." or "Well in my country we don't do that." Why didn't you know? Your airport of departure would have had some security, why expect none at Heathrow, didn't you check first?

And just for the record, you're not in your country; you're here in this one so abide by the rules. Remember the saying when in Rome do what the Romans do. Although, I don't think the Romans, who invented lots of things we still use today, invented air travel, although I could be wrong.

I'm standing at the archway, searching passengers that either set off the metal detector or are randomly picked out for searching when I noticed a middle-aged woman and her teenage son. The woman was French; I knew because I heard her speak to the loader. I'm not sure if her son had autism or not, although his behaviour seemed normal, neither of them spoke English, it appeared.

It's a strange phenomenon, but many French passengers I encountered at Heathrow could not speak English when it suited them. Yet, they knew every swear word and insult in English when they wanted to insult you. Life's strange quirk!

I'd noticed that the boy was wearing metal toe boots. These would set off the metal detector. I indicated to the loader that they would need to be removed. And I pointed to the passenger's shoes and mouthed the words, "Boots off." to which he responded with a nod of his head. See we work together as a team.

A female STL appeared at my shoulder. "Anthony love (she addressed everybody as love) why did you ask the loader to get that boy to remove his boots? You know the rules; we don't have to remove all footwear."

"No 'Pat' I know. But based on my 25 years working in the security industry, and my extensive experience of working here, I felt the boots offered a security risk as they are of the type that can conceal hidden contraband and dangerous items. And they're metal toed boots like workman's boots. They always activate." I said, "Why, is there a problem?"

She looked flustered, as I knew she would, and would probably have to go out of the airport to have a cigarette. It was her usual response to anybody daring to have an answer to her bullying attitude.

"DfT are monitoring you, so I wanted to know why you asked for the kid's boots to be removed."

"Just tell DfT to come and ask me. My experience in security and the decisions I make should be supported by management not deemed to be a fault. But hey, this is Heathrow let's not upset the passengers for the sake of security eh." I said and looked around to see if I could see anybody with security identity around their necks monitoring me. There wasn't anybody, as I knew there wouldn't be, it was just Pat trying to bully staff, sorry Pat wrong person to take on over security matters I thought to myself.

Things were now escalating at the loaders position. The woman had by this time, walked through the archway and not activated it. But her son was still at the loaders position and not understanding my colleagues request for him to remove his footwear. I am witnessing this at the same time as searching male passengers who have activated on their way through the archway.

"Just take your boots off and place them in this grey tray." said the loader.

"Eh?"

"Your shoes, please take them off."

"Eh?"

"Anybody speak French?"

"Veuillez retirer vos chaussures et les placer dans le bac gris." said a passenger who was in the queue behind the boy

"Veuillez retirer vos chaussures et les placer dans le bac gris." the helpful passenger said again.

"Je ne veux pas."

I got the gist of his reply, he didn't want to remove his shoes. I turned to the mother who by now had collected her belongings and was standing just behind me waiting for her son to come through.

"Madam! Do you speak English? Parlez vous anglais?" I was at the end of remembering my schoolboy French at this point.

"Yes." she said in that husky, sexy accented English that only Frenchwoman seemed able to do. How do they do that, it always reminded me of Brigitte Bardot or Leslie Caron?

"Could you please tell your son to remove his shoes and place them in the grey tray?"

"He will not take them off." Oh, I could listen to that accent all day.

"If he comes through the archway and it activates, he will have to take them off. It's better he does it that side rather than this side."

And with that, she walked back through the archway to talk to her son before either I or my colleague, could stop her. Great, now if she activates when coming back through the archway she'll have to be searched again.

She spoke to her son. I couldn't understand what she was saying, but he seemed to argue back. She grabbed a grey tray and threw it on the floor by her son's feet and walked off back through the archway where she hit the side of the machine causing it to activate, and her then requiring to be searched.

My female colleagues stepped forward and said "Madam you have activated the archway metal detector and I have to search you. May I search you please?"

"Je ne comprends pas l'anglais."

"What did she say?"

"She said she doesn't understand English." I said.

"What does she mean she doesn't understand English? I heard her talking to you in that bloody sexy accent they all use."

"Madam, you told me you spoke English." I said.

"Je ne comprends pas l'anglais."

"She's now saying she doesn't understand English. How very convenient."

"Recherché par mon ami." I said. It was about as near as I could get to explaining what was required of her.

It worked, she submitted herself to my colleagues being able to search her. At this point, her son, instead of taking his shoes off, decided to just stand in the grey tray with his arms akimbo.

Things were going from bad to worse. His mother on completion of her search then shouted and gesticulated to her son. He argued back. And in a fit of temper picked up the tray and threw it back on the rolling assembly line, took his shoes off and walked through the archway carrying them.

They activated, and we had to get the shoes off him and put them on a tray so they could be monitored by the screen reader. And I had to search the boy.

"Sir, may I search you?" I said not expecting an answer.

"Of course." he said in perfect English.

Have these two been taking the 'micky' out of us all this time? Both could speak English and understand it well yet we've gone through this rubbish. Why they would behave in this manner, was beyond me.

All went well from this point until, after the boy's search had been completed and he'd retrieved his shoes, his mother came up to myself and my colleague and said in that sexy husky voice in English "You are all dick heads and cochons."

My colleague asked what the woman had said, so I told her. "She said she was overwhelmed with our efficiency and kindness in dealing with her and her son today.

----

17 HISS AND TELL

The team and I were working in the staff search area on the ground floor of the departure lounge. It was always a busy site, as BA ground crew used this facility to enter the security area of the airport. It was their nearest entry point to work. They used it more often than just coming into work and going home at the end of their shifts.

If any of them were smokers and wanted a quick cigarette break, they had to leave the secure areas of the airport and go outside to the landside area to enjoy their habit. But this meant that they then had to come back through security before being able to return to their place of work.

Now, some of these workers would do their stuff in the apron area. Loading or unloading aircraft, refuelling or routine maintenance and then leave the airport for a quick cigarette and then back through security staff search and back to work. In an hour these workers would enter and leave the airport at least three times, and all would need searching. They appeared to have a perverted sense of humour in making security officers have to search them. I swear they used to have a sweepstake to see which of them could wind us up the most.

Most of the ground crews were built like Dockers. Huge men who were wearing shorts irrespective of the time of year; I think it was yet another competition amongst them to see who could stay in shorts for the longest period during the winter. And maybe it was a macho thing. Most were adorned with tattoos (usually in support of their favourite football team, sorry soccer for my American readers, things like Arsenal, Gunners, Hammers, Lilywhites etc.). And they had piercings which would activate the archway. There were many of them from the Indian culture. They would wear the gold bangle A Kara (I looked it up) it's a steel or iron bracelet, worn by initiated Sikhs, to identify a Sikh as dedicated to their religious order.

I think it had become something that all the younger Indians wore, whatever their religious followings, as a trend. They would never take them off so always activated. It meant that you could end up searching the same man three or four times in a half hour session on the archway. It was always a busy area. However, I had developed a great rapport with these men, and we had some wonderful laughs during our searching of them.

It was always busy as it was the nearest staff search facility to the staff buses that stopped just outside the terminal building opposite. And especially busy at the changeover of shift times from the earliest to the latest one.

It could be a stressful area to work in. Just to make it more interesting if passengers left the baggage hall without their personal effects, this was where they had to report to BA, to be allowed under escort back into the baggage hall to reclaim their belongings. There was a telephone on the wall near the entrance. It was a connection to BA ground support staff. The passenger would pick up the phone and be in direct contact with BA. They'd explain what they'd left behind, and BA staff would come to this area, on the Airside of the security lane, and inform us of which passengers could be allowed through the security process. They would be escorted into the baggage hall by the BA staff to retrieve their lost possessions.

But this was Heathrow, and it wasn't as simple as that as we found on many times.

On one such occasion, I was on the Archway with 'Rami', Stan, and Bubbles, at the loading bag searching position. When two large Africans, a man and a woman, walked into the staff search area. They approached the desk where the staff were queuing to have their pass scanned by the officer positioned at the scanning machine and sitting on a podium just for this job.

It could be a mind-blowing boring position, but very important as you took each member of staff's ID, checked for certain security markings and that the photo was the person who presented it to you (we got tested for this by STL's, and DfT so had to be alert).

The officer pointed to where the telephone was and said to the two Africans, "You need BA. Pick up the phone and tell BA what you forgot." It was such a frequent occurrence that many officers sitting in this position did this automatically. They looked confused, so from my position I said. "Have you left something in the baggage hall?"

The woman gave a sort of hissing noise with her lips that you hear many West Indian men do. But she said nothing; I think it's called 'teeth kissing'.

"If you've left anything in the baggage hall, you need to pick up that phone. When BA answer just inform them, and they will tell you what to do, ok?"

"Tsk, tsk." was all I got in response, it was this tooth kissing sound, not spoken.

The man must have understood as he turned and walked back to where the phone was and picked it up. We carried on with our jobs. We didn't take any notice of the couple. Usually, once they'd got in touch with BA, they had to wait until a BA member of staff came along and gave permission to allow the waiting public into the secure area.

Sometime later the BA member of staff appeared and said, "Are there any passengers waiting to be escorted in?" My colleague on the desk called for the passengers to come forward. They did, and he explained that they'd have to go through the full security screening process as if they were going to the departure lounge to catch a flight. He pointed to the queuing members of staff who were going through the screening process.

They queued and when they got to the loading position; the loader asked the same questions to them as she had to everybody else.
"Do you have any electrical items in your bags?"

"Tsk, tsk." or it might have been hiss, hiss.

"If you have any liquid's please remove them from within your baggage."

"Hiss, hiss."

They had loads of makeup, well she did anyway, and they had loads of electrical goods too. But they were ready to come through the archway.

"I bet she goes off and I have to search her." said Rami.

"Naw, it will be the bloke. Mind you, they both might go off. I think she'll have to come through sideways with her bulk."

"Yes, and look at that thing on her head. That must be two foot tall, what is it?"

"It's a head-wrap (dhuku) I think it's called, but I've never seen one that big before."

"It goes with the rest of her then dunnit; she's huge. But how did you know about her head-dress, Tony?"

"He's not the Messiah, just a clever boy." said Stan before I could say I'd looked it up on Google, which was the truth.

I beckoned the man through, and he did not activate the machine. As the woman walked through, I realised she still had a load of bangles on her arm, and sure enough, she activated the metal detector.

"Your customer Rami." and I moved aside. Well, she was big, and there wasn't enough room for two her size to stand side by side. I still needed room to beckon the men through the archway to keep the flow moving.

"Bastard!"

"Rami, I've told you before I saw my mum and dads wedding certificate, and I wasn't born out of wedlock, so a bastard I am not."

"And you're not the Messiah either, but you're a very naughty boy."

"Thanks, Stan."

With that Rami started her search, and I have to admire her, as she carried it out so skillfully given the size of the woman's' girth. She then had to use the metal detector on the woman who she still had other metal items on her person. But the search was completed after a professional and competent search. By this time the two passenger's bags had been taken off as they both contained items that could not go into the baggage hall. It was Stan's turn to carry out the search.

When the woman had completed her search, and collected her other personal effects, she stood along with her husband at the search desk area. Stan was busy when she started hissing at him, and it was loud. It must have been because we all stopped what we were doing to look at her.

"Hiss, hiss." she did it again. "Stan," I said, "You're being hissed at, or has a snake escaped from her bag?"

"Hissss, hissss." again but now with more urgency or anger, I wasn't sure.

"Stan, she is trying to get your attention you know."

This was the first time I'd ever seen Stan getting annoyed.

"Is she hissing at me?"

"Yup, I think she's trying to attract your attention."

"Well, she'll just have to wait until I've finished doing this one then, won't she?"

"Hiss, hiss." It was getting on everybody's nerves. But Stan completed what he was doing. And in his usual indomitable manner, he carried out the search of her bag. All the time being professional and polite. The rest of the team were by now trying to get Stan to crack, in a friendly way. I have to say I couldn't have searched as he did without losing it with our hissing friend.

"What the hell is all the hissing about?"

"Stan, are you taking the hiss outta her?"

"Naw, she's got Hiccup's but she lisps."

"Look," said somebody "She's getting smaller that hissing must be a puncture in her, Rami did you puncture her when you searched her?"

"Stan, you have a new friend there, that hissing means she wants to marry you in her language you know."

"No! It's a gas leak, take cover! She's gonna explode, take cover everybody."

But he carried on regardless, and to be fair although the two passengers couldn't hear the jokes going around. If they did, they said nothing nor reacted to anything. They stood erect in front of Stan starring at him as he conducted his search, with the occasional hiss at him. Stan was getting angry, every time the woman hissed you could see his anger rising. I'd never witnessed him getting angry before, or maybe he believed she was proposing to him, I don't know, but Stan getting angry was a sight to witness.

I said to nobody in particular, "You know this is gonna be a whole chapter in my new book. I'll call it Hiss and Tell. By the way, did I tell you I had a book published it's called 'A Turnkey or Not?'"

Rami responded with "Yes you did tell us about a hundred times so far this week."

"Stan," I said "Stan, you're not the messiah but you're a very naughty boy." and at that, we laughed, even Stan.

----

18 I KNOW I KNOW BUT HOW DO YOU GET OUT OF YOUR CAR?

I was working another plus shift that was working six hours before my official shift start time of 1215. I had reported for work at 0615, meaning I'd got up at 0430 to get to work for 0600 for my 0615 starts. Then I would work until my finish time of 2100, long days but overtime was needed by many of the staff and was also needed by management to make up for shortfalls in the staffing levels. And to cover for the poor staff rota system in place at the time.

Me! Well in my early years at Heathrow I needed over-time, so my wife and I could get back on our feet after losing so much money during our brief time in Spain.

I was at the bag searching position, in the North concourse on the Fast Track lane and the screen reader had rejected a passenger's bag for a search.

"Whose bag is this?" I asked as I held up the Louis Vuitton hand luggage.

"It's mine." said a female voice in a resigned but sexy tone.

I looked up to see a beautiful woman around mid-thirties in a grey business suit that showed her best features. Nice I thought to myself, it looks like a Chanel or Versace suit, nice, cost a lot of money. And she smelt of expensive perfume, Chanel number 5 or 19. I recognised the smell as both are my wife's favourite scents. She apparently spent a lot of time preparing for her trip to the airport and subsequent business meeting wherever she was going in the world.

"I'm sorry." I said, "But I have to search your bag. Please collect all your personal property and come around to the front so I can search your bag."

'Ok' she said in a really husky sexy voice. You know sometimes this job has some really good perks I thought to myself especially at 0645 in the morning.

"Do you have any sharp items in your bag; you know anything I could cut myself on?" I asked although we were supposed to ask if the passenger had any sharp items within their bags I liked to add a little extra to ease any tension that might be there, after all, it's not a pleasant prospect to have your personal property searched by a security officer.

"No, unless you included my nail files." now how many times have I had that said?

"I don't think they'd be a problem." I said, "But let's have a look and see what the problem is with your bag."

Due to the technology available to us, I already knew this passenger had left her laptop inside her hand luggage, and it was also inside a laptop bag. Yep, it too was a Louis Vuitton laptop bag. She had money, lots of it judging by her hand luggage.

"Would you please unzip all the pockets of your bag and open it for me?" We ask this because we have to get the passenger to open their property. If we did it and damaged a zip or a catch we would be liable for the repair. Whereas, if the passenger of the property opened their own bags and caused damage we weren't liable for the damage.

She opened her bag and said, "I don't know why my bag was rejected for search. You know I'm a regular traveller through here, and always travel 'fast-track' and business class. I know what to do at security, so don't know what's wrong."

"Let's have a look, and we can get you on your way as soon as possible."

Thanks to the technology available to us I knew that this passenger had left her laptop inside her hand luggage. And it was also still inside the laptop bag, and the screen reader had correctly rejected her bag for a hand search.

The latest technology Heathrow provided was an extra screen at the searcher's table to show why the screen reader had rejected a bag for search. So as a bag searcher, you knew what you were looking for, but the passengers did not know this. Often, I'd show this screen to them and say, "Look, this is why your bag was rejected for a search." and I'd show them what the screen reader had seen. Most would be amazed at what we saw in their bags. I thought it would help next time they travelled through the airport.

Which is what I did on this occasion saying, "It looks like you've left your laptop inside its cover, inside your hand luggage? I will have to search the whole of your bag, run a test on your laptop and rerun it through the x-ray machine. I also have to search the whole of your bag. Sorry, but that's just the regulations."

"Do you have to search my entire bag?" and she fluttered her eyelashes in that sexy way that women could do. Did they learn that at sex lessons while at school? Lessons that us poor males were not privy too I wondered.

"Sorry madam, the rules are quite clear."

"This is Fucking ridiculous!"

I must admit even though I was a man of the world and had spent 25 years working in Her Majesty's Prison Service I was always taken aback by a woman swearing at me. Especially this attractive business women swearing at me. Louis Vuitton, Armani, or Chanel does not excuse bad language when it's your fault, I thought to myself.

I'm sorry." I said.

"Well, it's fucking ridiculous. I travel regularly through here and never have had my hand luggage searched before."

"Sorry, but on this occasion, I have to search your bag and rerun the laptop through the system."

"Why? You know I'm a regular business passenger. The guy at the other end (referring to the loader) didn't tell me I had to take my laptop out of my hand luggage, so it's his fault."

'Yes, it probably is, but tell me are you a regular traveller?'

"You know I am. I'm a regular, frequent business passenger, always come through on fast-track, and never have a problem. I don't know why I have a problem with my laptop today."

"Really, as a frequent traveller you know leaving your laptop within your hand luggage is a no, no." I said.

"But the guy at the other end didn't say I had to take it out of my luggage, did he?"

"I don't know." I said "But you must know the rules as they haven't changed for ages. And after all, you took your liquids out of your bag. You already had them in the clear plastic bag as per the requirement. You didn't have to be told that, did you? In leaving your laptop inside your hand luggage, you must have known as a frequent traveller it would be picked up for a hand search. So, you can't blame the loader can you?"

"Oh, fuck off, you supercilious prick." she said, "Don't lecture me, do you know who I am?"

"No, and I don't care." I said "I'm just doing my job, and if you couldn't be bothered to take your laptop out of your hand luggage as the requirements demand, that's not my problem. Please refrain from swearing at me; I don't think your language is fair."

"You arsehole." she said "You lot think you're so clever. I earn more in a month than you get in a year, so who do you think you're talking too?"

"Personally, I don't know who I'm talking to. Except for a passenger travelling through Heathrow airport who forgot to take her laptop out of her hand luggage, and so had to have me search her bag because of her forgetfulness. Furthermore, she apparently thinks she's far more important to the world than me. Yet, she wants to blame security staff for her incompetence that's who I think I'm talking too."

"Fuck you, who do you, think you are? Your colleague at the other end didn't tell me to take my laptop out of my bag, so it's his fault, not mine."

Why is it when a passenger is told they've made a genuine mistake, it's never their fault but everybody else's? It's one of life's amazing idiosyncrasies.

"You're quite right, madam. My colleague at the other end is a complete idiot, for not telling you to take your laptop out of your bag. As you say, you're a frequent business traveller coming through our fast track lanes. I'm sure every other time you have travelled through fast track a colleague has advised you to take your laptop out of your hand luggage bag for security screening. I don't know why my colleague didn't so this on this occasion. Although I'm confident that when you dressed this morning, nobody had to tell you how to put your clothes on or clean your teeth, did they? But can I ask you one question?"

"What?'" she said, in an aggressive manner.

"Did you come here by a car today?"

"Yes, I used the M25 why?"

"Did you park your car in the T5 business park?"

"Yes, of course."

"Do you always park your car there as a frequent business traveller?"

"Yes, of bloody course, I always do. Why?"

I persisted, "Did anybody tell you how to get out of your car?"

"No, of course not. Are you stupid?"

"I'm not stupid madam, but then I too don't need to be told how to get out of my car in the business car park, as you don't. And also, I don't need to be told about the liquid rules, as you don't. I don't need to be told to take my laptop out of its bag and my hand luggage at airport security.

But you obviously do need to be told. So, I'm sorry but who is stupid madam, me or you?"

"Did you call me stupid?"

"Was it me who forgot to take their laptop out of their bag, or was it you?"

"Well it was me, but your colleague didn't tell me to take it out."

"You're calling my colleague stupid? No! Nobody needed to tell you to get out of your car at the car-park, did they? So as a frequent flyer why do you expect somebody to tell you what to do with your laptop every time you come through airport security? After all, you're a frequent flyer and a fast track business woman, surely you don't need to be told everything all the time? And you managed to get out of your car at the car park without being told to do so, didn't you?" and I continued in the manner we'd been trained. "Would you like me to repack your hand luggage for you madam, or would you prefer to do it yourself?" We always made the offer to repack the bag we'd searched, sometimes passengers insisted that we did, but that's another story.

I don't think I've ever seen such an attractive woman change so quickly. I saw her go so red that all her attractiveness disappeared. She grabbed the rest of her belongings and walked off muttering something like 'patronising bastard', but I'm sure she wasn't referring to me.

Oh well sometimes being polite and keeping calm does have its rewards.

----

19 HOWZAT

A well-known ex-International cricketer, one of the world's best spin bowlers during his long sporting, and who came from Australia, was a frequent flyer through Heathrow. He was travelling with his then partner and girlfriend, who was an actress and the ex-girlfriend of a well-known English actor who starred in film 'Four Weddings and a funeral'. She had become famous when she had worn a side pinned black 'Versace' dress.

Although I was at the back of the security machine at the searching position, my colleague a small young quietly spoken girl from an Asian background was going to carry out the search of this passenger's bag. My colleague was one of the most conscientious and patient security officers I had ever worked with. She never raised her voice much above a whisper, was professional when dealing with any passenger, was an exemplary member of staff, and a real pleasure to work with.

We'd had conflict when dealing with the girlfriend who always complained about having to take her shoes off when coming through the security screening, even though she knew she'd be asked to take them off. But hey, it's part of our job to take the flak from our passengers without complaint. However, on this occasion, this ex-sportsman's hand luggage was rejected. The screen reader saw that his bag contained liquids and therefore had to be rejected for hand search to investigate what the liquids were.

Our celebrity passenger who was travelling with his family - I seem to remember it was his son, and his brother kept making derogatory comments about why his bag had been rejected for a search. He said, "You've just pulled my bag off because my girlfriend made a fuss at the other end of the machine." referring to the fact that she had indeed complained at the front of the security screening equipment that she did not want to take her shoes off. This too was a regular occurrence, I had been at the bag loading position on several occasions when this female passenger had come through the security process, and on each and every occasion she had asked the same question "Do my shoes have to come off today?"

I had taken time to explain to her on the first occasion that she had confronted me over this issue "The problem is that as your shoes contain hollow wedges, and the clasps are made of metal. It's our experience that they activate when you walk through the metal detector, so to save you from having to be searched, and having to remove your shoes once through the archway, it would be better for you to remove your shoes before and the need for a search would not happen." I explained. "I would suggest you remove your shoes and place them in the tray for your own convenience."

But it didn't seem to stop her asking the same question whenever she travelled through the terminal wearing these same shoes. Oh well, you can take a horse to water etc. etc.

My colleague just continued with her job, and the celebrity continued,

"Son, she thinks I'm a terrorist. Hey, do I look like a terrorist?" he said shouting at my colleague. "I travel all over the world, and nobody has ever thought I was a terrorist before, I'm travelling with my son and brother, so do I really look like a terrorist?"

Again, my colleague just carried on with her job, but he continued,

"If you think I look like a terrorist you should start looking closer to home. There seem to be a lot of people working here who look more like terrorist's than me, you know. Have you looked in the mirror lately?"

At this point, my colleague had reached the stage of the search where she'd found a container with a clear liquid in it, so it had to be tested to see what it was.

"Sir," she said in her usual hushed soft voice "you left this liquid in your bag, and I have to test it." she explained.

"Christ," he said, "it's my contact lens solution. I am allowed that, you know."

Why he felt the need to tell my colleague whether he was allowed the liquid or not was beyond me. After all, we are the people who know the rules after such extensive training. We didn't need the passenger to tell us our job. On this occasion, the liquid container was 115ml in size and passengers were only allowed containers up to 100ml. It would have to be either voluntarily rejected for disposal by the passenger or refused authorisation by the security officer. It was always a bone of contention at UK airports, as in America these containers are sold in 115ml size bottles and allowed through USA airports but in Europe, we have the 100ml rules and cannot accept them, so this often became a point of conflict.

"It's contact lens liquid you know, not an explosive; can't you tell the difference? I would have thought you lot knew how to do your job."

"Yes, I'm sure you're correct, and once I've tested your liquid then, of course, we can tell the difference. However, it's in a container that is over the allowable size here in Europe." she explained.

He again turned to his son and said, "She thinks we're terrorist's." and he looked at her, and continued, "She should look closer to home."

At this stage I'd heard enough, I was so angry that he was making such comments to my colleague who was after all only doing her job to ensure him, his son, and his party would be safe.

I approached the celebrity and withdrawing a pen from my pocket,

"Sir, I believe you've travelled all over the world and especially the Indian subcontinent, so maybe if I give you my pen." At this point, I believe he thought I was going to ask for his autograph. I continued, "Perhaps with your vast experience of terrorist's you could draw for me what one looks like as that would be of some benefit to the whole security process."

He went bright red; I hope with embarrassment, so I continued, "And maybe in future before you start making such sweeping statements about my colleagues you will think what sort of example you are setting for your son. If you were my dad, I would be embarrassed to be with you."

And I turned away and asked my colleague if she was ok with how she'd been spoken to. She nodded her thanks, and I left it at that.

But really what gives so called celebrities the right to treat members of staff who are only doing their job, in that way? I was disgusted with him.

I hope next time he travelled through Heathrow he was a little more contrite, but knowing his TV persona, I doubt it very much. Which was a real shame as I admired his sporting achievements but as a human being he'd gone down in my estimation?

----

20 CELEBRITIES

Celebrities, you either love them, hero-worship them or loathe them. And we all have our opinions of them. Me, I treat them all the same, whatever my personal feelings. However, I've a soft spot for sports people. My first boyhood hero was Jimmy Greaves, a footballer for Tottenham Hotspur. I'd cycle 30 miles just to see him training at the then Tottenham Hotspur training ground in Cheshunt, Hertfordshire. This ground is now a Tesco's superstore, oh well times change. But my dream was to be a professional footballer and join my hero Jimmy Greaves.

We hero worship different celebrities for different reasons. And it's a healthy part of being a human being. Many of the staff at Heathrow worshipped Bollywood stars. You'd often see a cluster of Indian staff surrounding a man or woman, who'd mean nothing to me, but to them, they were heroes from a Bollywood film. I'd say, "Who was that?"

"Tony, you don't know who that was?"

"Nope, sorry."

"That's one of the biggest stars in Bollywood. It's Aishwarya Rai Bachchan; she is bigger than Julia Roberts to the Indian community." Or "That's Shah Rukh Khan, more famous than Brad Pitt!"

"Wow! I just wouldn't know."

Each to their own. But celebrities are made by us, the public, in whatever field they perform. I remember saying to Stan once, while we worked in the Windsor suite, "That's Elton John. I wonder if he will thank me?"

"Tony, why would he thank you?"

"I got him his knighthood."

"How!"

"I bought his records, and buying his records led to his knighthood and his wealth, so he should be thanking me, not the other way around."

"You know you're not the Messiah but you do have a valid point."

And to be honest, that's the way I feel. These so-called celebrities are only such because we, the public, have made them so. Not because of themselves, so maybe they should give us more respect, rather than expect it from us.

At Heathrow, we meet many celebrities coming through our security screening systems. I have had both good and bad experiences with them all. From Dame Shirley Bassey to Ainsley Harriot, Gold medal winning tennis player Serena Williams (London Olympics 2012) to Tara Palmer-Tomkinson. There was Pierce Brosnan, Naomi Campbell, Lulu and Whitney Huston (just before she died), and so many sportsmen and women I could not list them all here. I have seen them all and been privy to their behaviour.

One rule I was told about early in my career at T5, was that asking celebrities for 'selfies' was not allowed. If the celebrity was being escorted by a BA escort, then we could not engage in conversation with them, apart from in the usual manner we spoke to members of the public to carry out our duties.

Not sure why this was, maybe it had something to do with the BA escorting staff thinking they were celebrities themselves. Or maybe they were just guilty of 'elitism', I never knew and never cared. My philosophy was always the same; I treated people the way they treated me. I was always polite, but if they were rude, then 'the gloves were off', and although I wouldn't be rude to them, I would not make polite conversation either.

When travelling through T5, and as First Class or VIP's, celebrities would use the south concourse as this was where the dedicated fast-track lanes were located. The lanes exited the screening area next to the BA First Class lounge, so many celebrities used this option when travelling through Heathrow.

One celebrity who fell into this category was a famous British actor who had starred in several romantic comedy films including 'Four Weddings and a Funeral' 'Notting Hill' and 'Love Actually'. Funnily enough, my wife has a connection with the film 'Four Weddings and a Funeral', as one of her girlfriend's partners was the drummer in the band that plays 'Love is all around' at one of the wedding scenes in the film.

I was working the South concourse as the searcher on the archway metal detector (WTMD) when he came through the security lane. As he walked through, he activated the sensor. I stepped forward "Sir, may I search you?" It was at that moment I realised who he was.

"Yea, I suppose so." he said in a grumpy manner. He must have gotten fed up with travelling through all these different airports in the course of his work. But did he ever consider the people he was grumpy with paid his wages by going to watch him in the cinema? I doubt it, but if he did, he might not be so grumpy with airport staff.

"Do you have any metal objects on you?"

"Naw, oh I might, I have my mobile phone in my pocket, I suppose I should have taken it out and put it into a tray or something."

"Yes, sir. Now I need to take it off you and place it in a tray as it has to be put through our x-ray machine." I said as my female colleague put her hand out to collect the phone, to which he handed it over.

"Do you have anything else in your pockets sir, any sharp items I could catch my finger on?"

"No, oh I have coins in my pocket do you want them too?"

"Please, sir, them too. As they're metal, they too need to go through the x-ray machine."

He handed them over and assumed the position required to enable me to search him, but as I'd said before, I always try to be polite and make conversation. It's a good way to check if there are any hidden items in somebody's mouth, sorry old prison habits die hard, so as I started the search.

"Off filming anywhere nice, sir?" I asked.

He looked at me with contempt and said, "Naw, just going to New York to do voice overs, boring really. Just get on with it would you."

Whoops sorry, I thought, and I won't bother to waste my breath on you. I continued my search in silence until I had completed it, then said, "Thank you, sir, hope you have a good day."

He just walked past me mumbling to himself, "Fucking idiot!" or words to that effect. After collecting his personal items, phone, and coins went away in the direction of the First-Class lounge.

My colleague said, "What's his problem? What a grumpy git he was! And so, it stuck, every time I saw him again I always referred to him as grumpy Grant. Sorry, I like your films, but come on lighten up when coming through security.

He had just won his first World Championship in Grand Prix racing, and he was another person who came through the fast-track lane heading for the first-class lounge. He was travelling with a female, BA escort. It was a quiet period, and although I didn't have to search him as he went past, I said, "Good luck for this year's World Championship." He stopped and said, "Thank you very much. Are you a Grand Prix fan? I hope I don't disappoint you." and walked on. But as he got to the first class lounge he wasn't allowed in. At that exact moment, my female colleague and I were rotating to the back of the machine at the bag search area. As we got there, I said to him, "Won't they let you in? Maybe it's because you're too young."

"No," he said, "it's probably because I am black." and he laughed. As we weren't busy both my colleague and I stood there chatting with him, and eventually my colleague said, "Would you mind if we had a photo?"

"No, of course not." he said, and came over and put his arm around her, while I took a photo of the two of them.

His colleague then came out of the Lounge and told him to join her, and they walked back in together.

What a nice guy he was, and I've always been a supporter of him ever since, thanks to our own Grand Prix World Champion; you made my day on that occasion.

A well-known British comedian was travelling through the south concourse, and he was every bit like his TV persona. He'd starred in a program called 'Little Britain' and was a regular panelist on a UK show 'Britain's got talent (BGT)'. He was hilarious and exactly as he appeared on the TV; he asked lots of questions and seemed genuinely interested in how we all worked. Shortly after this, he appeared on TV with his famous co-star in a comedy show called 'Come Fly with Me' which was all about people in an airport. Although the show was filmed at Stansted airport, he must have obtained a lot of the material for the show from his journeys through Heathrow, because all the characters that appear in the show I had met during my time working there. Great show, great comedian, thanks for being you. PS. If you want more material for a follow up to the first series, come and read this book.

The Lord Mayor of London wanted to close Heathrow and build a purpose-built airport in the middle of the Thames Estuary. Yet, he was always his usual happy bumbling self when he came through the security screening system at Heathrow.

I was on the ticket machine, scanning passenger tickets and allowing them into the security screening area. The Lord Mayor of London and his entourage came waltzing in through the automatic scanning machines and joined the queue for fast track security and then through security lanes and into the First-class lounge. You could not miss the then Lord Mayor of London by his unkempt blonde hair, which was his most distinguishing mark.

"Hello." he said, "I'm Boris."

"Nice to meet you and I'm Tony, and you want to close us down and do me out of my job." I said to him.

"Ha, well, you all do a great job. Keep up the good work." and with that, he was gone along with his entourage.

Strangely enough, he had a great persona that made people like him despite his idiosyncrasies.

I was always pleasantly surprised by most of the celebrities that travelled through the airport. On one occasion a large, jovial celebrity chef came through my lane. He'd become quite a TV star but was best known for his cookery shows, 'Can't cook, won't cook' and 'Ready Steady Cook'. As he walked through the archway, it gave out its audible activation signal, and before I had a chance to say anything, he said, "It's my knees they always do that."

"Replacements?"

"Yes."

"Do you get any problems with them?"

"Apart from always going off at airports, no. They haven't even gone rusty from when I take a shower." he joked. He was a larger-than-life character, cheerful and chatty.

"May I search you, sir?"

'Of course. But just be gentle with me, I'm only a young 'un, well my new knees are."

As I searched him I engaged in conversation "I've met you before, sir."

"Really? Now, let me guess, I'm great with remembering faces."

"Ok."

He looked at me, thought about it, but said, "No, sorry, give me a clue?"

"The Oval last test match of the series versus the West Indies?"

"Yes, now I see you. I was going around the kitchens meeting all my old mates, as I used to work there years ago as a chef, and you were on security duty."

"Yes, that right."

"I never forget a face, and we beat the West Indies to whitewash them in the series."

"Yes, it was a great cricket match and a great day."

"Yes, and John Major, the then prime minister, turned up in his green jag. I always wanted that car you know."

"Yes, me too. Well, that's your free massage completed, and it was nice to meet you."

"And it was nice to meet you again too. (and he looked at my security pass and said) Anthony thanks for a nice professional search." and with that, he was off into the first-class lounge.

Another celebrity who arrived at Heathrow in a bad mood and maybe had had one too many drinks before coming through security. Who was a previous James Bond actor and had starred in that great movie 'Mamma Mia'. All I can say, and not to make any excuse for him, but his behaviour was appalling. Maybe he was a nervous flyer or something like that, but on arriving home that night, I told my wife about him and the way he had behaved toward us. She was so very disappointed, and upset, as she had the hots for him. Oh well, another illusion shattered.

I remember seeing Whitney Huston coming through the fast-track lane one day. And thinking to myself, oh my goodness, she has aged quickly. If that's what drugs can do to you, then I will never touch them. It was such a shame. She had a fantastic voice and was part of my growing up. Her music featured in my coping with life's crises that were thrown at me over the years. It was so sad when a few weeks later she died. What a great talent to have wasted her opportunity in life.

The dame of British pop music travelled through the South concourse. What a wonderful lady living up to her title of dame. From such a humble background of Tiger Bay, she had become one of the world's singing superstars and what a wonderful person she was too. So polite and respectful of the rules; I was on loading duties when she arrived with two BA personal escorts.

"Do you have any liquids, gels, or pastes in your hand luggage?"

"Oh yes, here they are in their plastic bag all ready for you." she answered in that so familiar Welsh lilt."

"What about any large electrical goods like a laptop or large tablet?"

"Ha ha, I don't use those things. I leave that to my managers; I can't be bothered with them all."

"I don't blame you for that. Can I see your shoes, please?"

"Of course, but they are flats so don't think they will be a problem." and she showed them by lifting her legs up in the air one at a time.

"No, they are fine, thank you."

"Thank you for being so polite and helpful."

"And thank you for your incredible voice. 'Diamonds are Forever' is not only one of my favourite all time Bond films, but your singing on it was fantastic, and made the film!"

"Yes, I enjoyed that song too."

"Nice to meet you."

"And lovely to meet you too. Thank you once again."

And with that she was off through the archway and whisked into the First-class lounge. What a wonderful voice and a wonderful woman.

On another occasion, while on tickets there was a commotion behind me. This is the area where passengers would queue to go through the security channels. An attractive, slim woman came rushing out of the security area, shouting and screaming all sorts of obscenities at the top of her voice.

As she pushed past the ticket gates the wrong way, I thought 'hey I was told those gates cannot go that way, so they got that bit wrong'. At that point, the female got past the gates through a gap. It showed just how slim she was as I'd thought you couldn't get a rat through there. She managed it, still shouting her obscenities and then throwing her handbag at me. I caught the bag as she tore across the concourse, although we were landside, I could not leave my post. I thought I recognised the woman but wasn't sure.

Here I was, sitting on a ticket machine with queues of passengers waiting to come through the turnstiles to go into the security screening area, with this passenger's handbag on my lap, along with her passport and her mobile phone. Who was she? Was she drunk? Or was she running away after an incident? Well, as I had her passport and mobile phone it wasn't difficult to ascertain her identity. She was the famous royal connected 'it' girl.

The next thing two STL's come from behind me and one said, "Anthony, did you see where that female passenger went?"

"Are you talking to me?"

"Yes, Anthony."

"Sorry, I keep telling you it's Tony. Anyway, she headed across the concourse towards the exit; I've got her bag, her mobile phone and passport, she threw them at me."

"Well, hold onto it. The police will be along presently to get the stuff from you." and with that they both went running of in the direction the female had taken.

"What was all that about?" I asked my colleague who was seated just along from me.

"Hang on, I'm listening on the radio. It seems she was trying to get into the First-class lounge and they refused because they thought she was drunk or drugged up. She had a hissy fit and went into meltdown and charged back out through security."

"How the hell did she do that? I thought these security lanes could only go one way."

"Yup, me too. Who was she? You got her passport, who is she?"

"Shit, she's you know, that one out of 'I'm a celebrity get me out of here'. The 'it' girl and socialite, with the double-barrelled name. I think she's related to the Royal Family"

"Oh her, she's probably back on drugs or drunk or something. If they refused to let her into the First-class lounge."

"Why is that?"

"Well, it's happened before with her."

A police officer approached me and said, "I understand you might have that passenger's personal effects. Can we have them?"

"Sure." I said, "You know who that was then?"

"Oh yea, we got a report about her and was on our way to assist the BA staff who she was abusive too." he said. "She was refused entry into the First-Class lounge due to her condition, then threw her temper fit and charged out of the airport."

"Celebrities eh, who'd be one." I said.

The next day there were headlines in the press stating it had taken twelve armed-police officers to apprehend this passenger and restrain her. The truth was that just as she departed the airport a police van containing twelve armed-police officers arrived and did apprehend the passenger. But they were only there because they'd just reached the changeover of their shifts and were taking over from the other twelve officers on duty at that time. But hey, why would the press ruin a bloody good story even if it wasn't true?

Celebrities, who'd want to be one?

----

21 INFAMY! INFAMY! THEY'VE ALL GOT IT IN FOR ME!

I was searching a passenger's bag, having gone through the usual routine of asking whose bag it was and if I could search it. I asked if it held any sharp objects and requested that the passenger open the bag. This was done as we had to get permission to search the bag before we could begin. We'd always get the passenger to open their bag just in case we damaged their property when doing so. Saves the company any insurance claims, although as over sixty percent of our passengers were not English, and spoke no English, this often proved a point of conflict. Management seemed happy to allow us, officers, to put up with it, while they avoided any clashes in the interest of good customer service.

As I searched, he said, "Are you the Tony Levy who has written a book?" I noticed who was asking the question. It was an elderly gentleman who along with his wife was happy to have their hand luggage searched. I thought, well at least this search should be pleasant compared to others I'd carried out today. They were both dressed smart casual and appeared to be a very nice elderly couple.

"Yes." I stammered suspiciously.

"The book on the prison service? You know it's called A Turnkey or Not?"

"Yes, why? Is this a wind-up by my colleagues?" I added, looking around to see if any of them were smirking.

"No. I bought your book on my Kindle, back in the summer, after meeting you here. I never thought I'd meet you again, so wasn't sure it was you."

"It's me. What do you think of my book? Please be honest; it won't affect the way I search your bag." I joked.

"I am enjoying it. It's great to see how an organisation like the prison service operates. We're not in the profession so we don't know what goes on, I'll put a review on Amazon when I've finished it."

"Great, and many thanks. It's appreciated getting this sort of feedback." and I continued to carry out my search of his bag. He'd left a bottle of water inside, and I explained that it was over-sized so would not be allowed through.

"That's ok. It's just a pleasure to meet you again."

"Well, thanks and have a safe journey. It's a pleasure to meet you both again too."

This had made my day. It made up for the stress that was going on at that time. Thank you, whoever you are!

An airport's a fantastic place for people and worlds coming together. I wrote my book while still employed in the prison service, but started the process of publication while I was working at Heathrow. I had to inform the management that I was going to have a book published, and it wasn't about working here, but my previous employment.

Funnily enough, the airport in-house magazine on hearing the news of my impending publication, asked if they could include a piece about my book, and take photos of me holding it outside the doors to T5. And of course, I readily agreed.

I remember another occasion when searching a passenger's hand luggage; I asked, "I notice you have a Kindle in your bag, what sort of books do you like to read?"

"All sorts but autobiographies are a particular interest of mine."

"Oh well, have you read my book?" I offered her one of my cards. I tried never to miss the opportunity to hand out my book business cards and tried to take an interest if passengers had kindles or books on their personal effects. And I'd turn a conversation around to books in the hope to sell my own to them. "I've actually had it published."

"What's it about?"

"It's about my 25 years working in the British Prison service."

"That sounds interesting." said her husband who wwas also at the search table."

Yes, it is."

"Is it available on Amazon?" he asked.

"Yes, it's under A Turnkey or Not? by Tony Levy."

"Ok, yes." he said, I'm just downloading it now, and will read it on our flight."

'Oh, wow many thanks. Please put a review, good or bad, on Amazon when you've read it."

"Yes, of course, I will." he said as I completed the search of his wife's bag.

Often, at the loading position, if I saw a passenger take out a kindle from their personal luggage I'd ask what sort of book they were interested in. And inform them of my published book and offer them one of my business cards.

I often heard my team mates ask the same questions, and try to sell my book for me. I got through a lot of business cards but not sure how many books I sold because of this. I'm grateful for their help.

In fact, it became a team joke that my colleagues would say to passengers, do you know this man, whilst pointing at me. He's a published author, have you read his book......thanks guys!

Whether I was at the loaders position or searching the hand luggage, I'd ask passengers what books they were interested in. And ask if they'd be interested in an autobiography and offer my business card.

Many of my colleagues would often ask me if I'd write another book. I'd say, yes but this one will be about working at Heathrow warts and all. They'd say, let us know when it's published as we want to read it. I would say, well I'd have to leave here first, and maybe move back to Spain.

I hope you guys are reading this now and are not disappointed, and it's still safe for me to travel through Heathrow or not?

The hardest part of any writer is to get their works published. Even JK Rowling had her first book rejected by many publishers before she became world famous. But then one publisher took a chance on her, and the rest is history. That she obtained that one willing to take a chance on her was amazing; I often wonder how those other publishers feel that rejected her now?

I wonder how many of my colleagues at Heathrow had skills and achievements that nobody knew about. I knew of another member of staff who was also a published author. She was one of our staff trainers; I believe her book was fictional. Then there was a colleague of mine whose wife was a published author, writing the second book at that time, I hope she was successful too.

Infamy indeed.

----

22 50 SHADES OF EMBARRASSMENT

What a beautiful BA Stewardess, I thought to myself, as I spent another day working at the UK's busiest airport. We get wonderfully attractive women passing through this airport every day. It gives the job fantastic perks with great compensations to an otherwise mundane and sometimes boring place of work, even though it carries so much responsibility.

This one was whisking through the airport like that scene in the film 'Catch Me If You Can'. When the stewardesses came walking through the airport in their red outfits with Leonardo Di Caprio to the music, come fly with me. Gosh, this one was a real stunner.

We are here to keep you all safe; safe in the knowledge that when you step onto your aeroplane, our security has been good enough to ensure you reach your destination, safely. We are professional at our jobs, but come on looking at the odd, beautiful woman or man, is a distraction we can all do with. As long as we're not compromising security.

I remember one occasion the England Rugby team came through the South concourse. I think virtually every woman in the airport was watching them walking around the shops, and probably some men were envious of the looks the players were receiving.

On a Friday lunchtime, we'd often see a celebrity couple from an ITV morning chat show program walking around the shops waiting for their flights back to Belfast. Everybody would look at them as they were always such a happy couple. It provided a lovely distraction from our mundane business, even though he was a mad keen Manchester United fan.

These were pleasant distractions and often helped to lessen the tension that could often occur after dealing with stressful incidents.

I was so engrossed in watching this stewardess, well, she had lovely legs and looked so good and attractive, and I wasn't the only person looking either. Many men's and even women's heads turned in her direction as she came through the security screening process; she was stunning. I hoped her bag would be rejected. I was the bag searcher on the security lane she was coming through. It would have been a nice distraction from carrying out the bag search. But no such luck, she and her bag passed through security with no problems.

I was watching her collect her personal effects when I suddenly realised that a passenger's bag had been 'rejected' by the screen reader. It was in need of a security search. At this particular time, it was my responsibility to carry out the search.

Shaking myself back to the job in hand I asked politely, "Whose bag is this?" A passenger standing on the other side to the machine said in a very effeminate voice "It's mine."

"Ok. It needs to be searched. Please collect your personal belongings and come around to the end of the machine where I can search your bag. Thank you."

"Ok, but I don't know what I have left in the bag."

"Well, just take a look and see."

"Yes, sure be my guest. There's not much in there to search, anyway. I'm on a 'jump' seat'." A 'jump seat' is when a member of aircrew is getting a flight to connect them to their aircraft of operation for the day. Although they get the seats for free as they are regarded as passengers, they have to go through the same security screening as all passengers have too.

"Oh, you're staff."

"Yes, me and Amanda." he said pointing to the lovely stunner I'd been looking at. At that point, she approached the search area and asked in a beautiful sexy voice "Simon, what have you left in your bag you dope?"

"I don't know, but this lovely man is going to search it for me." he said in his best mincing voice.

"Ok. Do you have any sharp objects in your bag? Anything I might cut myself on when I put my hand in your bag?"

"No, well only my nail file its metal, but it's allowed."

"Yes, it's allowed so no problem."

I started the search, taking each item out and placing it in another tray. I took out his steward's waistcoat, and a few personal items that I placed discreetly in the tray but under his waistcoat so nobody else could see them. We try to be discreet when dealing with personal items of clothing and other objects especially if they are of a sexual nature. I then took a book out of his bag and as I was a published author and always tried not to miss an opportunity to get a passenger interested in my book, I look at the book cover 'Fifty Shades of Grey'.

"Is this a good book?"

"Oh darling, it's filth. It's so sexy it turns me on just reading the pages. It's sex on words."

"Really, that good uh?"

"I read it to my partner, and it drives him crazy."

Wow, too much information for me. He turned to the stunning colleague "Amanda! Have you read Fifty Shades yet? It will turn you horny and get your love juices flowing."

Bloody hell, do I really want to imagine this beautiful woman becoming horny, and especially when trying to concentrate on my job.

Amanda said to him in that sexy voice (or was her sexy voice in my imagination) "Simon I found the book boring it's just porn, and I put it down around halfway through it. It's not my type of book."

"No," said Simon "you prefer the real thing anyway don't you; I saw you and that gorgeous man going into that hotel last time out. I bet you didn't need 50 shades of anything." and he giggled. She looked a little angry at him, blew him a kiss and said in a jokey manner "Fuck off you dirty pervert."

"Well, I saw him first and fancied him before you."

"Yes, well he's straight I'm afraid."

"Oh, you bitch." enough already! Do I want to hear all this? No!

I was getting a little embarrassed at the tone of this conversation. I continued my search and found a bottle of water inside 'Simons' bag.

"Oh, dear sir, this is the problem." I held up the bottle of water.

"Oh shit, how did that get in there?"

"It's your bag Simon." said the lovely Amanda.

"Oh yes, I remember. I was chatting up that lovely man on the flight from Glasgow. As he was getting off the plane, he handed me the bottle as he said he didn't need it. I must have put it in my bag without realising it. He had such a cute bum, you know, I must have been distracted. Just discard it ok."

"You're distracted by anything with a cock."

"Well said, Amanda - the ice queen." Ok, I've had enough now!

"Yes sure, I'll discard it, but I have to test it first just to make sure. Then I will dispose of it in the bin."

"Thanks, darling. You're very nice, you know."

I was getting even more embarrassed and felt he was trying to 'chat me up'. Just my luck, I have a beautiful woman at my desk and the gay man she is travelling with tries to chat me up. Oh well, it makes a change from being sworn at or treated with contempt.

I finished my search and said to Simon "Would you like me to repack you bag sir?"

"Oh no thanks sweetie. I can manage that myself. You should try to read this book though; it might give you some sexy ideas for when you get home." he said and winked at me.

As the two of them walked off to the shops arm in arm, they both turned around and blew kisses at me.

Embarrassed? You bet fifty shades of it!

----

23 THE 2012 LONDON OLYMPICS

What an event, what an experience, and to be an important part of the whole background to it was fantastic, not to mention the bonus we all received for the expected amount of extra passenger we'd experience.

The London 2012 Olympics was a world event and a fantastic one at that. And Heathrow Airport was to play a significant role in the overall success of this prestigious event for the UK and our economy.

Getting the thousands of participants, the background staff, coaches, and their equipment was a major logistical headache. The planning took years to develop at Heathrow. And we security officers would be small cogs in this very big wheel. Exciting? Yes, it was!

An extra 650,000 passengers were expected to pass through the airport during the Games. Visitor numbers would start to increase just as the holiday season, Olympic athletes, and delegations would also be arriving. All at the same time, so a busy period for sure.

Heathrow had unveiled a new temporary terminal building to cater for athletes and officials involved with London 2012. The terminal has been built for "Games Family" departures. It would be used for the three days after the closing ceremony on 12 August.

Over 10,000 athletes and 37,000 bags were expected to be diverted away from the other terminals during the period. Some 80% of Olympic visitors were due to arrive at the airport, with 13 August expected to be Heathrow's busiest day ever.

As security officers, we'd been given instructions we were not to approach any of the athletes and ask for autographs or obtain 'selfie' pictures with them. Although this was always the rule anyway, many of the staff just ignored this including the STL's.

Many times, throughout the Olympics we had unexpected encounters with VIP's and celebrities. I remember one such occasion. I was waiting to go home and catch up on the highlights of what was happening at the Olympics.

I was on a singleton post late on this evening. On a position called International backflow south (there was an identical position at the other end of the baggage hall North). My job was to sit in an alcove at a desk and watch the passengers come out through the customs hall with their personal belongings. I had to ensure that nobody went back into the customs hall. The rules of the UK Border Control staff were that nobody was allowed back in through this route once they'd left the baggage hall and gone through customs. The only exception was for medical staff on a 'shout', and then we had to log the incident.

If, as happened often, a passenger forgot to collect their baggage or would leave personal effects or something in the baggage hall, we'd have to direct them to a staff search area where BA staff would be called to escort the passenger back to find their missing items. This led to the occasional confrontation, given a passenger would be in panic mode when realising they had forgotten their luggage.

However, on this detail, I'd have been on this post for around 3 hours with no breaks (comfort breaks could be had, but you had to radio the duty allocator to get somebody to come and cover you. It could be touch and go whether a relief would come before you relieved yourself, more about that later).

I was hoping my night shift relief would come soon so I could go home. I always volunteered for this post whenever my team were on this duty line. It required that the post is filled at the end of the day's shift. Once the night patrol relief arrived, I could nip out through the staff exit and be at the bus stop before anybody else. This post was the nearest to the staff bus stop. This exit was used by authorised staff, and we were supposed to get them to show us their Identity passes before they could exit. Many staff and mainly BA cabin crew ignored us as unimportant compared to them and would often try to sail past us. Funnily enough, the Captains and Pilots showed their passes without question.

There I was getting impatient to go home. A female member of BA ground staff came up to my position with a passenger who I didn't recognise, but I wasn't really looking. She said, "Can I take this passenger out through the staff exit please?"

Without looking, I said, "Sorry, but you know the rules. Only staff with approved passes can exit this way."

"But this is a very important passenger."

"Sorry. Your colleagues have already tried that one on me before. I really can't let the gentleman out." I said. As I looked at him I thought to myself; I'm sure I know this geezer. But at that moment it didn't register who he was.

He then leaned towards me so I could get a good look at his face. He said in an easily recognised voice "I have the highest authority in the land. I'm trusted by her majesty the queen. There are a lot of press waiting for me at the main exit, and I don't want to become embroiled in the paparazzi at this time of night." Oh, my goodness, it was James Bond! Well I know it's not the real James Bond, he's just a fictional character. This was the actor who was now playing him in the films. And who I'd seen in the opening sequences to the start of the Olympic Games in that amazing Danny Boyle opening ceremony.

"On this occasion, I think I can make an exception." and I added, "I thought your opening sequences in the Olympics were fantastic."

"Yes, David and I (referring to David Beckham), had great fun filming that. The Queen was wonderful you know."

"Ok, I stammered." and allowed them through.

"Thank you so much," said 007, "and if you're ever in trouble don't forget to get in touch with James Bond, and I'll be over to help." he laughed, and off he went.

The whole encounter made a great end to a boring shift. When I was relieved by the night officer, I told them the story, and he said, "Did you get his autograph or a picture with him then?" 'Shit' I thought, I didn't even think about that.

I found out afterwards that many of my colleagues had completely gone against the rules. They were competing against themselves to obtain as many autographs and photographs of them together with the stars of the games and all the celebrities.

I was on tickets south when a well-known female tennis champion was coming through the area. She stopped at my desk and handed over her ticket, which I scanned and returned. She'd just won the Gold medal at the Olympics, for the female tennis champion. And she was returning home to the USA. I cheekily asked, "Many congratulations on winning the gold medal, do you have it with you?"

"Yes, I keep it with me all the time since winning it; it's precious to me."

"Could I look at it?"

"Sure." she said and reached into her handbag and retrieved the gold medal and handed it to me.

I was gob smacked; I never expected her just to hand it over. I was honoured to be allowed to hold it. I'd never seen a Winners Olympic Gold medal before, but the ones from the London Olympics were special. "Thank you so much. I hope you continue to be a world champion."

"Thanks. I intend to be around for many more years yet." she said and disappeared into the maze of the security screening lanes.

The lightning 'Bolt' also came through T5 on his way home from winning his three gold medals in the athletic sprints. He was so quick we all missed him. He was surrounded by so many BA hangers on that I didn't get the chance to even congratulate him.

It's fine protecting your customers; it's the BA ground staff's job. But come on, the man had just made Olympic history. All we wanted to do was offer our congratulations to somebody who'd made Olympic history in our lifetime. The escorting staff stopped us. He seemed very humble, and I'm sure he'd have stopped to chat to us all if he'd been allowed by the BA staff.

The strange thing about the Olympics, and the very generous bonuses we received for each day we worked during the games was that the terminal seemed to run not only smoother than usual, but it seemed less busy considering we were at the height of the busiest time of the year. I don't know why that was. I know many questions were asked of management about the amount of staff made available for the number of passengers travelling through the airport. It was expected that during the games Heathrow would experience its busiest day ever. It never did. The busiest single day was still July 31, 2011, when 233,561 passengers passed through the airport. I believe that figure has now been beaten.

But all in all, the Olympics passed through Heathrow very easily, and I think we helped to contribute to the incredible success of the 2012 Olympic games.

----

24 THE BEAUTIFUL STRANGER

Who was she? Who knows where she came from? We don't know. Where's she going? We don't know that either. What she does for a living's also an unknown factor. But she was a real beauty a real stunner, one that you looked at and could not take your eyes off her? You wanted to look and take her in, look her up and down and savour every part of her perfectly formed body.

Our eyes met across the concourse. I gave a slight nod of approval. She too gave a slight reciprocal inclination of her head. That beautiful wonderful sensual head. Was she appreciating my looks as I was of hers, or just acknowledging my looking at her? Was that smile one that says to yourself, 'I know you know how beautiful I am' or was it of inward amusement at the looks she attracted? Who knows? She was obviously used to getting those looks from complete strangers and liked it. She was stunning, of that there was no doubt, and she knew it. Not in the page three model sense but the English beauty sense. She exuded money and class. The way she held herself, she knew we knew, and she knew we were watching yet she appeared oblivious to our stares. She oozed sexuality, enough to turn anybody on.

Her sex appeal was evident to all who viewed her. And many did. Her eyes had that come to bed look in them, and you knew with her you'd have great sex. Looking at her that film with Gene Wilder and Kelly Brook, 'The Woman in Red' came to my mind, and I took a more intimate note of her.

Her ankles were small and thin; you could see this clearly despite the ankle length boots she wore. They had zips up the outside, black with just a hint of ornate metallic designer motifs. The five-inch heels accentuated the length of her long slender legs, up past her perfectly formed dimpled knees. I watched as she sexually unzipped each boot and took them off, delicately placing them in the provided tray like they were precious stones. Those long legs went upwards forever, boy she was a sexy woman of that, there was no doubt.

I continued my observations of her legs upwards until the start of her short flared black gypsy skirt which started about six inches above those lovely knees? How did she have those dimples on her knees like that? Those legs just went upwards and upwards and had an even suntan not too much and not too little, just enough to let you know that this girl bathed in the sun whenever she wanted to and had an even suntan. She wore no tights or stockings and didn't need to with that suntan.

I continued my assessment of her past that incredible sexy bottom, my how you'd die for a bottom like that. Then moving my glance upwards towards that slender waist of hers, perfectly formed in harmony with the rest of her body. And the belt wrapped around that thin waist, with the designer name-clasp in metal, showed her waist in the best possible manner.

Then again, moving my gaze upwards from her slender waist to her hips, which had just the right amount of movement to synchronise with the rest of her fabulous body. I continued my glance up to her breasts. She had a strapped thin V-neck, t-shirt, also black, that showed just the right amount of cleavage, clear evidence that no enhancements were needed. They accentuated her movements with every breath of air she took in and exhaled out. Not small, and not big, but from where I stood admirably formed, and pert. She wore no bra; she didn't need to. A necklace adorned her throat, and shone even from this distance; it shouted money at you as it glistened in the light. The earrings matched with the necklace; they hung down her ears towards her lovely neck.

Her long angular neck led to a flawless face. That she was a beauty was in no doubt. And she knew it and knew how to make sure everybody else knew it. Wonderfully structured high cheekbones with a slender aquiline nose gave her a classic look with just the right amount of thickness to her lusciously red lips. They shouted at you to be kissed, and I bet she used them expertly too. Oh, to be kissed by those lips, I longed for the opportunity. And her deep blue eyes with expertly manicured eyebrows spoke sexual expressions at every change of her face. Her long hair shone in designer flowing locks, and it was evident to all that a great deal of money, time, and care had gone into her hair to make it so attractive. It fell and swished around her slender shoulders in time to her body movements. A pair of designer sunglasses adorned her head as if they were part of it, like a Princess tiara put there for effect, and not a pair of sunglasses to be worn in bright sunlight.

Her arms like her legs had an even suntan throughout the length of them; she had slender fingers with well-manicured fingernails. No rings adjourned her third finger left hand, but on each little finger shone ornate gold rings along with a beautiful diamond ring on her right middle finger. This was no cheap designer jewellery but the real McCoy you could just tell. She had money or had money spent on her, yet she travelled alone. Perhaps going to meet her lover in some foreign country or maybe she had just left her him and was making a fresh start. Who knew, but she shone through the place. She lit it up as the stares came from all direction. She was a looker that was unquestionable, and she knew she was attractive to both men and women and loved the attention.

I realised my partner was speaking, "Sorry what did you say?" I stammered.

"I said, do you want me to ask her to take that belt and her boots off before she comes through the metal detector? She will go off when she walks through, and you'll have to search her, you lucky devil."

"Yes." I answered, too embarrassed to look at him. He must have known I was staring at this beauty, as he'd been himself after all my sexuality was no secret in this place.

He spoke to her, their eyes flirtatiously meeting. Then, using her well-manicured fingers, she removed first her belt and then her boots. Her height was reduced to its normal five-foot-seven, but this did not detract from her overall appearance of beauty and sophistication.

And then like a model on the catwalk, only she was not one, she swished through the archway without a murmur. The faint lingering smell of Channel number five left in her wake, well what else would this one wear. No indication, so no need to search her. What a shame I thought. I bet my colleague would have loved that job if it had been possible, but only women can search women at this airport. So, it would have fallen to me to carry out this search. But alas no!

She collected her personal effects and was lost in the maze of a busy international airport, leaving the stares of many behind her. Off to who knew where to a life of who knew what. Never mind, this was always the problem when you worked at one of the busiest airports in the world. People come, and people go, they make an impact and then are gone. Never mind, move on to the next passenger and continue to do my job.

As a security officer in one of the world's busiest airports, you meet so many beautiful people male or female, but I wonder if they know what you are thinking.

I hope not.

----

25 T5B

I only solved the mystery of T5B when our shift Rota's changed, and instead of working only in Zones 1.2 or 3 we were detailed to work in our teams in all three areas. I'd never worked T5B but had heard a lot about it. But it was the same as T5C, except our shift duties only placed us there for either a two hours stint or a long just over three hours at a time. But it was a great place for your team to interact with each other during the many long quiet spells that occurred when working in T5B.

All flights into T5B and T5C were long haul International flights. No domestic flights arrived or departed from either terminal. It amazed me that passengers would end up at T5B and claim they didn't know it was not for their domestic flight. How? I really do not know; maybe they fancied a trip along the little railway link and into the satellites of 5B and 5C. It created a huge security issue, when this happened, just to get the passengers back to the correct area they needed to get their flights.

Most of the flights into and out of T5B were to the Indian sub-continent and Canada. There was a daily flight that arrived from Canada and had a connection to India, and this was always a busy time for the security staff working at T5B, and vice versa. Many of these passengers apparently had not flown before or very infrequently as they never seemed to understand the security implication of not doing what they needed to do. Or maybe back in their remote parts of the world corruption played a huge part in their expectations of dealing with authority. Whatever the reason, I was always glad we had members of the team that could converse with the Indian passengers.

But dealing with these passengers was always difficult due to the diverse cultures and especially the various cultures within their own cultures. I was working the archway one day when a group of these types came through. All dressed in a similar way to what you'd imagine a cross between a Buddhist monk and a Japanese sumo wrestler would be dressed. They were on some religious journey or returning from the event. There were six men in similar attire, non-spoke any English nor did they seem to understand the Indian language that our colleague was using in trying to converse with them at the loaders position.

It was like a sketch from a comedy show. Now bearing in mind that these passengers were on an International transfer, and they had had to go through some security either in India or from whatever airport they had flown from first to get to Heathrow, they didn't seem to have any comprehension of what they needed to do. Our loader was speaking to them in his dialect, and they were just looking totally blank. He switched to English and said to me.

"Tony, some of these mountain men have strange languages that only they seem to understand, but as they're travellers, maybe using English would be better." and he turned back to them.

"Do you have any laptops or large electrical items in your bags?"

Silence.

"Do you have any liquids, gels, or paste, and if so are they inside your bags? You need to remove them."

Silence.

"Maybe they're a silent order." I said, helpfully.

"Naw, they were talking to each other."

"Maybe they're a silent order to non-believers."

"Piss off, I'm trying to explain here." and he continued to use sign language at them.

"Place your bags into the grey trays and remove your jewellery, please."

Silence.

It was going to be a waste of time anyway as they all had their religious bangles on their arms and they were never going to take them off; I knew I'd have to search them as they'd activate the archway. But my colleague manfully continued to try to communicate with them.

"Do you have any laptops or large electrical items in your bags?" He asked in both languages.

Silence.

"Oh, just put your bloody bags in the trays." and he handed each of them a tray which suddenly they seemed to understand what they had to do and complied. Great, we can get going now. Thank goodness, we were in T5B, and it was quiet, but we knew there were the usual long-haul flights due through at any time. That would be almost a whole jumbo jet full of passengers that would have to be processed. All again from the Indian sub-continent. That would mean lots of noise, lots of searching, and lots of protests. Oh well, once we got them through we would have nice quiet hours to relax and enjoy our time here.

But for now, these passengers needed processing. I looked at their footwear, flip-flops, so no problems with them having to take their shoes off. Thank goodness because by the look of them they looked marginally better than if they'd been in bare feet, but not by much.

I held my hand up in the internationally known stop gesture and asked my female colleague Rami to allow them through slowly one at a time; she stood in the middle of the archway on our side of the machine and beckoned the first one through Buzz, Buzz, Buzz.

"Sir, you've activated the WTMD archway, please remove your shoes." I was dreading this. By looking and pointing to his flip-flops and making the gesture to take them off. He seemed to understand, and removed them and placed them in the tray that Rami was now holding for him.

OMG the smell, I've never smelt feet so bad. When we were young, I shared a bedroom with my now deceased brother, and he had the smelliest feet I've ever had the misfortune to be in the same room as. But now I knew better; this man hadn't washed his feet for some time. I made a mental note to find out if the airport cleaners had forgotten to clean the floors for the last few months, for his feet to have been so dirty and smelly.

"Sir, may I search you?" and I stood, raised my hands in the International pose for preparing to be searched, and the man complied by copying my pose.

Shit, his armpits stunk. My goodness, the smell made me step back. And Rami had to hold her nose. Did these people never wash or had they had a terrible flight, I thought to myself. Now I wished I was wearing gloves. But I completed the search and Rami offered me the handheld metal detector as he'd activated the walk-through archway. I continued to use the handheld metal detector in the correct method. So far, I'd found nothing on him that would have activated the WTMD, and I know these metal detectors do not make mistakes.

At around his middle, the metal detector activated, informing me he had metal on his body, around his waist area.

"Sir, you have metal around your waist, can you please remove it?"

Silence.

"Sir, you need to remove the metal around your waist area."

Silence.

I gently lifted his upper garment which revealed a piece of string tied around his waist with what looked like a lump of metal in the small of his back with the string looped through it.

"What the hell is that?" I said to myself, pointing to the object. "Never seen anything like this. What do I do?"

Rami said, "I remember my grandma once telling me she thought some of these weird Indian mountain religions believed it to be sacred. And the sacred thread reminds a man to lead a regulated life with purity in his thought, word and deed."

"That's just great. Pity their religion didn't teach them anything about personal hygiene. But how do I process it? I think we need an STL just to cover our arses here, don't you?"

"Yes, Stan can you get an STL please?"

The STL was in an office just next to where our security lane was. There was all manner of communications equipment in that office along with all the cameras for monitoring the staff going about their work. We sometimes had an STL come out of the room and tell members of the team to stop using their mobile phones while on the machines. But many staff did it during the quiet periods, so we knew the cameras were watching us.

I explained the problem to the STL and also told him none of the men appeared to speak or understand any English or any of the Indian languages that any of my colleagues could speak.

"Ok, here's what we will do. I assume they're all going to be wearing these things, so we'll treat them all as though they are wearing these religious items. And we can just use the metal detector on them without taking the items off their person, okay?"

"Sure."

"But what is that smell?"

"Him well his armpits and his feet."

"Bloody hell, we need air freshener once you've processed them all."

"I need a shower once I've finished and some anti-bacterial wipes."

"Can you image the smell on the plane?"

"Well, would you notice it with the overwhelming smell of curry?"

"Probably not but they have to fumigate the plane, anyway."

"Shame they didn't fumigate the bloody passengers too."

I finished this search, and then Rami called the next man through, and we went through the same process again. And so on until the last man came through the archway and activated it. I completed my search, and he made the gesture of putting both his hands together in front of his face in the sign of prayer as each man had before him, but he then said in almost perfect English.

"Bless you and thankyou young man for your kindness today."

My mouth dropped open, and all of us on the machine looked at each other in complete amazement. I think it was my colleague who had all the problems; he was at the loaders position and was trying to communicate with them. He looked like he wanted to strangle this man. But we all laughed about it once I'd washed my hands in hot water and we cleaned all the equipment the men had touched.

We had many similar incidents while at T5B, many laughs and we often had passengers who wanted to argue or not understand the process. Even though to get to T5B or T5C they would already have gone through a similar security process at their departure airport. But it never ceased to amaze me how many of these passengers apparently didn't know about any security when coming to an airport.

I remember Rami once telling me that many of these Indian travellers were so used to a corrupt system they expected to encounter similar systems when coming to Heathrow. Many of them would just expect the staff to do everything for them rather than be expected to do it themselves and then get paid for their trouble. It is amazing just how different the cultures of our world are.

The mystery of T5B well and truly revealed, and it was no different to anywhere else in the terminal where you had to process passengers through the security screening process.

----

26 ROYAL SUITE

Tucked away on the south side of the airport is Heathrow's tiny sixth terminal - the Royal Suite used for royalty, visiting heads of state, and certain celebrities. It has its own stand and is only opened on special occasions.

The suite is within a purpose-built modern complex near Terminal 5. It can't be accessed by the public or seen from outside the airport's perimeter fence. It comes under the operation of Terminal 5 although for staff to report there for duty it requires a mini bus drive to get there. Funnily enough, it always seemed nearer to Terminal 4, but it was a nice tour of the interior of the airport apron areas whenever we were detailed to work there.

It was always regarded as a perk to be detailed the Royal Suite, and was often the subject of favouritism, as friends of the detailing staff and RA's often ended up being detailed the Royal Suite. In fact, because of these claims, our detail was changed so that every team in T5 was given one session on standby for working at the Royal suite during our new thirty-six-week shift-rota system. It still did not stop certain teams often being allocated the Royal Suite in front of the actual team's detailed rota to be there. And often the excuse was that if the correct team were detailed there, it would throw out everybody else's meals breaks. A rubbish excuse but management accepted it. However, the security staff all knew it was still the same 'friends' of the detailing staff that got the job.

As most of the detailing staff were from the same ethnic background and lived in the same areas, sometimes the same streets as the teams getting this much-wanted detail, I'll leave you to make your mind up about whether it was friends looking after friends. Or could it be interpreted as racism due to the ethnic makeup of the teams!

The Royal Suite's used by dignitaries like the Sultan of Brunei when he arrives on his private 747, along with other Heads of State and Royalty who use it. And it's used for the super VIP's, the Queen and Prince Philip; and by all the rest of the Royal family Prince Charles, Prince

Andrew, Harry and William, plus the prime minister, and visiting foreign presidents.

It's not to be confused with the Windsor suite which is also used by VIP's but is run as a commercial venture. Victoria Beckham was the first celebrity to use the Windsor Suite, and now many celebrities' use the suite.

Whereas the Royal suite is for the super VIP's which nowadays means anybody who has the money or status to arrive and depart from this exclusive part of the airport including the whole of the Liverpool Football team arriving late at night after a match played somewhere in Europe. And the Hull Football team in 2014 who arrived there before the FA Cup Final. Yup money really does talk.

John Travolta also used the suite when he arrived there with his wife over a Christmas period, some years ago. But although I was on duty in the suite and got to see him and all his family as they were escorted into one of the suites there, I never found out if he flew his own 747 jet himself or whether he was the co-pilot that day, but it was a great experience. As he was only arriving at the airport he and his family did not have to come through the exclusive security screening system; they only had to be scrutinised by the UK Border passport control system. We had to be there because their exclusive drivers had to come into the suite from landside to airside and therefore were subject to the security screening process.

This was often the case; we'd be sent over to the suite (when it was our turn on the rota) only around forty-five minutes before any arrival. And usually only because drivers or other personnel had to come into the suite from the landside of the airport.

The suites were fitted out in total luxury. Plush huge comfortable armchairs and settees were scattered in all the suites, and expensive pictures adorned all the walls. It was the height of luxury, all had private bathroom facilities with refreshments available and in one room was a Grand piano that one of the regular workers over there could play really well. He would often play on the piano once we had completed our jobs and were waiting for the transport to take us back to the main T5 terminal. It was wonderful, listening to his playing in that environment.

Every time VIP's or Dignitaries, and anybody else who wanted to pay the rate for using the suite and its anonymity was leaving the UK then they would require a security team on duty in the suite as apart from Heads of State or Royalty everybody leaving the UK had to go through the security process.

Once, just as my team were going off on our long break the RA said to us, "There's a late movement at the Suite, but it will mean working overtime."

"Yes, count us in," said Rami.

"If you want to do it, then you must all go together as a team otherwise I'll have to give it to another team. It's a late movement, might not get away until three or four a.m."

"Hang on you, said the whole team, what all of us?"

"Yup, that's the deal."

"But that's unfair."

"That's the deal otherwise it mucks up my boards."

"It's still unfair on the team, just because one person might not want to work overtime. And in my case, it means getting home in the early hours of the morning."

"That's the deal. Think about it and let me know when you come back from your break." and he smiled at us all, knowingly.

The team and I walked out of the RA's office and on to our break; I could tell the team were not happy with the arrangements as they knew that I didn't work overtime if I could avoid it.

Off we went to our break. I knew the others really wanted to go the Royal suite, after all, it was our team's detailed rota for going there. And it was a real perk to get off working the usual mundane security lanes, but they also knew that I didn't like to work overtime. The reason was simple because I'd already received my occupational pension from the Prison Service. And along with the current salary from Heathrow and the annual bonuses we received, and on this occasion, we were also getting a bonus for working during the Olympic Games, it put my earnings on the border of the next tax threshold and therefore meant paying a lot more personal income tax. Basically, if I worked too much overtime, it meant that I would be taxed more than what I got paid for the overtime. So, despite the inbuilt expectation that all staff would work overtime, I avoided it whenever possible.

As the team walked off, I stopped just outside the RA's door to text my wife, when I overheard an officer talking to the RA.

"Hey what's happening Bruv, with the Royal Suite gig?"

"I told Rami and her team about the late movement but told them the whole team had to go otherwise I'd send another one as it mucks up my board."

"Was Tony there?"

"Yup, and you know he won't do the overtime, so the gigs your team's. I look after you, don't I?"

"Yea Bruv respect, innit."

I was livid. We already suspected that some of the RA's seemed to favour this team. They were known on the concourse as the 'team'. Everybody seemed to know about the 'mates' arrangements, but nothing was ever seen to be done about it. But on this occasion, I was so angry to hear it going on.

I walked off toward the landside restroom as I wanted to chat in private to my wife, and I explained what I'd heard.

"You've got to do the overtime."

"I think so, just to show them they cannot get away with such underhand little schemes."

"Yes, I agree, and you have two rest days afterwards, so it doesn't matter what time you get home."

"You're right, just don't want to disturb you when I get back."

"Don't worry we can stay in bed the next morning."

"Ha, you mean you will." I laughed.

"Just let me know you if see anybody famous when they arrive."

"Ok, but I don't think it will be as late as the RA said the airport closes around eleven p.m. And they're not supposed to have any take offs during that time, so it must be a VIP arrival, and even then, the airport's meant to close. So, I cannot see it going on as late as we've been told."

"All right, I'll see you when I see you. Goodnight."

"Ok darling, love you, bye."

We arrived back at the RA's office from our breaks; I hadn't said a word to the team about what I'd overheard, nor had I told them I would do the overtime so as not to let them down. I thought I'd wait and see how the RA reacted when I said yes. In fact, I was looking forward to seeing his face and wished I could be there when he told his mate they wouldn't be getting the Royal suite after all. But for now, I said nothing.

"Ok, what's it to be?"

"Well, we want to go." and they all looked at me.

"Yes, I'm in too."

"Yea, nice one Tony. Thanks." the team said.

"Report to the Windsor suite for transportation to the Royal Suite in five minutes then."

"Sure, and thanks for making sure we could all go to the Royal Suite together. I so appreciate all your hard work you RA's do to look after us." I said sarcastically.

The RA looked daggers at me, and I just had to say

The RA looked daggers at me, and I had to say, "I might be old and need glasses, but I can see extremely well, even behind the scenes, and my hearing is excellent. Did I ever tell you I can hear three different conversations at once?" and I winked at the RA as I walked out of his office.

"What was that all about?"

"I'll tell you some time Rami honestly, maybe in my next book. Did I tell you I have had a book published?"

And in unison, the whole team said, "Yes, once or twice."

Once at the Windsor Suite, we boarded our transport a luxury Mercedes mini bus used for VIP's usually, but it was also used to transport security teams to and from the Royal suite.

Off we went on our magical journey through the maze of the unknown roads and lanes that weaved their way around this busy airport. We went down through tunnels underneath the runways and taxiing areas, along with a maze of lanes all complete with traffic lights and aircraft crossing points, around the other terminals and a complete circumnavigation of the newly being built Terminal 2 which looked impressive from our perspective. Over towards T4 and passed the massive new multi decked Airbus A380's belonging at that time to Virgin Atlantic Airlines. These aircraft were huge, how these things ever get into the air is beyond me.

How the drivers of cargo trolleys and the many apron security vans, along with the buses that transported passengers from one terminal to another knew all these lanes to use was beyond me. The road signs seemed to be in some code that only these drivers understand. Finally, we arrived in the parking area of Terminal 6 the Royal Suite.

A VIP manager, known to us as she worked in the Windsor suite usually, and was always good to us, said there would be tea and biscuits available in the back restroom. The movement wasn't for at least another hour so we could relax.

This VIP manager was beautiful and efficient at her job of being a VIP meeter and greeter but was never overly friendly to us security staff. Which was fine for us, but she said

"I don't think we'll be here much past midnight, but I'll book you in until at least two am as its overtime past your finish time of eleven pm. Is that ok?"

"Yes." we said as we tucked into our tea and biscuits, which to be honest was always the best thing about working in the Royal suite.

"It's an arrival, and there won't be any luggage, so the only movement you might get will be a driver to take the VIP to Claridges."

"Can we arrange for the ride back to take us to the staff car park, rather than back to T5 as it's so late and the buses from T5 run so infrequently at this time of night? It would save us a lot of time. I said

"Yes. I'll arrange for the driver to drop you off at the staff car park, sure."

"Thanks."

That was that. I think she must have told us who was arriving at the Royal suite. But I cannot remember who the passenger VIP was, so it wasn't a celebrity of any sorts. It was most probably one of the Saudi Royal families who often flew into Heathrow for few days on business and then back to Saudi Arabia.

As an arriving visiting member of a Royal family, his luggage was not subject to the usual arrival security issues, but a member of the UKBA had to come and check the arrival's credentials.

And that was that the movement and everything else was indeed completed by one am. And the manager had kept her word and booked us the extra overtime and arranged for the VIP transport to take us straight to the staff car park. I was home in my bed at two am with a few hours overtime completed. Good days work and a nice break to the Royal suite. Job done!

But to be honest, because of the perceived corruption of 'mates' getting this sort after break from the busy normality of the T5 concourse, I never enjoyed this perk.

----

27 MIND YOUR PEE'S AND QUEUE

We all need to go to the toilet; it's a naturally occurring bodily function of all animals, human or otherwise. But at least we humans have the choice of when to go and when to hold it in, or do we? Some cultures don't appear to have the same level of personal hygiene as we do and to be honest, I have witnessed this in some of the countries I've visited, but I suspect so have you.

But have you ever been in a long queue and been waiting so long you need to go to the toilet? 'Do I leave this line and go to the toilet? Or do I wait and hold it' it's a dilemma, it's also a long queue, and I would have to go to the back of it if I went to the toilet. Hold or go? Hold or Go? Dilemma!

This has happened on occasions, so what I try to do nowadays is look at the queue and decide whether I can hold the natural process up long enough to get through the queue, or not. I've learnt to go before joining the long line of waiting people. However, you're in a hurry and are already running late, running through your mind is I'm gonna miss my flight, so sod it, get in the queue and hold it in, you can do it.

But it doesn't always happen like that. Read on, and I will reveal what several people have done and the consequences of their action.

I was told about a passenger who pooed himself while waiting in the queue to come through the security screening process. He had obviously made the decision he could hold it until he got through the process. However, the urge must have been too much, and he carried out his need to go, resulting in the whole of his line having to be moved into other queues as he had left his deposit on the floor. It led to even longer waits for some of them. But what if you suddenly have an attack of diarrhoea? What do you do?

I heard of some women wearing burkas who had left deposits behind after coming through the WTMD but witnessed nothing like that during my time there. I don't doubt the staff who told me of these abhorrent events.

I was working on the archway on yet another busy day (T5 most days were hectic, and every day had its busier spells). There was a long queue of people at my security screening lane, and it seemed that I had to search virtually every male passenger that came through the archway. As I was completing a search, I noticed that an African dressed man with a bright floral shirt and black tracksuit bottoms was the next person waiting to come through the WTMD. I thanked my present passengers for his patience and wished him a pleasant journey. My female colleague, 'Elsa', on the archway with me, signalled this gentleman through. He activated as a quote search, just my luck, I've searched all these passengers, and now I get a quote search. You know sometimes I think these machines have got it in for me. And I stepped forward yet again to conduct another search. "Sir, may I search you please?"

"I no speak English." he said in very poor broken English. It was evident that there could be a language difficulty, so I adopted the pose I wished the passenger to assume, to enable me to carry out the search.

"Tony, I think he's peed himself."

"What!" I said as I turned to Elsa. We often worked on the archway together, and she could have a good sense of humour, at times, so I thought she was joking.

"He's pissed himself."

I looked at him. He offered no explanation or showed any signs of understanding what was being said, let alone made any acknowledgement of the fact he had peed himself.

"Are you sure Elsa?"

"Well, there's a wet patch around his midriff and groin area."

Oh, shit there was a wet patch, and he had peed himself.

"Can you get me a pair of gloves please?"

"Yes." she said as she asked for a pair of gloves to be handed over from the nearest security lane. She giggled "Rather you than me on this one Tony."

"Yea thanks, this is the second time in two days this has happened to me."

The passenger had not changed his expression at all and seemed to ignore what he had done. I know we have different cultures coming through the airport all the time, but to do this without even mentioning it, was either ignorant or maybe he was just too embarrassed to say anything, I don't know, but when this had happened to me previously, the passenger had indicated what had happened. I took that passenger to a private room to carry out the search and then allowed him to go to the toilets to clean himself.

"Sir, have you wet yourself?"

"I no understand."

"Sir, you appear to be wet here." and I pointed to the general area "Would you prefer that I conduct a private search?"

"I no understand."

What do I do without embarrassing the passenger? "Sir, do you need the toilet, WC, rest room, bog? A pee, err, err?" I couldn't think of any other way to ask him.

"I don't understand."

"I'm just going to have to search him here, aren't I?" I said to Elsa.

"Yes." she was always abrupt. But what else could I do, I knew in the Zulu and Afrikaans language 'toilet' was 'toilet' but didn't know where this passenger was from, so could not figure a way to communicate with him. I went about the search as best as I could but had to carry it out in a different order to what I was supposed to. I didn't want to search that wet area and then continue with the search, so I left that area until the end. To be on the safe side, I also used the hand metal detector on him, to complete a thorough search.

"Thank you, sir." as I ushered him on his way.

"Thank you. I no speak English." he said as he walked past me.

No, I thought, but you must have known you pissed yourself. At that point, we were due to rotate to our next position in the screening process. I hoped I didn't have any bags to search, but as I walked to the next position and took my gloves off an STL approached me.

"Tony, I've got somebody to cover for you I need a word."

"Ok." I said wondering what was going on.

"I was monitoring your search, and you conducted it all wrong."

"Yes, I know, but it was because of the circumstances."

"What circumstances?"

"The passenger had weed himself."

"Are you sure?"

"Do you want to feel his crutch?"

"No. I'll pass on that, it's just that DfT was monitoring you, and they wanted to know why you searched incorrectly?"

"Can I have a word with them?"

"I'll ask?" He walked off and moments later came back with a gentleman wearing the correct Identity denoting he was from the DfT.

"You wanted to know why I carried out the search in the wrong order?"

"Yes. I have to mark it down as a failure to comply. You know it's important that a systematic search is carried out in the correct order. When we witness it being done wrong, we have to step in and have you taken out of the line and retrained before you can work on a security lane again. Sorry but that's the rules."

"The passenger had peed himself and was still wet."

"So, what? You have to search people in the designated method."

"Sorry, I have to disagree with you, and I'll explain why, if you would let me?"

"Ok, go ahead."

"The passenger spoke no English so I couldn't get him to understand about private searches. Had I searched him in the correct order, I would have spread his wet urine all over his legs, and then I would have touched the handheld metal detector and spread any germs from the passenger's urine onto the equipment everybody has to use, which is a health and safety issue. Don't you agree?"

"Err yes. I would agree, and it's good to see security staff using their initiative."

"I carried out the handheld metal detector search not because there was any need to but to further ensure there was nothing metallic hidden in the passenger's undergarments, and his urinating wasn't an attempt to avoid being fully searched. And we're taught that in difficult circumstances we have to adapt our searches to comply with the security needs.

The STL had a smirk on his face as I completed my explanation. He knew I'd have the answer to any criticism when it came to security matters, as we'd often discussed how we should adapt searches to the circumstances.

"Well, thank you for your explanation, and I think that covers that nicely. You won't be marked down on that search in fact given the circumstances I think it was exemplary. Thank you, err Anthony." he said as he looked at my identity badge.

"That's what 25 years working in prisons does for you." and I walked off to go to the toilets to wash my hands and dispose of the gloves.

On another occasion, I had to search a male passenger in a wheelchair. He had a colostomy bag attached to him and the wheel chair; this was going to be a difficult search. My female colleague was assisting in removing items from the wheelchair and went to remove the colostomy bag when I said, "Whoa hang on don't touch the bag."

"Why?"

"It's a colostomy bag he has to have that attached to him at all times."

"What, even during a search?"

"Yes." and I said to her and then whispered in her ear, "It's attached to his bladder, and he will continually be peeing into the bag."

"Oh sorry, never seen one before. But how can you search him?"

"We just have to adapt the search as best we can, but as long as we are certain that we have done all we can to ensure compliance, that's acceptable."

"Oh, ok. I've searched wheelchair passengers before but not one with one of those things attached."

"We're going to get plenty of wheelchairs coming through when the para Olympics come here."

I carried out the search as best as I could, making sure every aspect of the security requirements was conducted. While searching, I noticed that the colostomy bag was leaking, enough to spill its contents onto me. And on this occasion, I wasn't wearing gloves, so over my shoulder, I said to my colleague, "Can you get cover for me for the next search? I have to go to the toilets."

"Why?"

"Because this passengers bag has a small leak and I've got it all over my hands."

"Oh shit!"

"No oh pee!"

----

28 PASSENGERS

Do you know what the most common sentence we hear at the security screening process is?

"In America" Yup, that's what Americans continually say to us "Well in America" or "In America" or "I'm American and in my country".

I hate to be the one to burst your bubble but this ain't America and therefore what goes on in America is America's business, not ours. This is the United Kingdom of Great Britain, and we have our standards so why you think that we should do what you do in your country is beyond my comprehension.

You may have imposed McDonald's onto us and the rest of the world, but our security is what we practice here, so why compare it to your own?

I was loading one late afternoon, the queue was long, and the airport was very busy. It was sweltering; sweat was seeping from every available part of my body. The air conditioning was useless (as usual), and an American approached my loading position.

"Have I got to take my laptop out of the cover?"

"Yes, sir."

"But in America, we don't have to."

"Yes sir, but this is the UK, and here you have to."

"But in America we don't, so why do we have to here?"

"Because this isn't America sir it's the UK."

"Well yes I know that but in America it's different so why here?"

"Because this isn't America sir I just told you that." I could feel the sweat beading on my forehead.

"But in America…."

"Sorry sir I am trying to point out that you are actually in the United Kingdom."

"Well, I know that but in America…"

I cut him short and held my hand up.

"Sir, this is not America, so it doesn't matter what you do in America does it?"

"Well no but in America, we don't have to."

"Thank you for your insight into the American Airport security system its much appreciated but don't you think that the management of Heathrow airports would have studied your TSA systems and adapted them for our own situation?"

"Well yes but in America…"

"With respect sir, I couldn't give a damn what the hell you do or don't do in America. I know what passengers have to do over here and it's take your laptop out of its case."

"There's no need for an attitude son."

Son! Son! I'm old enough to be his Dad not the other way around or was he complimenting me?

"Sir, I don't have an attitude, but I do find it tiresome that Americans come to the UK and then tell us what their security is like in America. I'm not really interested. I have a job to do here, not in America. So why would I care what you do there, it's not going to change my life now is it?"

"Okay, okay, I get it I'll take the laptop out of its case ok?"

"Thank you, sir, your cooperation is much appreciated."

"No need for sarcasm."

Bloody hell an American who understands sarcasm, well I'm surprised, I thought to myself.

"What about the Nook?"

"Yes, that needs to come out of its case too please."

"Well in America…"

"Sorry madam you've activated the archway metal detector and now need to remove your boots for us to scan them. As it's that area that has activated, my female colleague will search you."

"I'm not taking my boots off."

"Sorry, why not?"

"In America, we didn't have to."

"But you're not in America madam, and here you do."

"Well, I refuse."

"Ok, I'll get a manager."

I called an STL who happened to be female and very petite, but she would not be intimidated by aggressive passengers.

"What's the problem madam?"

"I refuse to take my boots off."

"May I ask why?"

"Because in America we don't have to."

"But madam you're not in America, and here you have to take them off."

"And what if I refuse?"

"Then you will be denied permission to fly with us today."

"How are you gonna do that?"

"Easy madam, we will call the police, and they will arrest you. Now can you remove your boots please?"

"Well, I don't have any choice, do I? But in America, we don't have to take them off."

"You do have a choice," I interjected, "but there are consequences to your actions, which I'm sure in America would be similar. By refusing a lawful request, you are in breach of security regulations, and as such can be arrested and removed from the airport. That is your choice if you refuse to remove your boots. However, if you decide in your own best interest to comply with my lawful request, then you will be allowed to fly today. Your choice, your consequences."

"Thank you, Tony. I couldn't have put it better myself." The STL said.

"This would never happen in America."

"No, and we haven't had the twin towers in London, so it shows differences between our cultures quite succinctly doesn't it? Now please remove your boots."

The STL gave me a sideways look as if to say, 'that was over the top' which it was but hey enough is enough.

The woman sat down and started to remove her boots but continued to mumble to herself.

"Well in America this wouldn't happen."

Some people do such strange things when confronted by airport security; I remember watching one woman on an unusually busy Sunday.

She approached our security lane along with her young daughter who was around 6 to 8 years old; you could see they were mother and daughter as they had identical features.

Both dressed smartly, but the mum seemed particularly agitated about the whole process. As she approached the front of the security lane, my colleague at the loaders position spent a long time explaining it all to her much to the impatience of many of the other passengers.

The daughter, on the other hand, seemed calm and as my colleague continued to explain and offer assistance to the mum, she turned to her daughter.

"Just go through the archway thingy and wait on the other side for me, please."

"Ok mummy."

"Once she gets through the archway there are some metal chairs she can sit on and wait for you." said my colleague.

"Sheila, did you hear what the nice lady said?"

"Yes mummy, I'm not deaf yet."

"Well, just do like I said and wait for me there will you?"

"Yes mummy."

"I'll inform my colleague to keep an eye on your daughter once she is through the system if you'd like."

"Oh, thank you so much, you are so helpful."

The young girl walked through the WTMD archway thingy collected her personal belongings and went and sat patiently waiting for her mum on the metal seats that were adjacent to the two security lanes.

My colleague told me about the little girl, and although I was busy, I managed to keep an eye on her. It's a trick I learned in the prison service, do one thing but watch other things going on around you. I can also listen to more than three conversations at any one time, so just goes to prove - men multitask when we want or need to.

The mum eventually finished at the loaders position and joined the queue for the walk-through metal detector archway. But as she walked through she activated the metal detector and had to be searched by my female colleague stationed at the archway. Those M&S underwired bras' get you girls, every time, honestly!

I was beginning to feel sorry for mum because she was now getting into a tizzy. However, the search went well and then she was through to collect her personal effects that had been through the X-ray machine and were awaiting her.

She was gathering her effects up, but in her haste, she kept dropping things back onto the tray on the lane belt. Eventually, she manged to get it all together and order was restored.

"Madam." I called, "Madam, have you got all your belongings?"

"Yes?"

"What about your shoes?" which were still in the tray.

'Oh my god, I swear I'll forget my head one day."

"Well, it's only your shoes today, maybe your head next time." I tried to joke.

"I hate all this security stuff nowadays; it makes me nervous."

"I know what you mean madam, and have a lot of sympathy for you, but it's just a reflection on the world we live in."

"I know. I never thought my Dad would have to fight a war so that we could live like we have to now."

"Yes, I couldn't agree with you more. Anyway, hope you have a pleasant flight, bye."

"Thanks for your help and understanding today, bye."

With that, she started to walk away from the security lane and bypassed her daughter who was still sitting in the same place watching my colleagues as they searched other passengers.

"Madam!" I called again, louder this time. "Madam!"

"Sorry! What?"

"Are you sure you've got everything you came with?"

"Yes, quite certain." she seemed to be getting a little agitated again.

"Madam, I think you may have forgotten your daughter who's still sitting nice and patiently where you told her to sit."

"Oh my god, oh my god! I nearly walked away without her; you must think I'm an idiot."

"No, just nervous and stressed just like most other people here, and when you get like that, you forget things."

"But my daughter? My husband will go mad when he finds out."

"Tell you what, I won't tell him if you don't." and I winked at her. "I don't think your daughter even noticed. She's so engrossed in watching my colleagues on the archway searching people. Maybe she wants to become a security officer here when she's older."

"Thank you so much for your kindness." and she started to cry.

'Madam, please don't get so upset. These things happen. We had one chap who left the security area without his prosthetic leg. How he managed to leave the area without his leg and then realise he had left it behind was beyond all of us at the time. But hey these things really do happen. Another time, a lovely attractive lady left her wig behind and never came back for it. You'd be surprised how many people leave their laptops behind and never come back to claim them. Stress makes us do strange things don't you think?"

With this, she started to laugh and I think was now realising that stress does make you do strange things.

"Oh, thank you so much for your understanding and kindness, it's so appreciated. I hope your bosses appreciates how kind you all are?"

"Well, that's a completely different story." and we both laughed.

183

A postscript to this episode is that the passenger took the time to walk up to one of the STL's and give praise to my security team and me for the help and understanding we'd shown towards her.

The STL came up to us afterwards as we were leaving on a break and told us about the compliment from the passenger, it was nice and unusual to get positive feedback for a change. However, the STL then said to me, "Tony, in future you need to keep your conversations with passengers to a minimum and get more searching done' and he turned away and walked off, as I bunched my fists up in anger.

"Tony, Bruv, don't do it. It's what that wanker wants you to do, he ain't worth it innit."

"Sir, do you have anything in your bag that you shouldn't have, like a knife or any sharp objects?" I was bag searching, and I had a group of youngish lads off on a stag weekend judging by the way they were dressed, and they all stunk of alcohol.

"Naw, don't have any knives but I have a gun."

"A firearm?" Shit my heart sunk, was he joking or was he serious.

"Just a moment sir." I removed his bag to a safe area and walked back to the screen reader and asked as I pointed to the passenger.

"Can you remember what you pulled his bag off for Steve?"

"Yeah, over-sized liquid's."

"Ok thanks, he said he had a firearm in his bag."

"Course not, he had liquids and looking at the state of them it's probably booze. Anything else and I'd have seen it."

"Ok thanks."

I went back to the search table and returned with the passenger's bag.

"Ok sir, I have to search your bag so could you please open all the zips and compartments for me and then allow me to search inside."

'Yeah sure, but do you want to know where the gun is?" and he turned to his mates, and they all started to laugh. One of them pointed two fingers at me in a gesture of a gun and said 'bang'.

"Well if it's in here I'll find it. But it's not a good idea to walk around an airport security area talking about firearms, is it?"

"Naw, it's much better, I suppose, to talk about bombs then."

"Sir, it's much better not to make those sorts of jokes full stop."

"Fuck off!" and he turned to his mates who all thought it was hilarious, and they all started to go on about guns and bombs and laughed about it. We were now getting some strange looks from other passengers. This was fast developing into a serious situation.

"Sir, could I ask you and your friends to be a bit more sensible while you're here. I don't want to spoil your fun, or your stag do, but you really have to be careful what you say to security in the airport. We are very sensitive about passenger safety."

"Guns and bombs guns and bombs."

I'd had enough and asked my colleague to call an STL who appeared quickly.

"What's the problem, Tony?"

"I've asked the passenger and his friends to desist from talking about firearms and explosive devices in voices that can be overheard. But I think they've all been on the pop already."

"It's not sensible lads, to go on about those sorts of things at an airport security, is it?" the STL asked.

"Who cares? Just get on with your job grand-dad, and we can get on with our drinking."

"How do you know I'm a granddad, have you met my family?"

"Fuck off; it's a joke."

"Obviously to you, but not to me. Now can I continue with the bag search or are you going to continue to make inappropriate comments?"

"You fucking jobsworths are all the same, who do you think you are?"

"I'm the person who is trying to search your bag so you can go safely on your way to your stag do."

"Well get on with it then, and hurry up and find the fucking gun."

"Right that's enough." the STL said at which point the whole group of them started a football like chant going on about guns and bombs.

The STL radioed for the police to attend and instructed me to stop the search, which I did. The armed police arrived very quickly and in numbers, and the officer in charge said to the passengers.

'Ok lads you've had your fun now it's our turn. These are real fire arms, and we're real policemen, collect your luggage and follow us."

"Where are we going then?" asked one of them.

"Not on your stag do now, are you?"

"What the fuck do you mean?"

"Due to your attitude, we feel it would not be safe for you to fly today, so you are all under arrests for security reasons. Now, do you think it's funny to behave this way?"

And with that, they were all escorted off to the local police station.

"Whose bag is this?" I asked as I was at the searcher's position in our security screening lane.

"That's mine." said a high-pitched effeminate voice.

"Sir, if you'd just collect all your personal belongings and come around to here, as I have to search your bag." Oh blimey, I thought to myself as I looked at the passenger. I've got this hairy-arsed Harley Davidson biker's bag to search, and he's got a voice like 'Tweetie Pie' or maybe

'Joe Pasquale'. Gawd knows what I'm gonna find in this search.

He was a big chap with arms like tree trunks and full of tattoos. His head was completely bald or maybe just shaved but full of tattoos. He had a huge horseshoe moustache with a long goatee beard.

The beard was gathered into a point as it rested on his chest. Each finger was tattooed with the words love on his right hand and hate on the left. He was wearing an open waistcoat showing his tattooed chest. And on each nipple, he had tattooed 'light' on the right one and 'bitter' on the left, along with a tattoo of what looked like a fantastic Harley Davidson motor bike. He was a big man, no really! The sort of man you called sir and hoped he didn't get offended, and just my bloody luck I got to search his bag.

He came around to the search area as he placed his giant boots onto his feet. Bloody hell, he must have been wearing size 15 shoes, I thought I had better be careful dealing with this one.

"Do you have anything sharp in your bag sir?"

"No." he said in his Tweetie Pie voice.

"Ok sir, if you could just open up all the compartments in your bag and I can have a look and see what's caused the problem." and added "Going anywhere interesting?"

"Oh yes." said Tweetie Pie "We're off to a gathering of our chapter. And then biking along the Costa Blanca and on to Barcelona where we're meeting up with a huge Harley group."

I couldn't help it, this voice that was coming out of this giant of a man, and with the reputation of Harley Davidson bikers, it was so funny to hear him. I was struggling to keep a straight face. But hell, what with the size of him I didn't want to upset this passenger for sure.

"Well, it sounds an exciting trip."

"Yes, well you know, plenty of booze, beer, probably drugs, rock and roll and hopefully plenty of sex."

OMG, this was just too much, hearing him say all this with his 'Tweetie Pie' voice. I couldn't contain myself.

"Sorry sir," I squawked, "I just need to get a tissue." and I turned my back to reach for some tissues to hide my barely contained laughter, only to see two of my colleagues already doubled over. 'Bloody hell' I thought, how am I going to get this search done?

I returned to the search, careful not to make any further conversation, which was unusual for me as I did like to talk to my passengers. Only I wasn't sure that if I spoke to this man and his 'Tweetie Pie' voice came out, I would burst into uncontrollable laughter.

"Sir, I've found the problem. You seem to have a few containers with liquid in them. Although they are under the 100ml size, as they were in your bag I have to test them."

"Ok, but they are just my 'lubes'."

"Your what?"

"My lubes. You know, they're flavoured to give sex a bit of a kick."

"You're lubes? What are lubes?" I asked in all innocence. Yes, I know, I've lived a very sheltered life, but I really didn't know what he was talking about. Apparently, my two colleagues did know as they were in fits of hysteria and seeing them just made me want to start laughing too.

"Well, I just need to test them to make sure they are ok."

"Ok." he squeaked.

That's it; this was the tipping point! His voice, the sex lubes stuff, I just couldn't hold it together any longer. And as I turned my back I started to laugh, so unprofessional I know but would could I do? I had 'Tweetie Pie' dressed as a hairy-arsed Harley Davidson biker full of tattoos, and I'm holding his sex lubes as I try to carry out the liquid test on them to ensure they were what he claimed they were.

Thankfully, I carried out the tests which were ok and returned the liquids to the passenger.

"Sir, would you like me to repack you bag?"

"No, that's ok."

"Well, thank you sir. Hope you have a pleasant flight."

With that, I turned around and approached my colleagues who were still laughing.

"OMG Tony, the look on your face when he told you what was in the containers! Have you never heard of that before?"

"No, never."

But the funniest thing was his voice, how somebody so big and butch could sound like 'Tweetie Pie' is beyond me.

"Oh Tony, I almost wet myself! I have to hand it to you (which started them both off again into fits of laughter) how you managed to hold it together was fantastic really."

Passengers, it takes all sorts, but I could never look a Harley Davidson biker in the face again without thinking of this passenger.

PART TWO – SECURITY OFFICERS

1 MULTICULTURAL SOCIETY

Multiculturalism is applied to the demographic make-up of a specific place, e.g. schools, businesses, neighbourhoods, cities, airports or nations.

Heathrow is itself a complete multicultural society; it employs people from different and varying cultural backgrounds, from the indigenous British people to the more modern of ethnic cultures and new and emerging countries. Black, White, multiracial, all sexual genders, Polish, Lithuania, Spanish, Portuguese, Indian, Pakistan, Turkey, and representatives from virtually every known country, and cultures have come to work at Heathrow. This in itself can be an area of concern. We all have different ways of life and cultures, which to the uninitiated can be a cause of conflict. So just imagine how our passengers feel as many of them come from hundreds of different countries around the world. Yet on arrival at Heathrow, we expect them to understand our culture and way of life.

Due to its physical location and therefore its recruitment area, many staff working at Heathrow come from the local catchment area. As this is in the inner London area, staff are from different ethnic backgrounds. Before working here, I never understood that even within a certain sect there were cultural differences. Many of my co-workers were from the Indian culture but what I didn't know was that India is one of the most religiously and ethnically diverse nations in the world, with some of the most deeply religious societies and cultures. There are Hinduism, Buddhism, Islam, Jainism and Sikhism, collectively known as Indian religions, all were represented at Heathrow. So, it could be a very confusing working environment for all the non-Indian cultures that worked there.

Not only were there these cultural differences but we also had language difficulties from various cultures travelling through Heathrow and its terminals.

There has to be tolerance and understanding on both parties. It's no good if as a member of staff, you are confronted with non-English speaking passengers, and you expect them to understand what instructions you are giving them. Likewise, with our facial and hand expressions, what we mean by one hand gesture can be an insult in another cultures interpretation of that same gesture, it can be the same with our tone of voice. This is a real area of conflict but can be simple to resolve in most instances.

You put your hand up, palm out, facing another person and they know immediately that means stop. You stand with your hands on your hips, and everybody understands that is aggressive. There are many more hand gestures that are universally understood, some good some insulting and some downright rude, but we all know what they are, and hand gestures play an important part of working as a Security Officer.

My team and I were detailed to work in Terminal 3; this was often a detail my team got sent on. We were sent to T2, T3 and T4 when operational requirements deemed it necessary the same thing for the other terminal when T5 needed extra help (often the case).

Off we go on the tour of the inner roads of Heathrow, to go from one terminal to another. We have to use the transport that passengers travelling from T5 would also use to gain access to other terminals should their flights be from another operator other than BA as T5 was exclusively BA (or Iberia).

Arriving at T3 our identity details were taken by the RA's, and they establish if we had had any breaks and what time we had them. Often as it was towards the end of our shift, we would be due another break so we'd then be sent on an immediate break to come back and finish our shift in this terminal. It wasn't too bad because the RA's tried to get us off the machines before our finish time and in time to get back to T5 at our usual 'shoot' time. It worked out great on some occasions as the timing of the transport back to T5 could mean we'd get off before our usual shoot times.

I was on the archway searching a passenger, and I noticed I was being monitored by one of the T3 STL's. Now why he would monitor me was beyond me, I get monitored in my terminal often enough so why here, and surely, he should be monitoring his staff.

"May I search you, sir?" I said, and I stood in the arms outstretched position with my legs slightly apart as we'd been trained to do. Not just with non-English speaking passengers but to everybody just in case we were confronted with a deaf or hard-of-hearing passenger, and it would let them know they needed to be searched.

I complete my search, and the STL approached me, getting a replacement for me on the archway and taking me to one side to give me the feedback from the search. He said "I was monitoring you just then and have to say your search was text book. The way you spoke to the passengers was brilliant, and you developed such a good understanding of each other despite the fact the passenger doesn't speak English. That was exemplary; I wish my staff here were that good." Great, I thought, hope his feedback gets back to my STL in T5.

"But," he continued "You failed to get the passengers permission for you to carry out the search on him, so I have to mark you down for that. You must always gain permission for the search before commencing your search, you know?"

"What? What are you talking about? You know the passenger spoke no English and once he followed my visual example of how I needed him to stand to conduct the search that is illicit permission by his actions."

"Sorry, what's your name?" and he looked at my ID badge. "You have to gain verbal permission before you can ascertain you have the passengers' permission to start the search".

"And just how do I achieve that if the passenger speaks no English?"

"Well, that's your problem."

"Ok, so every time I'm confronted with a passenger that doesn't understand me or maybe the passenger is deaf, I have to gain verbal permission before I can search him, is that what you are saying?"

"Yes."

"Even if, by standing with my arms in the search attitude, the passenger copies me, I still have to gain verbal permission?"

"Yes."

"Suppose he gives me an answer, but I don't understand his language, then what do we do?"

"You have to gain verbal permission."

"Suppose the passenger is a deaf mute, then what?"

"You have to gain verbal permission."

"You're an idiot. Do you know what you just said; I have to gain verbal permission from a passenger who is a deaf mute? Well, that should be an interesting medical advancement."

He went a slight shade of crimson "You still have to gain verbal permission."

"I tell you what I'll do in future, every time I'm confronted with this issue, I'll stop the flow of passengers call an STL and let the STL gain verbal permission. That would make me popular with all the STL's in T5, and I'm sure over here you must be used to officers doing that then?"

"All officers working here have to gain verbal permission before commencing the search."

"What Tesco branch did you come from before working here?"

"Don't talk to me like that!"

"Sorry," I said "but you're an idiot, what you're saying is complete nonsense, and you know it. Now either mark me down and go away or take me off your machines and send me back to T5 where at least the

STL's know what they are doing."

With that, I walked back to my position on the archway. I said to the female officer next to me "Is that STL for real?"

She laughed and said, "I heard what he was saying. He's a moron. You know here in T3 eighty percent of passengers are non-English speaking. We all have to use hand gestures to be understood. That STL is an idiot so don't worry about him."

"No, I won't, and there are a few hand signals I'd like to give him too."

But it got me wondering about how we approach, and how we're perceived, by foreign-speaking passengers. I always tried to keep a calm voice and used what I hoped were non-aggressive hand signals and smiley expressions to communicate.

Many other cultures use the English language to communicate. However, foreign travellers can interpret tone and sound of how they talk differently. Despite our training on dealing with cultural and religious differing passengers, it was not always easy when under pressure to remember it all. Diversity was a regular part of our on-going training.

Telling somebody to remove their shoes can sound different to asking the same person to remove their shoes.

'Take your shoes off, place them in the tray' can sound harsh and commanding especially if you are pointing to the shoes and the tray at the same time as speaking. And to a tired passenger, it can sound rude and uncaring.

"Please remove your shoes and place them in the tray my colleague is holding." said in a softer tone, is a much more professional and sensitive way to approach a passenger. It's not always easy when throughout the day you've said the same thing more than a hundred times. And, of course, we all get exacerbated, but that includes the passengers as well as staff.

Some cultures speak in what they feel is an authoritative professional manner, but to a passenger (and some of their colleagues) it sounds demanding and rude. I worked with many colleagues from Eastern Europe who spoke in this manner. Maybe it was the way they were taught English, or maybe they thought it sounded authoritative, but it always sounded like they were angry or aggressive.

"Alright, bruv?" What! Why! Bruv! I had no idea when this form of greeting took over from standard 'hello', but every male officer from under the age of 30 seemed to greet each other in this manner. None of them were brothers and certainly not any of them mine as my brother died years ago. So why greet each other in this manner. Another example of the multicultural ways of Heathrow. And I suspected that in most inner-city areas of the UK, this was also the usual greeting within a certain group of younger men.

They'd say 'Alright Bruv' and then shake hands, now where did that come from? Was this yet another inner-city form of greeting misinterpreted by the youth of today as some secret signal? Or was it a cultural thing giving out secret signals of what street or part of London you came from? It was alien to me yet an acceptable part of Heathrow life. I never got used to being greeted with 'Bruv' and shaking hands; I didn't know where their hands had been in the first place so was sceptical of shaking their hands. Especially as I'd seen many examples of poor hygiene when using the toilet facilities.

It became evident that my colleagues who lived in London used a language unique to themselves, but for others, it was very confusing.

'Innit' how many times did I hear my male colleagues use this at the end of a sentence? For instance, 'How you doing today innit' or 'Hi Bruv is all allright innit' and it was a definite male thing to say. You never heard the woman speak in this manner. What a strange phenomenon.

I've travelled to many other countries where English is not the first language and seen different cultures. Including visiting the USA who although they speak English, it isn't the English I was taught. But you find out what the rules are for that countries way of life before travelling there. After all, you wouldn't take your car to France and expect them to be driving on the same side of the road as here in the UK, so why go there to their airports and cities and expect to be greeted with the same language and culture as your own.

But this is just a part of living in a modern multicultural society, and in working in such a diverse place as Heathrow Airport. It's not bad; it's not wrong it's just different and takes a little getting used to if you've lived in a small village in the Home Counties of the UK like me, then after several years away, coming back to work in the huge cosmopolitan city that is London.

Whether you're a travelling passenger or a Heathrow worker, we should all strive to be more understanding of each other's cultures and languages and try to make using the airport a less stressful environment.

----

2 Patrol

Patrols! I loved them, the best part of my rota, but for many, they were an excuse to skive off, sit on their arses all day, and do nothing. But not me, for me they were great.

The first time I was detailed to patrol was during my first week live on the concourse and because I didn't have a team to work with I ended up working with a lovely woman 'Mandy' who was great in helping me to understand what was required on this duty. We got on great, and I'd like to think we became good friends and reliable colleagues, due to our first working day together. The day passed quickly. We spent so much of the day chatting about our respective partners and past lives. It's hard to believe just how much walking we had to do on this particular patrol day.

There were two different parts to the duty and over the next few months they became more involved and complicated. On this first patrol, we had both a paper trail and a 'control track' electronic 'tagging' (or pegging points) system and set route to follow. We had to use the handheld monitor to electronically accept that we'd found the designated 'pegging' points on the set route. Eventually, all the paper routes were dispensed with in favour of the electronic routing systems.

Mandy showed me how to use the electronic (control track) machine and follow its instruction along the routes to each tagging point. These patrols took us down corridors, along back alleys, and through the maze of what makes up the airport behind-the-scenes routes and alleyways. We went down into the bowels of the airport to areas I never knew existed, let alone could ever find my way there again.

We had to complete three of the selected patrols to follow and then do as many of the paper routes as we could. And then return to the office to download the information from the control track device on completion of a patrol so that the central computer could ensure we'd carried out the correct patrol route. We had to arrange our meal breaks ourselves, so when on patrol you were your own boss and responsible for your actions. Great, I thought, this will suit me, and it always did.

Mandy explained that when patrols were paper often officers would just tick that they'd completed the route without even moving out of a rest room. Hence the electronic system was introduced. I was amazed that staff would do that as there were around six thousand five hundred cameras located around the whole of the airport, and within the terminal building, cameras could trace your whereabouts easily. These people sat in a rest room doing heaven knows what all day, it was beyond me. I witnessed it happening shortly after this first patrol.

We completed our designated patrols, had also had our two meal breaks, and we'd started on the paper routes, Mandy said, "Tony, you try to follow the paper instructions, and I'll just keep a watch to see if you go wrong."

"Ok." and I thought how difficult can this be, just follow the instruction, but how wrong was I.

Half an hour into the first paper patrol I was hopelessly lost. I'd taken Mandy down to levels I'm not sure she even knew. The instruction read like this: follow the route to the end of the corridor, turn left at the end, past the Gents toilet turn right, and so on. Easy, except at the end of the bloody corridor, there was no left turn. The route jinked right, and sure enough, there was a 'gent's' toilet but again no right turn, only a left turn, was I doing this route backwards? I had no idea.

"Sorry, Mandy, I'm lost."

"Ha-ha, I think I am too. Do you find the instruction helpful?"

"They would be if they'd been written in English. Who the hell wrote these?"

"I think they were written from the original builder's plans. That's why 'Carol' is converting all the patrols to the electronic system." (Carol was not a security officer anymore but she had taken on the role of converting all the paper patrols onto the new electronic system. I became good friends with her, and she always knew when I was on patrol, that although my work had to be checked, it didn't need to be).

The instructions were hopeless, but somehow, we completed our tasks, except one, as we'd run out of time. But I'd completed my first ever patrol duty, and loved every minute, and couldn't wait to do it all again next week.

However, the next day I'm working on the fast-track security lane in the South concourse when an STL approached me and said, "I need a word with you."

"What now?"

"Well, I didn't mean next week." These STL's really knew how to talk to their staff respectfully, as I found out quickly. NOT!

"I'll need my position covering."

"Just come with me now." he said sternly. This was my first experience of an STL. He didn't bother to introduce himself, so I didn't know who he was, however, his reputation was soon revealed. Known as 'Sly' he was a real pain at times, although towards the end of my time there he must have realised that I was an efficient and conscientious worker and we got on much better. But we did have many run-ins.

"Sorry." I said to several of the team "But he's ordered me into the office."

I followed him into the office, which backed onto the South concourse rest room. And I didn't realise how thin the walls were as everything we said must have been heard by the staff in rest in there.

Without preamble, he pointed to the paper patrol we hadn't completed the previous day and said, "Where were you at this point?" pressing his finger at the paper instructions.

"I have absolutely no idea."

"What do you mean 'no idea' did you do the patrol or just sit in a tea room?"

"How dare you say that? If you think I didn't do my work, go check on the security cameras, and you'll see me walking past them."

"Never mind about that, I want to know where you were?"

"I have no idea. In fact, if it hadn't been for Mandy I would probably still be down in the bowels of this building trying to find my way out."

"So, you don't know where this point is?"

"No. This is the first patrol I've ever done. You tell me where I was?"

"Why would I know?"

"Well, you're an STL, I assume you know what these patrol routes are?"

"No, that's why I'm asking you."

"How would I know, this is my first patrol? I've only worked here live for two days, so how would I know?"

"Well, I need to know where you were. The TDM needs to complete all the paperwork, and we need that information."

"Then I suggest both you and the TDM get off your fat arses and follow the instructions I tried to follow. Then you will see where the hell I was, won't you? Now if you'll excuse me, my team's running one officer short due to your ordering me to come into an office without covering my position. That's really doing your job properly, isn't it?" With that, I walked out of the office and back to work.

By the time our team was sent on our first break, the story of my chat with the STL had spread all around the terminal building. As I said, the walls in the office were paper thin, and my conversation with the STL had been overheard by the staff who were in the room on their breaks. I think this is where I got my reputation as someone who would stand for no nonsense and speak his mind to STL's. My motto was and is, that you earn respect you cannot expect it just because of rank and position, and I still believe in this philosophy today.

Several days later I located where Mandy was working, and I told her about the meeting with the STL. She said "Don't worry about Sly, as soon as he's under pressure he turns on staff. But I understand he picked the wrong one with you, so well done for standing your ground, and don't worry about it." So, I didn't.

The next patrol, on the following week, I was teamed up with a male officer 'Tan'. Now as we had to check both Ladies and Gents toilets, it made part of the patrol impossible. And to make matters worse the electronic system broke down, so we had to follow the paper routes only.

Almost as soon as we started this patrol, Tan needed to make a phone call, and off he went to the nearest rest room. For the first hour, this was the pattern we followed. We'd walk around following the paper instruction and then go off to a restroom, and I'd wait while Tan made a phone call. It was pretty obvious that he was running his own business and working at Heathrow, as in fact many of the male officers were doing this too. But I was getting indignant about all his phone calls and stopping off in rest rooms, so I said to him "Tan do you have a problem with working with me or something?"

"Naw Bruv, (my first experience of being called bruv) I got a business to run innit."

"What while you're working here?"

"Yes, and I have to make these calls."

"Yea, but we have to do the patrol too."

"Naw Bruv, we walk around for a few of them and then just come in the restroom and tick all the boxes. They never check, and they never know innit."

"Well, that wasn't the case last week I had a run in with Sly over it."

"Sly? Don't take no shit from him Bruv."

"Sorry Tan, I can't work that way, anyway I have to do my job properly."

"That's up to you Bruv, but I gotta make these calls."

"I'll tell you what, you make your calls and I'll do our jobs."

"Aw bruv, don't be like that."

"Sorry Tan." and I picked up the patrol notes and radio and continued to do the patrols. He met up with me later, but after our lunch break, our patrols followed the same pattern. I thought, never again will I allow my patrol partner to do this sort of thing again, At least we completed all our patrols without mishap.

One of the strange quirks of the early patrols I carried out, was that until the change of zonal working to all areas working, we were detailed patrols every second day on our rota of four on and two days off. So, we did patrols at least once a week, great I loved them.

On completion of your patrol, you reported back to an STL, who checked your patrol paperwork to make sure it was correct and then you had to wait in the restroom until all the 2100 shifts were allowed to go home. This was usually around 2030, but on one occasion the STL said to us at around 2020 "Ok, you can go home now. Thanks for all your work today."

And we left the rest room and walked past all the other 2100 finishers, one of whom was a 'Bruv', and he shouted out to the STL, "Oh what's going on with this lot being allowed a better shoot than us?" It was rich coming from this officer who the previous week when he was on patrol, was allowed to leave at 2015. And as he walked past us still working he stuck two fingers up in the reverse victory signal and shouted out "Nite nite mugs."

So, it was ok for him to get better shoots as he was one of the Bruvs but not for the rest of us. Ironic, but that's how the system was corrupted here.

The patrols eventually changed to all electronics and then a new development was the jetty patrols. You were informed via your radio of an incoming aircraft stand number, or arrival gate. Which gave you a window of opportunity to go to that gate number, and when all the passengers had disembarked, you had to check all the length of the walkway and jetty, up to the aircraft and around the empty aircraft general area before the next group of passengers arrived, to board the aircraft. But these patrols, which I loved, meant you did a lot of walking as you had to cover arriving aircraft from all the of T5's terminals. You could be sent from T5 main arrival gates to T5C and have to be there within a short timescale. Although the controlling dispatcher had the overall picture to make the logistics workable it was often the case that they directed us to the jetties too late to check them or too early as the disembarking passengers had not left the aircraft.

These patrols were busy, but I loved them.

----

3 SCREEN READING? NO, BOOK READING

I was working a six hour plus shift before my actual start time, on a Sunday, the overtime payments were worth it. But it just so happened that this was a very quiet Sunday. Quiet days did not come around very often. Usually, February was our quietest month, but I think this was October which also tended to be a little bit quieter.

Anyway, it was quiet. I was working on the North concourse which made it even more unusual for it to be so quiet, and I was at the bag searcher area. I was glancing around looking at my colleagues going about their business and making mental notes of scenes I thought might be worth including in this book when I spotted a male colleague of mine sitting on the screen readers position about three security lanes from where I was standing.

'Shit,' I thought to myself 'what's he doing, is he reading a book! Naw, he can't be. How can anybody do that when screen reading? No, I must be imagining it.'

"Jack." I called to a nearby colleague "Can you see that officer on lane 11?"

"Yes."

"Is he doing what I think he's doing?"

"Dunno, what do you think he's doing?"

"Well, from here it looks like he's reading a book."

"Looks like it, donit?"

"He can't be, can he?"

"Dunno, and don't want to know. Sorry 'bruv' not getting involved innit."

"What do you mean not getting involved? He's not looking at the machine he's reading a book."

"Tony, bruv, keep out of it." I'm not his bloody 'Bruv' and don't want to be, so why he kept calling me that was beyond me. But I ignored it.

"What do you mean keep out of it? He's not watching the screen. Anything could go through that machine. I can't just stand here and do nothing; I've got to report what I'm seeing to an STL."

"Well, that's up to you bruv, innit."

I'm not your bloody brother, I thought. I was getting angrier at what I was seeing. I left my machine and approached the nearest STL.

"Sorry to interrupt." I said, as there were two STL's deep in conversation, "But I'm sure I can see an officer on lane 11 sitting at the x-ray machine reading a book."

"What! Where!" said one of the STL's.

"Lane Eleven, over there." I pointed in the general direction of Lane eleven.

"Don't talk daft." said the other STL.

"Well, just look for yourselves. He's still there and is definitely reading a book whilst on the screen."

"I can't see him." said the second STL.

"Well, I can." I said, "It's that White lad over there." again pointing to Lane Eleven.

"Yes, well thanks, but just go back to your lane, and we'll investigate, but I'm sure you're mistaken." said the second STL.

"I might have to wear glasses, but I'm not mistaken. That officer's reading a book while on screen reading duties you can see it from here."

"Just let us deal with it. You've reported it, now let us do what we have to do, and you can get on with your job. Don't you have a passenger bag to search? If not, I'll bring one over to you."

I couldn't believe it; you could clearly see this officer reading a book while supposedly on screen reading duties. Yet I was being dismissed as if nothing was happening and my conscience could not let this happen. I walked back to my position as a bag searcher still incredulous as to the second STL's attitude.

"How did you get on Bruv?"

"That other STL didn't seem interested, and please stop calling me bruv. I only ever had one brother, and he died years ago, so I'm not your Bruv and have no wish to be. Sorry, but no offence, I've had enough of being called bruv by you lot."

"Tony bruv just calm down. I don't mean anything by it you know that, innit."

"Yes, sorry, but I'm furious at the attitude of these managers to what I've just witnessed, and nobody cares about it. But you're still not my bruv."

"Listen, Tony, you've got no chance."

"What do you mean, no chance?"

"That Bruv you saw reading a book, is mates with the STL you spoke too. Do you really think they'll do anything about it Bruv? It's all like that over here; don't know where you worked before but T5 is full of mates and Bruvs looking after each other. That STL plays five-a-side football with loads of the Indian officers on an evening, then they all go down to the local pub for a drink innit."

"You mean some of the white officers are also part of the Bruv culture?"

"Yes, mate, they all live in the same area and most in the same streets as each other, so they all look after each other black, white, or brown they all stick together and help each other."

"So, why are you telling me this?"

"Tony, you're a great mate to have on the machines, you don't stand for no nonsense from the passengers but you ain't never gonna beat this lot. Believe me; it's just the way it is here, innit. So, it's not worth getting het up over."

"I can't do that, and just accept what I see, no way."

"There are some battles you ain't never gonna win especially here mate."

"That's as maybe, but I will not stop trying. I have to live with my conscience."

"That's why I love working with you Tony; you are a legend bruv."

I was incredulous. I'd witnessed a sackable offence being committed, and reported it to the Managers only to be apparently ignored. No, this cannot be happening, surely not, what about passenger safety? What about professionalism? I was gob smacked. To find out my colleagues could be this unprofessional. No, I couldn't accept what I'd witnessed. That could be my family boarding a plane that this screen reader had not bothered checking the passengers bags on his screen, thus compromising their safety. No, it couldn't be allowed to happen. I wouldn't let this go.

I spotted another STL and called him over and explained what I'd seen.

"Tony, are you sure you saw the officer reading a book?"

"Yes, certain."

"He wasn't looking at a mobile phone?"

"No, but if he was, it's surely the same thing, he wasn't watching his screen."

"But was his machine running at the time?"

"Of course, it was. Look I could clearly see from here. Look for yourself. You can see a machine running from here. We're only three bloody machines away for Christ sake." Yes, I was getting exacerbated with it all.

"Ok. Let me go make some enquiries."

"Get that bastard off his machine for the safety of everybody, please? I pleaded with the STL.

But then I noticed that the lane had been closed down, and the staff were disappearing back towards the RA's office. And I thought nothing will be done now. But if I ever saw that officer again I would approach him and confront him with what I saw. I was livid.

Later the STL came back and explained that he couldn't find out what team was on that lane at the time.

"Look it's easy, ask the RA. He knows where he placed each team throughout the day. It'll be on his planning board, so they will know what team was where."

"Yes, but then we would have to assume it was any of the males on the machine. The RA's can tell us what teams were where but not who was on what piece of the machinery at any given time."

"There are only three males to each team, and the one I saw was not from an ethnic background. He was white, so that should make him easy to identify."

"Sorry, but I think they were all white officers on that machine;"

"No, they were not. I know the loader was Indian, I recognised him from when he worked overtime on lates. We worked a lane together once."

"Well, you identify the team, and I'll take action."

"As I don't work earlies usually and am here on overtime, I don't know the teams so I couldn't identify them."

"You know one officer, you said so."

"No, I said I recognised one officer who was Indian, as I worked with him once but I don't know his name, do I?"

"Without that, I can't do anymore." he said and walked away.

I was amazed, not only had I witnessed this gross misconduct but had reported it correctly. It had been ignored twice, and I'd almost been made to feel guilty about reporting a fellow officer.

I'm sorry but misconduct in any form is wrong but this just smacked in the face of safety for everybody working here or travelling through the airport.

This event made me question what I was doing working here. In fact, I used to tell my colleagues that should I ever travel through this airport I would not feel safe. I remember saying to a colleague once, "I hope my children and grandchildren never travel through Heathrow after what I've witnessed here."

I realised that these sorts of incidents were rare and most staff were very conscientious and treated the job with the utmost responsibility and were great at their jobs of protecting the public.

But it was a shame I couldn't find my book reader again. Although I'm not sure how I would have approached him if I'd recognised him. It left a bitter taste in my mouth for the rest of my time working at Heathrow.

----

4 LEFT HOLDING THE BABY?

As security officers, we get some strange requests, and it's often at the loading position that we get them. We try to be sensitive to single parents travelling with their offspring. It's a difficult enough task to travel on your own with children but to arrive at an airport and have to go through the modern security screening can be very difficult.

Unfortunately, some of my colleagues have never heard of the word sympathy and think single parent travellers should sort themselves out with no assistance from any member of staff.

I worked with several colleagues who offered no sympathy or help in these cases. Not very compassionate, professional or humane, but it takes all sorts I suppose.

On one occasion, I was at the loaders position when a young mother approached with two young children of around four and five years of age. Both girls were at the time of similar ages to my granddaughters and grandson, and I could understand the difficulties. She was struggling as she also had a young baby in tow of around six to nine months old. I explained everything she had to do to get through the process.

I said to the two girls, "Going anywhere nice girls?"

"We off to visit daddy."

"Oh, that will be wonderful for you and daddy."

"Yes, but we have got to go on an aeroplane a long way."

"What country are you going to then?"

"I fink it's called Africa."

"No," said the older girl "I keep telling you it's South Africa, Africa is all jungle, Daddy works in a big city."

"Wow, South Africa, that is a long way!"

"And it's a big surprise, so don't tell him were coming."

"Ok, I promise."

I noticed the woman was struggling with the baby and the push chair, so I said, "Would you like me to help?"

"Oh, thank you so much." she said with that so noticeable South African accent and promptly handed me her baby. So, what could I do, I held the baby as I was used to holding babies from holding my grandchildren.

I called across to the two officers on the archway "Can I let this lady put her pushchair through the gate, and you can search it? She's struggling to get it to collapse." We often had this problem, and I was always happy to allow the chair through our gate. And we searched it rather than putting it onto the security lane as a lot of these chairs did not collapse down small enough to go through the x-ray machine.

My colleague on the archways looked at me and said, "No, the bag searchers doing nothing he can sort it out his side."

I was taken aback "Oh, ok." You miserable bastard, I thought to myself, let's hope you never have children and have to do this sort of thing. But some of the staff didn't have any compassion for the passengers travelling with young children.

Here I am left holding the baby when I notice a nice warm feeling coming through from the little boys' one-piece fleece suit. Thankfully not leaking through, but you know when a baby is peeing.

The passenger finished organizing herself, and she took her baby back "Madam I think your boy has had a little accident. You might need to change him when you get through." and I pointed the nearest toilets where they had baby changing facilities.

"Oh, thank you so much for your help. He's a little water fountain, didn't have this problem with the girls. Anyway, it was so kind of you to help, not like last time I travelled through here."

She walked off with the two girls, carrying the baby boy, and the smallest girl turned around and put her fingers to her lips, "Shush, please don't tell daddy we're on our way."

"I promise."

"I wouldn't have held that baby for her." said the female officer on the archway.

"Why not?"

"Suppose you had dropped it."

"It was a little baby, and why would I drop him?"

"Well, I wouldn't have done it."

"Well, let's hope you never have babies and need to travel through Heathrow then." miserable bitch, I thought. We do employ some nice staff.

I'd like to think I was always considerate for passengers that needed help. But on the other hand, once a passenger was unnecessarily rude I'd then offer no help whatsoever. But to see staff that wouldn't help regardless, I found hard to comprehend.

Many of my younger colleagues would never hold a baby; I remember one of the younger men saying, "I wouldn't hold anybody's baby."

"Why not?"

"I just couldn't do it."

"Don't you have any young babies in your family?"

"Yea, but I ain't ever held one before. I wouldn't know what to do with it."

"You just hold the baby in your arms and make sure you support the neck."

"See, that's what I mean, wouldn't know what to do with it, really I wouldn't."

"You're just apprehensive about it."

"Naw, I'm shit scared." he laughed, but we both knew he was serious.

"So, what would you do if a passenger just handed you their baby?"

"I don't know."

"Well, let's hope it doesn't happen then."

"If it does, I'll just call one of the girls to help me out."

"Let's hope they're not scared as well."

"Naw, they got their natural mommy thingy inbuilt don't they?"

"Not all women."

"Well, let's hope all the ones I work with have that mommy thingy working for them." and we both laughed about it.

But some of my colleagues really were that concerned about holding babies. I hoped they would get used to it in the future, after all, I was that scared before I had grandchildren of my own.

"Madam, what are you doing?" I almost shouted at her in panic as she went to place her baby in one of the grey trays. I was at the loaders position, and a man and woman carrying a baby had approached my position in the security lane.

"I'm putting my baby in the tray."

"Yes, but why?"

"Well, so you can search her."

"I only want you to place any large metal objects and all your liquid's, gels, and pastes in the tray, not the baby." I laughed.

"So, what happens with my little girl?"

"You carry her through the WTMD with you."

"No, I don't want her going through the metal detector."

"I'm sorry why not?"

"Those rays are dangerous, aren't they?"

"Madam there are no rays when you walk through the archway. It just detects metal objects. But the grey trays go through an x-ray machine. I'm sure you wouldn't want your baby going through that machine." and I pointed to the x-ray machine.

"Oh, I thought it was the other way around."

"Really?"

"Oh, you must think I'm stupid!"

"No, just another stressed-out passenger having to go through this security stuff, and I can understand that."

"Thanks anyway for your understanding, but how silly of me." and she looked at her husband who hadn't said a word, and gave him the baby. "You walk through with her, and I'll do the other stuff with this lovely man's help." and pointed at me. The husband did as instructed. And the passenger completed her tasks, placed everything into the trays, and took her turn to walk through the archway.

Can you imagine what would have happened if the baby had gone through one of the x-ray machines, let's hope it never happens?

Not all passengers were happy for staff to hold their babies, and quite rightly so. It could be difficult to find out who would or wouldn't want you to hold their babies, and so I never offered unless the passenger asked for my help.

On another occasion, a woman came through the archway carrying her young baby. My female colleague went into what I can only call a typical mummy meltdown, even though she was in her early twenties she reacted to the baby as most women seem to do.

"Oh, how old is the baby?"

"Just over three months."

"She's gorgeous."

How women always know the sex of a baby without looking always amazes me.

"Oh, would you mind if I held your gorgeous baby?"

"Yes, I would."

"Oh, ok." my colleague said somewhat taken aback.

"I have to search both you and the baby." If the baby was this young irrespective of its sex, we usually let the female on the archway carry out the search unless the passenger insisted the male officer did the search on a male baby.

"Yes, that's ok, but you cannot hold my baby, sorry."

"No, that's ok I respect your decision, and I will be as careful as possible during the search of the baby."

"But I don't understand why you have to search my baby?"

"Well madam, as the archway activated as you walked through carrying your baby we don't know which one of you activated it, so the rules are both have to be searched."

"Ok, but I don't know what you think you will find. I mean do I look like a terrorist?"

"Madam, you don't look like a terrorist, and neither does your baby, but we (and she looked at me as she said this) don't know what a terrorist looks like do we? So we have to be sure and carry out the search. Unfortunately, it's the law for all airports."

"Well, let's be honest it's a stupid law."

"It probably is, but we have no choice. So, may I search you and your baby?"

"Yes."

"Ok, I'll have to search you first then the baby, ok?"

"Yes." she said and then handed me her baby to hold.

It can be a weird experience with passengers at an airport. Now why she suddenly handed me her baby to hold I've no idea as she had refused my colleague permission previously. I must look trustworthy.

I put it down to the stress of travelling through an airport; we all do and say things that in our usual situations we'd never say or do. I wonder why this phenomenon happens.

But here I was left holding the baby.

----

5 HOLIDAY TO SPAIN

A good security officer is never noticed but a poor one will be and will tarnish everybody else the same way.

I was travelling through Heathrow T5 on my way to Alicante with my wife for a holiday. British Airways had recently taken over the routes of British Midland, and this route was one of the routes that BA decided might be profitable to schedule to run from Heathrow. It was not profitable, and it was switched to their Gatwick service. But at the time it was perfect for me, for two reasons, one as a member of staff I could park my car for free as one of our staff 'perks' and two it was an opportunity to fly BA from my own terminal.

What I wasn't expecting was how we'd have to deal with security travelling as passengers. The boot was well and truly on the other foot. Our time of travel meant that we'd be going through the security process around about the time my team and many of my colleagues would be on duty. In all probability, my colleagues would be the ones who'd process my wife and me through the security screening process.

I'd informed my wife of everything that would happen while going through the screening process. However, what I didn't prepare her for, and nor was I prepared for, was the rudeness of one of my colleagues.

We arrived at the car park after an unexpectedly pleasant journey down the M25. After parking the car and unloading our two cases and hand luggage, we got on the courtesy bus and arrived at T5 as passengers for the first time. You'd think it would be easy to be a passenger when you already work at the very place, but no, nothing is that simple in life, and especially at Heathrow Airport.

We walked over to the nearest BA check in desk, only to be told that we couldn't check our cases in until two hours before our flight time. I'd thought cleverly that if we got to the airport early, we could get rid of our cases and go through to the departure lounge, have a meal, stroll around the shops (something that when working there I never got time to do) and soak up the atmosphere of T5. But no, we couldn't check in until two hours before our flight. Damn!

What could we do now? I spotted one of the BA staff I knew reasonably well and approached him, explaining that we were travelling as passengers today and that we couldn't check in our cases as it was too early. He arranged that after a short wait we could check in our cases sooner than the two hours, thanks, BA ground staff.

Having checked in our cases, we now approached the automatic ticket machines of the South concourse. I chose the South as I knew it was usually quieter and easier to get through than the very busy North and so it proved to be.

We ignored the advice to go to the North security area, and we went through the South instead. We'd already met some of my colleagues, on the way there. They were just arriving to go through the staff search area and off to work, so after some quick introductions, we went through to the scanning machines.

"Hiya Tony bruv, off on your holiday's innit bruv."

"Yes, we're going to Alicante then on to our home in Spain."

"You got a home in Spain? Awesome, bruv innit."

"Yes, and so convenient to fly from here."

"Great mate, bring us back some nice weather."

"Yes, we'll try."

"Tony, why did he call you Bruv?"

"Jac, I don't know. They all greet each other that way, for some weird reason but I don't know why."

We went through the ticket machines and into the security screening area. It was busy but not so bad and we were placed into a queue by the roving 'Clio' "Wotcha Tony mate, off on your hols then?

"Yup."

"Bit busy at the moment, but here I'll get you both into the shortest queue ok mate?"

"I bet you say that to all your favourite people. Yes, brilliant thanks, Tom."

Job done, and we were in a queue that seemed to move smoothly. We shuffled forward getting all our liquids ready in their already packed clear plastic bags. I'd warned my wife not to wear anything that wasn't easy to take off and that all her jewellery would need to be removed. We weren't taking laptops or other electrical items, so getting through should have been relatively easy. I pointed out various colleagues and where things were, like our restrooms and things like that, and then it was our turn at the loaders point.

"Hi, Tony."

"Hi Sue, this is my wife, Jacinta."

"Hi, Jacinta. Tony's told us all so much about you, but I can see none of it's true."

"What's he been telling you all?"

"I told them you were twenty-two stone and built like a brick shit house and I was scared of you."

"Typical, he always does that!"

"Well, he lied, although if I were him, I'd be scared of you after telling those lies." and we all laughed, this was going easier than I thought.

We joined the queues for the walk-through metal detector, and there was a long line of mainly women, as the men were being called forward, so I walked through the archway and no activation, thank goodness. I didn't recognise the two officers on the archway. It was still early, so I assumed that both were workers on the early shift as I'd not meet them previously. I think they were getting impatient to be relieved so they could go home as they both appeared short of patience with the queuing public.

My wife was waiting in a ragged queue as it seemed the poor female officer on the archway appeared to be getting all the activations, and she was on some personal go slow. In fact, her speed was such that I thought she was on a go stop let alone a go slow. However, the male officer had by now run out of males to call forward so he must have thought he would assist his colleague.

"Oi you lot, form a proper queue." he shouted at the women.

"Oi, I said a queue." and he made hand gestures to suggest the women stand in a ramrod straight line. I was gob smacked at the way he was shouting and gesticulating to the waiting women and female children and thought that's no way to talk to passengers like they were cattle or something.

I stood waiting for our hand luggage to come through the x-ray machine but was horrified at the way this officer was shouting and gesticulating to the patiently queuing women. How dare he shout at them like that. My wife made a gesture as if to say, "What on earth's his problem, who does he think he is?" and I had to agree with her.

While I waited for my shoes to reappear from the X-ray tunnel, I said to the loader who I also didn't know, "Do you think your male colleague should talk to passengers in that way?"

"And who are you?"

"Oh, just a TDM from Terminal 3. If I weren't catching a plane to go on my holidays, I would be complaining to the TDM's here about his attitude."

"Oh sorry," she said, "I didn't know you were staff."

"That doesn't matter does it, but the way he's speaking and shouting at the passengers is unwarranted and unprofessional, and you can tell him that from me."

"I will, but are you going to complain?"

"Don't have the time at present, so it's his lucky day, but just tell him about his attitude, would you?"

"Yes, of course, have a lovely holiday."

"Thanks." and I collected my shoes and personal effects and waited for my wife to come through the archway. She gathered her belongings, and we walked off to look around the shops of T5.

My wife said afterwards "He reminded me of an Indian version of 'John Cleese' from a sketch in a Fawlty Towers episode."

"I don't know who he is Jac; I've not seen him before, so he must be on the early shift."

"Who did he think he was, talking to us like that?"

"I don't know. I've had my run-ins with passengers but what he did was out of order."

"What were you saying to that other officer?"

"I told her I was disgusted with the way the male officer on the archway was speaking to staff."

"What did she say?"

"Well, I told her I was a TDM from Terminal Three and was going to complain about the officer. And she got a little worried, so I said as I'm on holiday I'm not going to waste my time, but that she should tell that officer what I said and who I was."

"Didn't she know you worked here as an officer?"

"No."

"But they'll see you when you come back to work."

"Yes, but like passenger's who only notice bad and rude staff, security staff only notice the bad passengers. So, when I come back to work and am back in my uniform, I could go up to them both, and they wouldn't even recognise me."

We enjoyed the rest of our time in the terminal. We walked around the shops then went to have a meal in what turned out to be the most expensive tapas bar we've ever eaten in before and since, along with the most expensive bottle of white wine.

I don't know how you regular passengers could afford to travel through T5 because we couldn't at those prices. Thankfully, our plane was on time, and it wasn't long before we were off on our holidays leaving T5 and all its hassle behind.

As we took off, I was reminded of that Elton John song 'Daniels flying tonight in a plane I can see the red tail lights heading for Spain'.

----

6 STAFF SEARCH

Who searches the searchers? We do! Who searches us? We do! Everybody who enters the security screening area of an airport has to be searched. There are no exceptions save visiting Heads of State or member of the Royal Family; everybody else is searched.

The Department of Transport (DfT) is responsible for the security of UK airports. Their policies are implemented at each airport by airport security staff. Airlines and travel companies don't set these rules.

The staff search area could be more stressful than working on the main concourse, but it could also be a quiet area in which to work. Hence it became a popular escape from the always busy main concourse.

There were two main areas for staff to be searched, one I have already talked about down on the ground floor where passengers who had forgotten their luggage had to go to gain access under escort by BA ground staff.

This was also the area where a member of BA staff was found to be carrying an unlawful weapon hidden in his hair. There was no real terrorist threat to this man, but he claimed he carried the knife for his own protection, but who knows. He was sacked immediately on discovery of the knife.

There were also two other areas because of the location of the staff's duties which took them down into the tunnel under the main runways. It was where you found the area of goods inwards; there had to be a staff search area down there too. This area was often closed due to staff requirements on the main concourse, but this too was subject to the agreed flow rates but for the goods that came in or went out of the airport.

Everything coming into the airport including humans had to be searched. Down in the bowels of the airport, you could have a long boring detail of several hours and time could drag, but at least as a team, we would keep ourselves occupied by various methods.

There was another area on the ground floor, as passengers and staff arrived outside at the many bus stops and underground railway station, and this facility was only open during certain hours to coincide the busy shift start times. It was located at the north end of the ground floor through a hidden door, near a public toilet.

But the main area of staff search was behind other hidden doors on the top floor as this staff search facility led the staff immediately onto the concourse. So, most retail outlet staff used this area, as did BA ground staff, and nearly all security staff, black Jax, purple Jax and all managers. It was by far the busiest area to work in with searching staff.

This was where I was working with the team on a busy Sunday afternoon. We had completed the busiest period of the changeover of staff shifts, with many staff entering the area for searching. Both sides of this facility were working, and now we were entering a slightly less busy period, but Sundays were no different to any other day of the week at staff search.

"Why has my bag been pulled off for a search?" said a lovely-looking member of BA ground staff. She was wearing her regulation uniform, but the skirt seemed a bit too short, and her shoe heels appeared to be bigger than usual. However, she did have lovely legs so why not show them off?

"You've left a liquid in your bag." I said as I was at the searching area, so it was my job to search her bag.

"No, I haven't."

"Well, let's have a look and see, shall we?"

"You security, you're all the same. Petty bloody jobs worth's the lot of you."

"Yes, I'm sure you're right, but this is one jobs worth that is going to have to search your bag I'm afraid."

"Do you get some kick out of picking on BA staff?"

"Of course. Our machines know when it's a BA member of staff's bag, so it automatically invents stuff for us to search."

"You do it on purpose."

"Look, I'm sorry but what is your problem?"

"You lot. What do you think you're achieving?"

"Sorry, I don't know what your problem is but my job is to search bags that have been seen by the X-ray operator to contain items that need checking. So really, what is your problem with that? You know you have to come through security to get to work, so what's your problem?"

"I'm running late for work."

"Well listen, don't take it out on me. You should get here earlier; you know you have to get through security."

"Oh, fuck off patronising me and just search my fucking bag will you!"

"Sure, but there's no need to swear at me."

"Fucking jobs worth!" the attitude of some staff, when they have to be searched, was amazing at times.

I started the search and found what the screen reader had seen and the reason this member of staff's bag had been rejected for search.

"It seems you have this in your bag." as I produced a half litre bottle of water.

"So, what?"

"You know what, it's over the size limit."

"How come yesterday I was allowed it, and today I'm not?" It was one thing that passengers used to say to us. And yes, yesterday they got away with it, but today they didn't. I think it's like the speeding in a car syndrome, you know 'officer I was speeding yesterday but you didn't stop me so why did you today'. The truth is that they didn't get away with it yesterday or the day before, but they use it as an excuse to justify what they've done in the hope they can get away with it today.

"I Dunno. What member of staff allowed you to take water this size into the security zone yesterday and I will report them and get them sacked?"

"Well, I don't know, you all look the same in uniform."

"Yes, and you all look the same when you're trying to get stuff into the airport you know you're not allowed. So please stop being stupid and patronising towards me."

"Did you call me stupid, you fucker?"

"Sorry to point out the obvious but you know you cannot bring water in this size container into the secure zone of the airport, don't you, and please stop swearing at me it's unnecessary?"

"Well, of bloody course."

"Yet you tried to bring just such an item into the secure zone?"

"Yes."

"Well then, who is being stupid you or me? Why didn't you put your hand up and say oops I forgot, instead of going on the attack and having a go at me?"

"You fucking bastard."

"Again, please stop swearing. And for your information, I know my parents were married when I was born. A fucker I might be but a bastard I am not. I will have to discard your oversized bottle of water."

"Wanker."

"Have you been watching me in the loos then?"

"What do you mean?"

"Well, if you think I'm a wanker. How would you know unless you have hidden cameras in all the gent's toilets? And even then, you would be wrong in my case. However, I know some of my colleagues might be wankers, would you like an introduction?"

"You think you're so smart with your sarcastic humour, don't you?"

"Thank you. At least you recognised my sense of humour which is lacking in yourself. To be honest, I was just politely taking the piss at your utter stupidity. Now I've finished my search, so please go away. And I hope you have a great day, as you've so far made mine so nice with your charm and use of the English language. I hope you're politer to your customers."

With that, she gathered up the rest of the contents of her bag and stormed off to her place of work where she would be yet another pleasant face of BA workers dealing with their passengers. Oh, if only the passengers saw the side of BA Ground crew we saw.

"Tony, one of these days you will be sarcastic to the wrong person." says bubbles.

"Yes, possibly but not to someone like her who thinks she can do what she likes and treat all of us with contempt because she works for BA and the rules don't apply to her for sure."

It goes to show that when you do something wrong and know you're in the wrong, you take your frustrations out on the person who has revealed your misdemeanour, and that's the same whether your staff or passengers. Strange world airports they really are!

During a quiet period, both Rami and I was on the WTMD, and we were just chatting. I was saying something about how I got annoyed at all the favouritism and 'Bruvs', and she said, "Tony I don't know why you get so uptight about it all."

"It's because I cannot stand by and see what I consider to be injustices."

"Buts it's just life."

"Doesn't mean to say we should accept it does it?"

"But it gets you frustrated and annoyed, is it worth it?"

"No sometimes maybe not, but it's in my DNA. Maybe it's something to do with my Jewish background, and what the Nazi's did to many of my relations I never knew. I don't know, but I can never witness this behaviour and just stand by and say nothing, and accept the injustice of it all. Even in the prison service, I was the same, and funnily enough, that's why I received so much respect from the prisoners, more than my peers."

"Don't get me wrong I admire you for it, but I couldn't be bothered."

"Do you think I should allow passengers and staff to be rude to me?"

"No, that's different. I love it when you're around, and a passenger gets angry because you will support your colleagues openly and argue back with a passenger rather than call an STL. I admire you for it, but this is different."

"Why? Why should we accept injustice in any form whether it is from passengers or our colleagues?"

"The passengers deserve it if they're rude to us, but the Bruvs it's just not worth it."

"If a passenger's rude then the gloves are off, I would never intentionally be rude to the passengers unless they are rude to me first, then its game on. But I feel the same with any injustice I see whether it's here at work or on the roads or in supermarkets, I can't stand bullying in any form or guise."

"But you won't change what's happening here."

"No, I know, but I won't walk willingly to the gas chambers like during the war I will go down fighting for my rights against what I see as injustice."

"I do admire you for it, but it's not my way."

"Don't forget you are from a similar ethnic background to what is going on here so maybe it's more of an acceptable way of life to you than to me."

"Yes maybe, I don't know, but I don't think I could stand up or be bothered to stand up against some of what goes on here."

"Maybe not but sometimes due to the situation you find yourself in, you might have to stand up and be counted, and at some period in your life you will face that dilemma believe me."

"I don't think I could."

"Each to our own Rami, each to our own." and I still haven't changed, just ask my wife.

Wow, this was getting heavy. And it wasn't like our team to have these sorts of conversations, but thankfully it was halted as another female member of staff came through the archway and activated. She was beautiful and stood in the correct stance ready for her search.

"Come on then Tony; you can do the search."

This officer loved to flirt and tease. I'd seen her do this with many of my colleagues. Although why she'd want to go through this routine with a man old enough to be her grandfather, I didn't know.

She was attractive with a fantastic figure, and many of the males working here had the hots for her. She was young and vivacious but to be honest; I never liked this up-front sexuality. I was and still am a prude where it comes to this open talk.

"Over to you Rami." I said as I got a bit embarrassed.

"I won't make that same offer again Tony." she said, laughing knowing I was getting more embarrassed.

"No, but I bet you say that to all the boys."

"Not all of them." she said and winked at the officer behind her, who I knew was her boyfriend.

"I'm old enough to be your grandad."

"Oh, I don't know, I'll try anything once." and she again winked at her boyfriend.

"You're old enough to be everybody's grandad." said Rami.

"You're not the messiah Tony, and you're not even going to be a naughty boy." pipped up Stan, and we all laughed.

Overall staff search was marginally better than working on the main concourse. We still had confrontations, but the staff were much more compliant than the passengers, and we had our fun moments. I was amazed at the diverse and often surprising things staff would try to bring into the secure area knowing the items were not allowed.

----

7 TOILET BREAK! TOILET BREAK!

There appeared to be an amazing phenomenon amongst many staff, or maybe it was an illness exclusive to Heathrow, particularly from an Indian background, but the amount of staff that needed to go to the toilet on numerous occasions during a two-hour stint on the security lanes was incredible. In fact, even stranger they always needed the toilet when they were in the loaders position or the bag searchers position and always managed to return to the security lane they were working on exactly at the time they were due to move around to the next piece of equipment. Absolutely amazing, and this strange medical condition seemed to affect the Indian culture more than any of the other cultures that worked at Heathrow.

Now I know if you have to go to the toilet and have held going for as long as possible then you really need to go. I've been in a similar situation on some occasions, but the frequency of some of my colleagues and their need to go to the toilet was incredible.

However, due to the tight staffing levels, there were never any spare staff to cover for comfort breaks when they were genuinely needed. It led to some serious issues for staff. I remember hearing about a member of staff in another terminal who needed to go to the toilet and had asked several times for an STL to get somebody to cover for him. The poor man peed himself and went off sick with stress. I believe he was trying to sue the company, and it served them right if he did.

Having said that, the staff didn't help themselves. I understood the need to go if you really did need a toilet break, but some colleagues and particularly the 'team' used to take it in turns to go off for cigarette breaks. They would illegally go out of the airport through the tickets machine area and across the concourse to the exit where there was a designated smoking area. Then come back as if nothing had happened, meanwhile the position on their machine; usually the bag searchers position was not being covered leading to many irate (and rightly so) passengers, who would then look at other members of staff and ask why their bags were not being searched.

There was one position on the machine which was designated to carry out random trace swaps, which was a DfT requirement. We used what looked like a magic wand with a white circle on the end to take a passenger's bag or laptop and go over it in a zig zag swabbing motion, then test the swab (the white circle) to see if it contained explosive trace.

I was on a machine doing such a job when the female officer on the bag searched position said to me, "I'm just going to the toilet, be back in a moment."

"Who's going to do the bag searching?"

"Who cares, I'm going for a pee." With that, she walked off the machine and instead of heading towards to the toilets she skipped under a barrier and walked out of the concourse back through tickets. I thought, she's going for a cigarette break and didn't even bother to get her position covered, how can she do that? But then I realised she was in the favoured 'Team', and they did whatever they liked and got away with it.

Meanwhile, the passengers were queuing up and getting annoyed at the unnecessary delay. An STL appeared "Where's your bag searcher?"

"Not my bag searcher. I'm doing random swabbing."

"Well, stop that and bag search."

"Hang on, what about the swabbing? If we miss the random targets, the DfT will make us search every bag again like last time."

"I don't care; I want the bags searched."

"Well, why not stop this lot from getting away with murder and going off for fag breaks without permission, instead of having a go at me?"

"Yea, just do the bag searching, will you?"

"Of course, but you need to get a grip of this, you really do."

"Yea yea yea."

"Whose bag is this?" I said and searched the bags. The honest truth was that nothing was ever done about the members of staff who just walked off the machines, despite that fact that management had CCTV cameras, and that this particular team never seemed to search a bag as they used this ruse often to avoid it. You cannot disguise the smell of somebody who's just had a cigarette; the smell lingers so recognisably.

I asked one of them once why this happened and he said, "I'm not getting my hands dirty and having all that aggro when searching them. So, I don't do it if I can get away with it."

"Yes, but your colleagues get it in the neck, and we have to do your work for you."

"Well, Bruv, who's the mug then innit."

After that, I avoided ever working on their machines as I was never going to allow this to happen to me again. I know many other members of staff did the same thing, talk about good teamwork and sticking together.

You can understand why passengers got annoyed when they saw a member of staff doing nothing yet their bag was waiting to be searched and they had a flight to catch. I witnessed a colleague standing on a machine that had broken down, and their belt had stopped running. The engineers were working on the machine, and the lane was closed, so they had no passengers and were all standing around doing nothing. Two walked off to go to the toilet or make a phone call or something. My machine was full of waiting bags to be searched. I was working as quickly as I could (which was a mistake according to some of my colleagues, as they deliberately took their time as they could only search a few bags in their designated time in that position of the process).

A passenger approached the officer on the other machine that was still doing nothing, and he said, "Is there any chance you could search my bag as my flight has already started to board?"

"Naw mate, nuffing I can do bout it."

"But you're doing nothing."

"Not my machine mate, not allowed."

"Even if I'm going to miss my flight?"

"Not my machine mate."

"Well, that's very nice of you, and you call yourselves professionals."

"Don't like it, don't fly from ere again innit mate."

"You idiot."

"Don't insult me. I'll get you chucked out for causing issues ere."

"You lot make me sick. I'm paying a lot of money for my family and me to fly through here with BA. And you lot are so lazy I'm going to miss my flight and the kids their holiday. All because you cannot be bothered to help out, amazing, totally amazing."

"Yea whatever mate, should ave got ere earlier then."

"I did, but your security queues took over an hour, and now all these bags being searched by this officer (he said pointing to me), and he has loads to search, so it's your system that seems to be at fault, doesn't it?"

"Dunno mate, not my problem."

Ok, I'd had enough now. I stopped my search and said to the passenger, "Sir, if you'd like to walk over to the STL standing over there wearing the fluorescent jacket and explain about your flight I'm sure he'll help get your bag searched quicker to ensure you get your flight."

"Oh, okay thanks very much." and he walked over and explained the problem. The STL came over and took the passengers bag and went off to find a lane that was not busy to get it searched quicker so he'd not miss his flight.

Later the same passenger walked past my machine and said, "Thanks so much for your help it's good to see some of you care about us passengers, not like some (as he pointed to the still empty lane with the same officers just standing there) thanks again."

"No problem sir, hope you have a good flight."

My colleague opposite looked at me with daggers. And I thought, you lazy bastard what was wrong with helping out a genuine passenger and relieving some of the pressure on your colleagues, but I knew the answer, I wasn't one of the Bruvs.

The toilet situation became so bad that an extra team of staff were formed. I think four to a team who wore high vis jackets and were assigned a particular group of machines to be available to cover for these much-needed toilet breaks. It used to annoy me whenever I was given this detail, as I'd often see officers after I'd covered them walking off the machine in the opposite direction to the toilets and be on their mobile phones, with no intention of going to the toilet. Management could see all this and ignored it. It was no wonder many of the staff didn't get on with one another.

On one occasion, I'd relieved every one of the 'team' and had spent more time on their machines than they had. And one officer, every time he got to the searcher's table, off he would go to the toilet, yea right. I called an STL and said "I'm not staying on this machine any longer. There are other members of staff who genuinely needed to go to the toilet yet so far I've covered every position and covered every person here and not one of them has gone to the toilet."

"Well, stop covering them then."

"If they ask for a toilet break, we have to go there. But you know exactly what's going on, and you need to have a word with them."

"Yes, ok." but he never did.

It got so bad that when some staff were detailed this toilet break position, they refused to wear the high vis jackets. They stated that, as they were dirty it was against health and safety regulations to wear them, but the real reason they didn't wear them was to avoid having to cover a toilet break.

The powers that be realised what some staff were doing, so they made all those on this particular detail have to wear a coloured lanyard around their necks. It lasted a few weeks before all the lanyards disappeared and we were back to square one. Nobody in authority ever really addressed the problem.

So that was toilet breaks, but I don't want to get bogged down in talking about them!

----

8 OVERTIME

Overtime, oh a magic word for many of the staff at Heathrow, and indeed there was an expectation for staff to work it. It was an unwritten rule you would be available to work overtime from time to time.

In my case, as I'd already received a pensionable income from my HM Prison service days, working overtime was a costly tax heavy imposition. Working overtime took me over the tax-free threshold, and it worked out that it would cost me money in paying more tax than I'd earn from the overtime, so I avoid working it. But many staff relied on working overtime.

Often subtle pressure would be placed on you to work overtime. The 'Manpower' (the tick in centre staff) would telephone you usually at home and say, "Overtimes available tomorrow." or "We need these shifts covered." They would often text message you with the same request even when you were on holiday. But I understand their difficulties. We had similar logistical issues in the prison service.

Manpower would get the next few days staffing requirements and realise they were short of x number of staff (we were nearly always short of each day) due to sickness, holidays or often because of the way staff could carry out shift swaps. The staff could make shift swaps with each other, with no prior consideration to the requirement of that day's gender mix. Which often meant we'd either too many males on shift at one time or too many females. The shift balance would then be wrong, and the Manpower team had the desperate job of telephoning all staff to match the extra staff needed. A thankless task for them to have to carry out, but they did their best, to cover the shortfalls with overtime.

We needed the same number of males to females to work the security lanes. The gender balance was critical. So why you might ask were these types of shift swaps allowed? The answer is easy, and we had these same problems in the Prison service and quickly learnt that any shift swap, if it was to be allowed, had to be between the same genders or not at all. But that would not resolve the fundamental problem evident from the opening of T5.

At Heathrow and in particular at the opening of T5, the logistical planning was of such an amateurish level or past custom and practice had led it to becoming so chaotic that maybe prior planning had never happened. You need three female officers and three male officers to run the machines, whatever the time of the shifts, simple. Then you need to consider annual leave entitlements and not allow the ratio of the genders to have more leave than each other at the same time. You then build in the x factor of anticipated sick leave, into the equation to cover short falls. You cannot account for the day to day unexpected sickness or short notice annual leave, and that is where any work involving shift patterns has its weakness, but it can be managed down to an acceptable level. Not at Heathrow.

There was a known shortage of male officers working all the early shifts. And the reverse was true of all the late shifts, so we already have an inbuilt imbalance, and the Manpower team were already under pressure to get males in on overtime for the early shifts and the opposite for the afternoon shifts.

Now let's add to that and allow too many of either gender annual leave at the same time, and just to make it more difficult let's allow male staff to swap shifts with female staff, and vice versa and there you have it, recipe for disaster, and it sure was.

The way to resolve the problem was to take a sticky plaster to cover the hole. It was built-in that there would be an expectation for staff to work overtime, to cover the shortfalls, and many staff worked overtime. There was a national cap (working time directives) on the amount of overtime staff could work, which had union agreement, and could not be breached. But this was Heathrow and it could, and would be breached and often, but given the work we do, I always thought this was a dangerous route to go down.

Just to put more strain on the inherent problems of shift imbalances, due to the 'mates' and 'Bruvs' system of working which extended into the personnel department, staff could put in for shift rota changes, from late to early and vice versa. And it seemed they had gotten these rota changes fairly easily. Right from the start even if they had got the shift gender mix balances correct, they were already taking that balance apart by looking after their mates and granted these shift rota changes without consideration to the balance of the genders, the changes made.

By the time I started working there; staff could apply for shift rota changes but would have to wait until there was a vacancy in the requested shift rota patterns. Many of the women preferred working early shifts if they had young school age children. And many of the younger men preferred to work late shifts, so they could go out at night after work and sleep late the next morning before coming to work.

When a new starter was given their shift pattern and team to work with, there didn't seem to be any consideration to the balance of genders within the team. It appeared to be an exercise to put 'bums on seats' irrespective of what 'bum' was going on what seat.

I might have gotten this all wrong, and if so I apologise, but this is my impression of what I witnessed while working there.

You couldn't work overtime on both your rest days as it was inbuilt into the computerised system you had to have at least one rest day in every seven days worked (I think it was seven, but as I didn't do it, I never found out what the limit was).

Many of the staff used to book annual leave and provided you worked a different shift to the one you'd booked annual leave on, you could come in and work overtime. This seemed perverse and in my former employment when this scheme would have been called 'Spanish practice' and have been outlawed, but again this was Heathrow.

"You mean I can book a week's annual leave, but work overtime on each day, provided I don't work the shifts I should have been on if I had been at work?"

"Yes."

"That's surely illegal?"

"No. You're not working the shifts you have annual leave for, are you?"

"Well, no."

"Well then, you can come in and work overtime."

"So, I'm getting paid twice for the same days' work?"

"Well, yes, and no. You're getting paid for the shift you've taken as annual leave and getting paid for the overtime you've worked."

"But both are on the same day. We'd never have gotten away with that in the Prison Service for sure."

But here at Heathrow, it was 'custom and practice' as was the shift swaps and the imbalance it created between the genders in the teams. No wonder Manpower's jobs were so stressful.

Eventually, a block was put on opposite sex shift swaps, which didn't go down too well with the staff but it was understandable. The imbalance of the ratio of male to females for all the shifts was never solved, well how could it be once it had been established in this manner.

I did sometimes work the occasional overtime shift, especially in my early days until I realised the full tax implications. To be honest, overtime was so easy. On one occasion, I worked a 'plus six'. This was six hours overtime before my actual start time of 12:30. I was starting work at 06:30, as I was working six hours, I was entitled to one break and also had to have at least thirty minutes break before the commencement of my actual shift.

"Does this mean I will have to finish my overtime shift by 12:00 mid-day?"

"If we can, we will get you off by then."

"Great." I'm already being paid thirty minutes for not working, yes; I'll have some of that! I thought to myself.

I worked on a machine for an hour then was sent on a forty-five-minute break. On returning from my break, I was sent to a broken security door to sit there and wait for an engineer to arrive and repair the door. Yippee, no machines on a busy Sunday morning great. Two and a half hours later I was relieved and told to report to the RA's office. They gave me two radio batteries and said, "Take one to T5B and the other to T5C, collect all the dead batteries and bring them back here, don't take all day but grab a cuppa if you want."

Off I went with my batteries; I thought it's a nice day why not walk the length of the underground walkways rather than take the transit trains packed with passengers? I took a nice leisurely stroll first to T5B swapped the batteries and collected the dead ones, then continued my walk to T5C and repeated the process. I didn't bother to stop for a drink but walked back along the walkway back to the RA's office.

"That was quick."

"Really? I didn't stop for a cup of tea, but I walked to both stations and then back, so I hope that was alright?"

"Walked! You walked all that way, bloody hell Tony your fit."

The RA looked at her watch and said, "Well it only took you forty-five minutes. Other staff would have taken ages. It's now 11:30, so you might as well go on your 'in betweeny' as I can't use you for anything else. Thanks for your help today Tony. See you later."

And with that my overtime was complete. Let me get this straight, I was working a six-hour overtime shift on double pay yet I had a forty-five minutes break, and now I was given an hour's break. I have actually worked for four and a-quarter-hours and during that time was only on the machines for one hour at the start of my shift. Well, if this is overtime bring it on.

That was why working overtime was so popular. Although on some occasions you ended up on the machines for the whole of your shift, it was after all only for four and three-quarters hours at most on a six-hour overtime gig.

The most sought-after overtime was Christmas and New Year, but you had to put your name down for it months in advance. And again, it appeared that some staff were looked after more than others for this lucrative extra overtime pay.

Many of the staff didn't celebrate Christmas especially if they were from the Indian culture. And what they used to do was apply on the first day of the annual leave application date. Once the leave was confirmed they'd offer their annual leave as a swap to somebody, who didn't want to work that day but had been detailed to work on their shift pattern and had been unsuccessful in their application for annual leave. Then after getting the swap, the same member of staff would apply for an overtime shift different to the one he had booked his (or her) annual leave for and then get paid at the double overtime rate for working the hours they would have done, anyway. Spanish Practice but it went on all the time.

Every Christmas I was employed at Heathrow I was on the rota to work, and every year I applied for annual leave and never got it. Once, I got a swap with a colleague who didn't celebrate Christmas. But to be honest Christmas day was an easy day's work as there were hardly any passengers travelling. It was a quiet and easy but boring shift to work as was Boxing Day and New Year's Day.

I asked Rami, "Why do so many of the Indian lads want to work Christmas day?"

"It's double pay for doing nothing."

"Don't they celebrate?"

"No. In our culture, we don't celebrate Christmas. It's a Christian festival, so, why would we?"

"Well, I'm Jewish but my wife is not, and we celebrate it with our children and grandchildren."

"We don't, so it's worth us working it, don't you think?"

"Yeah, definitely. No wonder 'Vishi' asked me if I wanted to swap my

Christmas day with him."

"Vishi always gets swaps for Christmas and New Year. There's usually a queue for him to swap with them. Otherwise, he gets overtime anyway."

'Yes, from the Bruvs. No wonder!'

But Manpower were always desperate to get staff to work overtime. I

was still getting text messages about its availability six months after I

left Heathrow and came to live in Spain. Oh well, and I thought it must be because I was popular!

----

9 THE REST ROOMS & STAFF CANTEENS

No book of mine would be complete without a chapter about what goes on in staff rest rooms. Heathrow is no different; it has many rest rooms and staff canteens. But the staff canteen services at the Terminal must be mentioned, so I've combined the two in this chapter.

There were at least five rest rooms throughout the whole of T5 and at the other two satellites, T5B and T5C; there was one each. All these rest rooms were airside of the terminal. However, there was one restroom on the landside, and I used to find this area a refreshing escape from the monotony of the other main rest rooms. Mainly, because the TV in this room often wasn't working, this was a blessed relief.

All the rest rooms had free tea and coffee machines, and another for purchasing small snacks like crisps and chocolate bars. Again, these only seemed to work Monday to Friday lunchtime. They were always either empty or broken on a weekend, fantastic that, don't you think?

There was a rest room on the South concourse and another on the North, the other one was referred to as the new rest room, and it was behind the International arrivals hall. These three rooms always had TV's blasting out monotonous repeats of either Friends or the Big Bang Theory or How I Met Your Mother. Whereas the rest room landside seemed to have either BBC news or films playing whenever the TV was working, which was rarely, especially towards the end of my time working there. I think somebody either stole the batteries from the remote-control unit or stole the remote and the connecting cables as it did not work.

Unless it was the Indian Premier League of Cricket when every television was playing the matches, perfect for cricket fans lousy for those of us who were not interested. The strange thing was that if you were working the early shifts, then all these televisions seemed to broadcast BBC news or Sky news, yet as soon as the late shifts came on duty, the televisions broadcasted the entire American so-called comedy shows.

I remember once, during a hours break around seven pm there were ten to fifteen officers crowded into the restroom and Friends or Big Bang Theory was being broadcast, and a colleague of mine said, "Don't you find this funny?"

To which I replied, "Absolutely not, what's funny about it?"

"Oh, come on Tony you really don't find it funny?"

"No! American humour is not funny at all to me."

"It's great. I could watch these all day, couldn't you?"

"No, and it's all canned laughter anyway, what's funny about it? I've never understood American humour; give me Morecambe and Wise or Only Fools and Horses anytime."

"Who?"

"Exactly and do you know what the biggest selling comedy show in the USA is?"

"No."

"Faulty Towers and they only made thirteen episodes of it, and it's still as funny today as it was then. This crap will be forgotten and binned in two years' time let alone last as long as Faulty Towers."

"You're getting old Bruv innit."

"I might be, these shows all seem the same, The Big Bang, How I met your mother, Friends. The same so-called humour and I'm sure the same actors in each, no definitely not funny."

And then Stan said "Tony, you're not the Messiah, you're a very naughty boy." and we all started laughing.

The younger staff all appeared to have this obsession with these crazy American so-called comedy shows. It amazed me then and still does today, but I suppose it takes all sorts of humour to appeal to all kinds of people.

The rest room was where I first offered my philosophical view of what was wrong with the world today. Stan and I, along with a few others were chatting about what was going wrong with our society and who we blamed for the decline in our standards. I think there had been a news flash on TV about some atrocity that had taken place in the USA or Turkey or somewhere.

"I blame the Government. They've made all our lives to easy, and we've become a nanny state."

"No, I blame the schools. There's no discipline in them anymore."

"No! No! No, it's the parent's fault they don't take responsibility for their childrens behaviour."

"Naw, it's all America's fault. Tony always says it's America that causes all the problems, don't you Tony?" This was said, I think, to 'wind me up' as I often said it was all America's fault.

"McDonald's." I said as everybody looked at me as if I was mad.

"McDonald's, as in the burger places?"

"Yup."

"Why do you blame them then?"

"I don't blame them 'per say' but what they stand for."

"Well, what do they stand for then?"

"Fast food fast service, in and out, nobody sits down and talks to each other. I blame their philosophy of in and out service for the breakdown in family values. And that has led to all the other values going wrong with our society, and there are McDonald's all over the world."

"I still don't understand what you mean Tony?"

"Ok, when I was growing up in my formative years, we all sat down for family dinners, no TV, no radios. We had time to talk. We learnt how to hold a conversation and listen to other people's views. There were no distractions, no mobile phones, in fact, we didn't even have a telephone in those days."

"Was that this century then?"

"Yes, of course. This was in the early nineteen sixties, but what we learned was valuable lessons in tolerating other people's views. We had no instant TV live news, or Internet, we either heard about what was going on via the radio or read it in the newspapers. And over a family meal, we could talk the event through in a reflective fashion."

"Bloody hell, I can't believe it was really like that then."

"Yup, we didn't even have Google to answer all our questions."

"I cannot remember a time we didn't have mobile phones."

"Stan, I believe you."

"No mobile phones, no internet, no TV, it must have been awful."

"Maybe, but our standard of behaviour was much better it seems looking back now. Look at what do you do today, rush into to McDonald's grab a 'big mac' and off you go about your business. No time to sit down and chat, no time for yourself to allow you to view what's going on in a calm, logical manner. Everything is rush and tear. Our pace of life is so much quicker, but our quality of life has deteriorated. We don't get time to tolerate other people's behaviour because we have to rush off to our next important bit of life. So, yes I blame McDonald's philosophy for it all going wrong in the world."

The restroom was silent as I think others actually thought about what I had said.

"I think you're right Tony, about the breakdown of society, but not sure you can blame McDonald's for it."

"Ok McDonald's and America."

"Tony, you're a very naughty boy and maybe you are the Messiah after all." pipped up Stan and we all laughed.

All the rest rooms had the internal intranet system so we could log into our personal areas where we could check our details and leave entitlements or order our uniforms and request annual leave. The South concourse computer always seemed to be broken. Come to think of it half the PC's in the new rest room never worked, anyway. Yes, another example of good communication for staff and this was usual for Heathrow. They were all supposed to have TV screens linked into the Heathrow staff information system; again, I think only the new restroom had a screen that worked intermittently; none of the others had screens that worked at all.

When the new computer systems were installed, it was being hailed as the best innovative idea for improving the communication to all staff. All restrooms were to have the new equipment so any member of staff could access their personal records, leave, sickness monitoring, staff reports, etc. They replaced the old computers with nice new ones. In, the south concourse rest room it took nearly another year before the computers were connected to the system. Great piece of kit for the staff I must say.

During one shift, I was sitting having a cup of tea in the South rest room, and on noticing that nobody was watching the television, I asked, "Is anybody watching this?"

"No." said one, the others just ignored my question and continued to chat amongst themselves. As I couldn't find the remote control, I unplugged the TV only for the officer sitting in a comfortable armchair to say, "Oi, I was watching that!"

"Well, you might have been watching it, but you couldn't hear it as your snoring was louder than the girls in the corners chattering."

Another time, after a hectic first stint on the machines, we'd been sent on a break. The rest of the team went to the landside rest room, but I remained in the South concourse and used that rest room as did Stan. The two of us walked in, Stan straight over to the tea machine to get tea for both of us and me to sit down in a comfy armchair. There was an almighty argument going on between staff, with the telly also blaring out in the background, it was like bedlam in there. Some rest I thought to myself. Stan brought the tea over as the argument raged. I'd had enough and shouted out to the two protagonists "Oh you two, can you please shut up!"

"What, who said that?"

"Me, I don't know what your issue is but just pipe down. We could hear you two arguing from outside so the passengers must be able to hear you too, so just calm it."

"What's your problem bruv? Was just having a discussion."

"No, you're having an argument, and we can all hear it. If you want to swat handbags at each other take it outside of the terminal and leave the restroom as it is. You know there's a clue to what this room is for, it's called a REST ROOM, so just bloody well rest will you and let us do it too."

Stan pipped up, "Tony you're not the messiah, but you're a very naughty boy." and I looked at him and laughed.

The most important function of the restroom was for staff to arrange their shift swaps with each other. The notice boards were full of requests - if colleagues could swap with them on different dates. When I resigned, things had changed, but until then you could swap a shift with either sex. This defied logic, as you could end up and often did with too many males or female staff on duty at the same time. For instance, a team of six needed three males and three females to run, so if two males had swapped shifts with two females, you ended up with five females and one male so the security lane could not run. It meant more pressure for the RA's sorting out the correct gender mix, yet management just could not see that this was a problem. Mind you, their gender mix for all the shifts was completely wrong, and eventually, they had to admit the problem and take drastic action to rectify what they'd allowed to happen. Again, this would never have happened in the Prison service, yet I used to call that service inept, oh boy how wrong was I?

There was a strict rule that the only language we could speak while at work and this included when in the restrooms was English. It was a rule that would never be upheld as it seemed on some occasions that English was the minority language for staff. Often you would walk into a restroom and listen to the babble of so many languages. It was like a day working in the United Nations building or the EU building in Brussels, but it added to the spice of life (no pun intended).

One time, I was looking for my mate 'the silver fox' known as 'Naz', we'd worked together in my first team, and he was a bit older than most of my colleagues but still younger than me. Mind you; it would have been pretty difficult to find staff older than me.

As I walked along the short passageway into the restroom, I noticed that there was no TV blasting out. Oh, that's a rarity, I thought to myself. As I opened the door, I noted that there was not one Indian officer in the room, what's going on then? Is it a special holiday and they have all got together to celebrate? But I thought, this is very unusual, everybody's white in here, not one other ethnic group. Until I realised that all I could hear was Ukrainians talking to Ukrainian's in their language, Polish staff talking to their fellow Poles in their language, and Spanish also talking to their Spanish colleagues. Oh well, I was the only Englishman in the room, once again.

Now, where has my mate 'Naz' gone? I wanted to thank him for bringing back that lovely purple pashmina for my wife, from his holiday to India.

The staff canteens appeared to cater for every ethnic food requirement except basic English food. Yes, you could get an excellent English breakfast, but only up to 11 am in the mornings, after that it was either lunch or dinner food available up to around 8 pm. Not a lot of good if you were, and it often happened, given a break after 8 pm then no food in the canteens was available. Another brilliant piece of staff care. The nearest you could get to plain food was jacket potatoes with a filling, usually lukewarm baked beans, well as the joke goes they always 'luked warm' to me.

It was a Sunday; I think I was on a patrol day and had walked past nearly all the canteens. I'd noticed that all were advertising a typical English

Sunday Roast lunch, great, excellent, I thought. About time, a typical English Sunday Roast just what I wanted. My mouth was watering at the thought of roast potatoes, vegetables, and roast beef with gravy. How wrong could I be?

I had planned my main break to work out what was the best canteen to go and get my Typically English Sunday roast, and decided the canteen behind the UK Customs Hall south usually offered the best warmish food, and besides which I thought the landside canteen had gotten fed up with my complaining about their cold food, and after my experiences in the prison service I really didn't trust what they would do to my food.

I was at the counter when one of the serving lads, also of ethnic origin said, sorry, all the roast beef had gone, but they had chicken instead. Ok, I thought, I'll have chicken, it's still a roast dinner. Don't get me wrong; I didn't eat Indian food because in the past curry powder and my stomach didn't get on and I'd had some terrible reactions to eating it. I loved spicy food particularly Mexican. I was never sure what caused the issues but thought it better to avoid eating Indian food. I have to say nowadays I eat Indian food and it's wonderful, and I've not had any allergic reactions, so am upset about what I missed out on for all those years.

I collected my dinner and sat down, the roast potatoes needed a chisel to obtain entry into them, the vegetables had been steamed into oblivion, and the chicken was tandoori. I took my meal back to the counter "What is this you are serving up?"

"Typical English roast dinner."

"What part of England did this come from Luton or Bradford?" both places are renowned for having large Indian communities.

"Don't you like it Bruv?"

"Where do you want me to start? The chicken is tandoori, and I'm allergic to Curry powder."

"Don't be silly, no-one's allergic to curry powder."

"I am, and the potatoes are so hard I need a chisel to cut them open."

"They can't be that bad."

I tried to stick my plastic knife and fork into the potatoes, and both implements broke in half. "Not that hard, what bit of not that hard don't you understand?"

"They'd be alright if you had metal knives and forks."

"Yes, but we are not allowed metal, that's why you only provide plastic. And what have you done to the vegetables, they're tasteless?"

"Nobody else is complaining."

"That's because they all had curry."

"I can do a curry for you too if you prefer?"

"I told you, I'm allergic to curry powder, didn't I?"

"Oh, yeah, sorry bruv don't know what else to suggest."

"Well, for a start I'd suggest you tried to make edible food for a change. I work long shifts and need decent food once in a while obviously this is not the place to get that, so I won't bother to eat in the canteen again."

"Your choice bruv, but M&S are expensive." There was an M&S food store on the landside, and many staff would purchase food there and take it to the landside staff restroom where there were microwave ovens to cook their food.

"You know what, it's worth the extra to eat good food. I used to be a food lover until I came here to eat."

That was the last time I attempted to eat in a staff canteen at Heathrow. My wife used to cook roast dinners and make sure there was enough left over for me to bring to work the next day. And I'd warm my food up in the provided microwaves. But for many who had to rely on the canteen food, I felt very sorry, as they must have gone hungry frequently, or were just used to eating the terrible food the staff canteens provided.

----

10 SHOOTS

I always thought a shoot was an association football term when you shouted to one of your players 'shoot', in the hope they'd hear and would attempt a shot at the oppositions goal in an attempt at scoring a goal. Or, wasn't a shoot those little green things that prize open the earth and grow into plants, or trees, but not at Heathrow.

At Heathrow, it had become custom and practice for you to be told you could leave work and go home before the end of your shift time. And it was the colloquially referred to as a shoot, I, however, knew the terminology for this sort of thing as a 'flyer' but here it was a shoot.

"Why are these flyers known as shoots?"

"Obvious Bruv innit, we get to shoot off work before the end of our shift."

"Oh yea, obvious." and that's what it was throughout the whole of Heathrow airport. It had become an expectation you would receive a 'shoot' before the official end time of your shift.

The real problem with this system was that the early shifts got no such shoot as their finish times coincided with one of the busiest times for the terminal and therefore all security lanes were operational. If your finish time was 14:00 and the next shift start time was 13:45 by the time the RA's had assigned each team their security lane and by the time that team had walked to the lane it often meant you got off work just before or even dead on your finish time. There seemed no inbuilt handover period. I was told it was inbuilt into the system. But I witnessed no possibility of this being in place. There was also the time some teams took to walk from the detail office to their lane of operation; I had seen snails walk quicker and particularly when you were waiting to be relieved by the night shifts and were the last teams waiting to go home.

"Oh look, here comes the creeping death squad."

"How do they manage to walk so slowly?"

"I timed them, it's taken nearly ten minutes to get from the RA's office to this lane, and we are three lanes from the bloody office."

"How do they do it?"

"Practice."

It led to animosity between the early shift, the late shift staff, and the night shift staff, even though the early shift and the early early shift staff got paid a significant higher shift disturbance amount in their monthly salaries.

I worked overtime sometimes by coming in on a plus before my actual shift and found the animosity to be open and often hostile when early staff found out I was a late shift. The late shift staff was also referred to by the early staff as the kids, and the earlies wrongly assumed that all the younger members of staff worked the lates so they could go out clubbing after work and sleep in the next morning before their start of shift. It was probably true for some of the younger staff, but if that is what they want then why not.

But it did appear that the early staff was of the more mature nature than the late shift staff. I was amazed at the different attitude between some of the staff working these two shift patterns. Having worked these early shifts, which meant I had to get up around 03:30 to get to work by 05:00, it was nice to mix with similar-aged staff. I made several friends on these shifts, but it would not have suited me to do them all the time.

Of course, the early shift finish time of between 12:30 and 14:00 due to those times being some of our busiest times meant that any decent shoots were never possible. When I worked these shifts if you were given over fifteen minutes shoot then you had done well as most of the time it was five minutes. The lates often got thirty minutes, and depending on the team you were with, that could sometimes be as much as forty-five minutes.

I remember once working with the 'Team', and we were given a shoot so early that I arrived home before my official shift finish time, and that was after a forty-five minute drive home. Obscene really but that was what happened.

It was a recipe for resentment and animosity between the early shifts and the late shifts as was bound to occur with this expectation of receiving shoots by the late shifts.

I remember being at a meeting of selected staff and managers when the subject of shoots was brought up. One officer said, "It's unfair the way the shoots work. We should all be given the same time at the end of our shifts for shoots. Why should some staff get off earlier than others?"

"I don't think this is the correct forum for this discussion." I said and the TDM who was chairing the meeting agreed.

"What do you mean bruv?"

"In my last job getting off work at your finish time was a perk. So why are you complaining about getting off work earlier than your finish time? It's a perk, not a requirement."

"Because others are getting off earlier than my team. You know what's going on here Tony."

"Yes, I do and to be honest we don't want to go down this line here."

"Oh, and why not?"

"Well to be honest, if I were management I'd be saying if you want everybody to have the same finish times as each other that's simple, nobody will be given a shoot from now on." and I looked at the TDM who said, "Tony's spot on. I can stop everybody getting shoots from now on if that's what you want, but you are complaining about a perk and not a condition of your working contract you know?"

"Yes, but it doesn't seem fair."

"No, it's not, but it depends on the shift you're working?" Said the TDM.

"And who your friends are." said the officer.

"Yes, but that's something else not for this meeting don't you think?"

"What do you mean?" said the TDM.

"Well, we all know what goes on here with the corruption and the mates looking after their mates, don't we?"

"Look, we're talking about shoots, and if the RA's give me five minutes of a shoot, I'm not going to complain that somebody else got ten minutes. It's daft! In the Prison service if this went on it was called 'Spanish Practices', and if the press ever got hold of it, then there was hell to pay from the Ministry of Justice. In fact, over one hundred prison staff got sacked for getting so called perks that had become custom and practice. We don't want to go down that line here, do we?"

We all agreed. But the irony of getting shoots was that on the few occasions I did get a superb shoot of over thirty minutes, the bloody M25 was blocked by accidents, and I got home later than if I'd finished at the correct time. I think that's called 'Sods law'.

----

11 UK BORDER CONTROL

The UK Border Agency (UKBA) was the border control agency of the Government of the United Kingdom and part of the Home Office that was superseded by UK Visas and Immigration in April 2013. It was formed as an executive agency on 1 April 2008 by a merger of the Border and Immigration Agency (BIA), UK visas and the Detection functions of HM Revenue and Customs.

On 26 March 2013, following a scathing report into the agency's incompetence by the Home Affairs Select Committee, it was announced by the then Home Secretary Theresa May that the UK Border Agency would be abolished and its work returned to the Home Office. Its executive agency status was removed as of 31 March 2013 and the body was split into two new organisations; UK Visas and Immigration UK Visas focusing on the visa system and Immigration Enforcement, focusing on immigration law enforcement. Before this in April 2012, the border control division of the UKBA was separated from the rest of the agency as the Border Force. But it's still referred to as the UKBA.

The agency managed the UK Government's limit on non-European economic migration to the UK. It was responsible for in-country enforcement operations, investigating organised immigration crime and in detecting immigration offenders including illegal entrants and over stayers. The body was also responsible for the deportation of foreign national criminals at the end of sentences.

The agency's E-borders programme checked travellers to and from the UK in advance of travel, using data provided by passengers via their airline or ferry operators. The organisation used automatic clearance gates at main international airports. The UKBA is an integral part of any port of entry into the United Kingdom and indeed at Heathrow, although absolutely nothing to do with the Security aspects of the airport, it plays a big part in the smooth running of the airport as a whole.

Unless you are catching a connecting flight, your first stop after arrival at any of Heathrow's terminals will be passport control. There are two queues at passport control one for European Union (EU), European Economic Area (EEA), British and Swiss nationals, and a second for all other nationalities.

At, the passport desk a Border Force officer's job is to ask to see your passport or travel document and any supporting documentation necessary for your visit here. However, despite the vital work they do they can also cause absolute chaos. Particularly during the busy periods at the airport when flights have been delayed, and several long-haul flights often arrived close together. You could have upwards of a thousand passengers disembarking their respective aircraft and all heading towards the already queuing masses in the Passport control area. There was in place an agreement that no passenger would have to wait over twenty-five minutes to get through the process. This target was often missed.

This would often lead to the UK press producing headlines like 'Furious travellers complained they had to wait in monster queues at Heathrow Airport. Or 'Furious passengers complained of long queues at Heathrow immigration yesterday amid mounting fears of a shortage of border guards'. And 'Weary passengers, many of whom had arrived on long haul flights, claimed they were forced to wait for over an hour in what was branded an absolute shambles.'

Sadly, these instances were all true. I know because as a security officer we were often called on to assemble orderly and safe queuing systems; however, the abuse we'd get from the passengers was incredible to witness. Funnily enough, the new Purple Jacketed Heathrow Ambassadors seemed to be in the front line of much of the abuse, but they did an incredible job of keeping the masses in some order.

I remember once there were several of us detailed to go down to the customs hall and help with the rapidly increasing queues of passengers waiting to go through the Boarder Control. It was the third instance in recent weeks where people arriving had criticised long lines at passport control in UK airports. This was amidst the UKBA's growing internal row over crippling cuts to their numbers.

It was absolute chaos when we arrived in the hall; we were directed to assemble tension barriers along the whole route of the queuing passengers. My goodness, these queues went back so far, and as other aircraft arrived and disgorged their passengers who were then coming out of the jetty tunnels and joining in wherever they were, irrespective of the already long formed queues, there was tension and unrest in the air.

For once, the contingency plans were working, and it didn't take long before we'd organised our barriers into a safe method of getting new passengers to be shepherded to the back of the increasing line of passengers. The purple jacketed ambassadors were giving out bottles of water to the waiting masses and refreshments were organised.

Most passenger behaviour was good given the circumstances, but there were some that I'm sorry to say were terrible, and especially to their fellow travellers. I remember one man in particular. I was holding the queues along with two other colleagues, all of us wearing high Vis jackets, when this smartly dressed man in a grey business suit, detached himself from the crowd and walked towards the customs hall. We were supposed to hold the passengers back and allow a few through at a time as the long lines of queuing passengers eased through the Passport officers desk after being checked. These long queues zig zagged backwards and forwards in the customs hall before the UKBA desk could be reached.

"Sir, I'm afraid you need to wait until we can get you into the customs hall."

He went into a purple rage "I've been fucking waiting long enough! I've got to get to an important meeting."

"I appreciate that sir, but all these other passengers have important things to do. We're doing our best to get you through fast."

"It's not bloody well quick enough, is it? Get more staff down here you bunch of morons."

"Sir, the delay is at the UKBA desks and not by us."

"You're all the same; you're all in uniform. What is your problem?"

"The problem is sir, that UKBA are taking longer than usual to carry out their security checks and because of several flight delays that have all arrived here at the same time. It's added to the problems. Now, please return to your place, and we'll get you through as soon as we can."

"I think you must be deaf as well as daft." Strange thing to accuse me of. I knew I wasn't deaf as I could hear his ranting alright, and I knew that well, maybe, I might be a bit daft from time to time, but how would he know? So, I said, "Sir, I'm not deaf as I can hear your rantings over and above all the other noise here. So, would you return to your place in the queue please?"

"I don't give a shit I'm going through now!" he shouted, and I heard him easily thus confirming that I wasn't deaf.

"Sir, please have consideration for your fellow passengers who are all in the same position as you."

"I couldn't give two fucks about these other idiots patiently waiting here. I've had enough of this, and I'm going through."

I pointed at the huge zig zag queue in the main hall "What, you're going through that mass of people because you think you're more important than them? I don't think so, sir!"

"And you're gonna stop me, are you?" he said taking an aggressive stance towards me.

Ok, now this had become a confrontation, and the man was getting aggressive.

"Sir, please calm down, we're doing our best. However, that doesn't mean I will not call the police to arrest you, and then your precious meeting will be delayed longer. I don't take kindly to being threatened (and I looked him up and down) by the likes of people like you, who think you're more important than anybody else. Now go back to your QUEUE!" I said in a raised voice.

At this point three STL's appeared and thankfully one of them 'Mo' was a huge mountain man, his shoulders were massively wide, and I knew he was also a martial arts expert.

"Do we have a problem here sir?"

I think he suddenly lost all his aggression when he saw 'Mo'. "I have an important meeting and need to get through this lot!" and he waved his hands all around.

"Yes sir, and so does everybody else. Now, you're going to go back to the queue and wait like everybody else, until my officers can call you forward, do you understand?"

"Yes, but I really need to get through."

"I'm sure you do, but sir, please consider the situation. It's not ours in the making, its UKBA, so please be our guest and make a formal complaint to them about these delays in their service?" and with that Mo walked off and winked at me as he went past.

I returned to my position very near to this passenger and tried to make conversation with him.

"Is there no way you can contact the people you need to see by mobile phone, sir?"

"No, my bloody phone won't work in here."

"Sir, would you like to use my phone? If your meeting is so important, mine will work here."

"What, you'd let me use your phone?"

"If it's an emergency," I said, "We would do everything we could to help."

"Well, that's very kind of you. I appreciate that honestly, I do." Well, what a turnaround in attitude from him.

I allowed him to use my phone, and as he handed it back, I was given the signal to allow the next batch of passengers to join the main zig zag queue. This included the gentleman, so off the group moved and as they did so one young family of four approached me, and the woman said, "Thank you so much for all your efforts, especially for how after all his insults (pointing to the Gentleman) you went out of your way to help him. I'd have told him where to get off."

I laughed and said, "All part of our service. Hope you get through soon, bye." and I waved to her two young children, who'd been waiting patiently.

There were interesting headlines in our national newspapers about the massive delays on this particular day, one of them said this:

Some passengers caught up in yesterday morning's hold ups vented their anger at Heathrow Airport Security Staff, but immigration is the responsibility of the UK Border Force. Many complained to the airport, but the responsibility falls with Border Force.

Please remember that when travelling through Heathrow the Border controls are not run by Heathrow security but by UK Border Force.

There was also an occasion when we were forewarned that UKBA would go on a work to rule.

"They're off again! Bloody UKBA it'll be the usual chaos, and we'll be in the firing line Tony, you watch."

"Naw, they're on a work to rule. That means they have to work properly and not at their usual snail pace. Passengers will get through quickly; you mark my words."

And sure enough, that's exactly what happened, they went on their work to rule and passengers got through immigration quicker than they ever had before.

Well if that's a work to rule, then let's hope UKBA hold more of them. We all laughed at that one, thanks, UKBA.

----

12 BLACK JAX TO PURPLE JAX

Black Jack is an "aniseed flavour chew" according to its packaging. It's a chewy, gelatin-based confectionery. Black Jack is manufactured under the Barratt brand in Spain. In the 1920s Trebor Bassett made them, and the wrapper showed gollywogs on it. While still manufactured under Tangerine Confectionery, Black Jacks have been rebranded from Barratt to 'Candy Land' and the packaging, most notably the outer box, has been redesigned.

No, they're not, honest! When I started at Heathrow, many of the mundane jobs necessary for the smooth running of the terminal were carried out by a group of contracted staff known to all and sundry as the 'Black Jax' see I told you they're not a chewy sweet.

The Black Jax job was to hand out the plastic bags as you walked up to the security staff at the tickets area of the departure lounge. They were also there in the same sort of area in the International transfers area of the terminal, to remind passengers of all the security information they would need as they walked from their arriving aircraft into the security screening area and into the departure area to get their connecting flights to their final destinations.

They played an important part of the whole security process and maybe due to their unrewarding efforts of trying to inform passengers about the allowances they could or could not bring in through the security screening process; it made our jobs at the loading position a little easier.

I had often sat at the ticket machines watching them approach passengers and ask if a plastic bag was required, or try to inform passengers about the liquid rules. Despite the sixteen information boards relaying this information, only to be often rudely brushed aside by impatient and uncaring passengers. You all know who you are!

They also helped out in the security lanes by helping passengers into the queues for their respective security lanes and through the screening process. I felt sorry for these workers as they carried out a thankless task with little recognition of their efforts. I was embarrassed by the attitude of some of my colleagues towards these hardworking members of the team.

During their time at Heathrow, I became friendly with many of them and always appreciated the work they carried out.

The London Olympics changed all this. The black Jax were removed. I don't know if they lost the contract, or the company just re-organised and morphed into the new one, or were taken over. But I know many of them moved to the new company and told me of the better job opportunities now offered to them by the changeover.

So now, although doing a similar job, they changed from wearing their black jackets to new purple jackets and trousers.

The Ambassador Service as it was now called, was set up to provide an enhanced multi-lingual and cultural interaction of face-to-face customer service standards to the worldwide passengers as they arrived, transit and departed the airport. The aim was that of creating a blueprint for exceptional service. All the Ambassadors had high grooming and etiquette standards, and their primary role was that of providing assistance and information through their expert knowledge of the passenger journey to ensure the service was delivered at the highest level. This is taken directly from their advertising blurb.

And it went on: Assisting and engaging with passengers with preparation for security areas ensuring passengers carried through regulation items only to reduce the amount of baggage checks and carrying out queue management for a quick and efficient flow management and transition through to the departure lounges.

They were there to provide help and guidance to passengers at the automated ticket systems, enhancing the technology and increasing passenger throughput into the departures halls reducing the need of several manned desks.

The Hosts had to demonstrate and communicate a good understanding of the passenger process, assist passengers with the use of CUSS (Common

User Self Service) kiosks for quick and efficient check in process. They helped to manage the concourse queuing areas to ease the pressure, organise and control passenger flow.

Hosts welcomed premium passengers and managed access to the arrival and departure Fast Track services to ensure all guests were security compliant. They were also in positions in flight connection areas and needed to have knowledge of airlines and terminal transfer information to ensure passengers were directed quickly and efficiently for onward travel.

Uniformed mobile host specialists, were situated in the arrival and departure halls to provide knowledge to passengers, and those who come to collect passengers, and they were there to answer the frequently asked questions and supply information on flight arrivals or departures. They also were to provide local transportation knowledge, know about the airport terminal, transfer/connection, and to give assurance to passengers.

Wow, a tall order and it sounded fantastic on paper, but I'm not sure that was what they did or was it just their recruiting information. In reality, they were there to do what the Black Jax did but they also now needed to speak different languages especially during the London Olympics. They provided valuable help to security staff in relieving some of the pressure of dealing with the day to day issues passengers encountered.

Although Heathrow targeted recruiting 1000 volunteers to help with the Olympics many of these were then recruited into the ranks of the newly formed Heathrow Ambassadors.

During flight delays or cancellations due to bad weather, these purple Jax seemed to be in the front line for much of the abuse received from passengers. It was a shame, as they did an incredible job of keeping the masses in some order.

Just as a postscript to this chapter and the previous one there is a common link, UKBA started to recruit more staff. They had to have a degree to qualify to apply for the job, but one of the Black Jax that I became friendly with, was a young tall and handsome Indian lad, who had many academic qualifications. I think he wanted to become a lawyer but couldn't get a position, so he worked as a black Jax to earn money while he continued his education. However, when the situation changed, and UKBA started recruiting more staff, he applied for and became a member of the UKBA. I often saw him at Passport control doing the very job that he'd spent hours previously in keeping the queues for passport control orderly.

A strange twist of fate!

----

13 LIGHT DUTIES

My foot problem had got worse, and after two weeks of complete rest, I was still in a lot of pain whenever I had to stand up for any length of time. My doctor had recommended I wore my own footwear and went on restricted duties, so I requested it and was granted light duties.

I hated it from the off, not only did I have to work with all the shirkers and con merchants but the actual duties were boring too, mind numbingly so. If you couldn't work on the security screening lanes, then light duties meant working on the ticket machines, on the main concourse or singleton posts guarded security doors that had faulted, or on the international or domestic ticket areas. Boring!

There were many genuine members of staff who like me were conscientious, but due to musculoskeletal problems needed to be taken out of the line and work in areas of low impact. But there were some who shouldn't have been on these duties and certainly not for the time they had been.

I ended up working with one such officer frequently. We were working at the tickets desks in the International transfer hall, which was within the immigration hall area. Our job was to sit at a desk each and take the passengers boarding cards off them, scan their tickets in the machines, and then allow them into the queues for them to go up to the security screening area. Then there were purple Jax to advise these passengers of the security screening process.

Many of these passengers would arrive through the domestic arrivals. Then they'd have to go through our security where we would take their photograph and then they'd be allowed up to the security screening lanes before entry into the departure lounges.

The rules for domestic travellers were that any passenger on a domestic flight had to be photographed before being allowed into the International Departure lounges.

This could often be a point of conflict as many arriving passengers didn't understand why when they left their departure airport and had been subject to security, they then arrived at Heathrow and had to do it all again. Despite how many passengers were told this and then told what to expect going through security by the black Jax/purple jax, they still ended up at the security screening lanes with item on them that they'd been informed would not be allowed.

My colleague, a tall, slender Indian lad in his mid to late twenties said, "Hi I'm Vijay, who are you?"

"Tony, I've worked here a few years now, but not seen you before?"

"Oh, I've been around but was off sick for, so am now on light duties, what about you?"

"Yes, me too. I have this thing called plantar fasciitis."

"Planter what?"

"It's called plantar fasciitis, but it's known as policeman heel." and I explained my problem to him, while we processed passenger tickets and took photographs when required.

"Is it really that painful?"

"What do you mean?"

"Well, you know, are you really in that sort of pain? I saw you walking over here very gingerly, so I guessed you had some foot problem, but that sounds horrible."

"Yes, it's bloody painful, believe me. When I wake up at night and need the loo, I feel like crawling to the toilet to avoid the pain I know I'm gonna get when I put my foot down on the floor."

"Hell, sounds bad."

"Yup, but what about you? What have you done to yourself?"

"Oh, I hurt my leg." and he showed me his leg which had a bandage on it, he pulled the bandage down, and there was a small mark with bruising around it on his ankle.

"How did you do that?"

"Oh, playing five-a-side football with the lads."

"What, with the lads from here?"

"Yes, we play two nights a week after work." I'd heard about this officer; he did have a reputation for being one of the 'Bruvs' who enjoyed avoiding work. He'd hurt his ankle playing football, had gone off sick and had come back and managed to get put on light duties.

"Bloody hell my seven-year-old granddaughter would get a knock like that playing football and still be playing the next day. And you went off sick and are now on light duties, how do you do that?"

"Easy bruv." and he rubbed the side of his aquiline nose in that knowing manner.

"What have your doctors said about the injury?"

"I haven't seen a doctor."

"How did you get on light duties then?" I could feel my indignation rising and prickling me.

"Just told them I needed it, they said to make an appointment with Occy health (Occupational Health)."

"Yes, I did the same, but when did you see them?"

"Well, I haven't yet."

"What! And you still got on light duties, how?"

"Told them I needed light duties until my Occy health appointment."

"So, when's that?"

He told me the date of his appointment "It was the earliest I could get."

"Well, I still don't know how you got a date so long in advance. I telephoned them, and they gave me an appointment the next day, not in three weeks' time. I don't know why you have to wait so long." I think my old management hat was coming on and I was indignant that somebody could get away with this with nobody checking-out his story.

"It's not what you know; it's who you know if you know what I mean."

I was so angry at the front of this officer, boasting about abusing the system. Then I thought it's not my place to get indignant and annoyed if the company are stupid enough to be so lackadaisical about it. But my DNA doesn't work that way; my view was why should he get away with abusing the system at the expense of others, just because he didn't want to work on the concourse and saw this as an easy life.

At this juncture, another officer came along and told Vijay he was relieved to go on his first break.

"I'll probably see you around Tony if we're both on light duties."

"Yes probably, but I hate being on light duties so don't expect me to be on it for long."

"Naw mate, keep on it as long as possible. It's cushy and beats dealing with passengers on the concourse." and he winked at me and his relief and walked off.

"I see you've met Vijay then Tony?"

"Yes, just now, don't know how he gets away with it."

"He's one of the Bruvs mates and plays football with the STL's."

"Yeah, nuff said."

I worked with Vijay a lot while on light duties, and on every occasion, I felt myself bristling with indignation about how he'd gotten away with the light duties. Especially as he got better and longer breaks, with better shoots than everybody else. But I suppose good luck to him if he could get away with it.

There was a rumour going around that the company had sacked him, but all the paperwork had been carried out incorrectly, and they then had to reinstate him. I think it made him feel he was untouchable and to a large extent that was the case. But once again it showed just how unprofessional the company could be with individual members of staff. However, I was and still am not sure if this rumour was true or not.

Eventually, he'd been off sick and on light duties for so long that he had missed his annual DfT test and had to go back to the training system and be retrained before he could return to working on the concourse. I thought that would make him feel guilty but not a bit of it. He was so proud that he would still have to remain on light duties until the company could fit him into a training group, which they eventually did but it was another few months before he was back working full time on the concourse.

Another time, I was sent to an area known as 'swing gates'. We had just introduced a new system of moving clean passenger to other terminals and also moving them from their arrival areas to either exiting the terminal or going through customs to collect their baggage or making connection flights from T5. These changes affected flights from Dublin which although technically outside of the UK but in the EU and therefore subject to the same rules as all EU flights; they were always put on stands in an area that was difficult logistically to get to their next ports of call.

Our job was to sit either side of these electronic gates and allow passengers through if they needed to get the transit buses to other terminals. At the North end of the Terminal and the south end were another set of gates for the Dublin flights. You check the passengers onward flight details etc. and then swipe the electronic system which opened the gates to allow them through. Again, a quiet position and as you had a glass partition between you and your colleague not much conversation went on unless the gates had to be opened.

There were other functions to be carried out, but this happened so infrequently and was complicated due to security implications. I cannot reveal what the function was, so will leave it as a mystery.

The RA asked me one afternoon, "Tony, are you swing gate trained?"

"No, not yet."

"Oh damn, not supposed to send untrained staff down there."

"Yes, but is the other officer that's there trained?"

"Oh, yes."

"What's the problem? They can show me what to do, come on it can't be that difficult. I already know about checking their onward ticket information, it's just when the flights from Dublin come in. How difficult is that to know?"

"Yup, you're right. And you're intelligent enough to pick it up no problem. Ok, you're off to swing gates South, tell Vijay he'll have to train you."

"Ha ha Vijay's down there, why am I not surprised?" and off I went on the little walk around the concourse down the stairs and off down to the swing gate position.

I arrived at the swing gates, and Vijay said, "Tony, have you been trained on the new swing gate system?"

"No."

"Didn't think so, but don't worry I'll show you what we have to do." and with that he did.

I have to say it was easy. Why we were making so much fuss about staff having to be trained by the correct staff was beyond me, but I suppose it covered management in case something went wrong. If you'd been trained, then there was somebody to take the blame, but if you'd not been trained, you couldn't be blamed. But it was not a challenge to understand how it all operated. Although I'd heard of some staff refusing to work there, as they'd not received the correct training. Or was that the excuse just so they could be 'bloody minded' about it and think they were making it awkward for management, I don't know.

We'd been working there for about an hour when a female member of staff arrived and informed Vijay he'd been relieved for a break, and off he went. I'd not met this officer before.

"Have you been trained for swing gates?"

"Yes, Vijay trained me earlier." and with that, she snatched the radio from me and called up the RA's office.

"Hi, its 'Rachel' I'm down at swing gates with, what your name?" she asked me.

"Tony Levy."

"With Tony Levy, he's not swing gate trained, and I'll not work with him down here." and she then turned and said "Nothing personal mate, but I ain't working with untrained staff. I don't trust those fuckers in the office and am not getting blamed for something going wrong."

I shrugged my shoulders and said, "That's up to you, but we've had only one flight come in since I got here, so I don't think there is an issue, do you?"

"Yes, I don't trust them upstairs. And I ain't gonna work with untrained staff, are you also on light duties?"

"Yes."

"Well, that's definite then, no way." and she again used the radio "Allocators from swing gates receiving, over."

"Yes, go ahead."

"Are you getting a replacement for Officer Levy down here?"

"Yes, affirmative, and on way."

"Ok, out." and she turned to me, "Somebodies coming to relieve you ok?"

"Yes, if you're not happy then it's for the best, but I think you're unfair to both me and the RA's."

"To be honest Tony, I couldn't give a shit what you think I'm not working with staff that are on light duties and untrained."

"Well, to be honest, I don't want to work with staff like you who are awkward and unreasonable. I don't know and don't care what your issue is with the RA's or management, but apparently, you think you're special, and under those circumstances, I wouldn't want to work with you, anyway."

"How long you worked here?"

"Long enough to see many people like you and I was in senior management in my previous jobs, so I know what people like you are all about." and with that, I closed the partition between us and waited for my relief to arrive.

It was nearly forty-five minutes later that the relief officer arrived and in that time, we didn't process one passenger, so I don't know what this officer's problem was. But hey 'this is Heathrow' and some staff would do nothing to help management in any way, so maybe you could understand management's attitude towards its staff after all.

I was so glad that after some weeks, although not fully healed, I was reporting back to full working fitness and getting off this, for me hated, 'light duties'.

PART THREE – THE MANAGEMENT

1 MANAGEMENT

I do not doubt that what I write will be derided and denied by the senior management of Heathrow Airport. Any dissenting voices are treated in this way in any big organisation, but coming from the background of Her Majesty's Prison service and the public sector that is often publicly criticised, I can only say despite its problems the Prison service's efficiency could be an example to many private businesses in the UK including Heathrow.

I must point out that despite these issues the majority of staff and particularly the security officers were conscientious and understood the importance of their role in keeping the public safe. They do a wonderful job under extreme pressure, and I have nothing but admiration for them for making and keeping Heathrow one of the safest airports to travel though in the world.

At Heathrow, lower level managers seemed to have been chosen more for their customer service skills than their ability to manage staff; this was an alien concept to me. If you're given a position of authority over staff, then your ability to manage those people must be a priority. At Heathrow, this seemed not to be the case. Some managers had management of people skills. My final Manager was one such person, but most of the staff that became Duty Terminal Managers seemed to come from either Tesco's customer service backgrounds, or call centres or DIY stores. This is fine if we were dealing with a customer base, but as the passengers coming through the security operations at Heathrow were not our customers but customers of British Airways, I couldn't understand the predisposition to employ managers with only customer service skills.

I remember a day when the latest new Director of Operations for T5 came onto the concourse to view his new empire; he lectured a group of us security officers in the reasons that the flow rates were so important. I couldn't help myself and said, "Excuse me, but what does that say on my

ID badge under my name?" as I pointed to it.

He replied, "Anthony Levy."

"No, below my name."

"It says Security Officer."

"Exactly, so you worry about your bloody flow rates, and I'll worry about the passenger's safety."

It didn't go down too well, I could tell by his reaction, and some of my colleagues looked at me.

"I cannot believe you would talk to the Terminal Director in that way."

"Why not? Our job is security, not customer service if they want to employ customer service staff then let's stop all this crap of trying to make the airport safe. Stop wasting all that money training us to the levels we need to be at and let the terrorists just blow everybody up."

Melodramatic I know, but the bottom line is that as Security Officer's our job is security. And as we provide a service on behalf of the safety of the passengers, we do not have any customers. That's the function of British Airways and all the other airlines that pay Heathrow to provide security for their passengers.

"What background are you from?" the director asked me.

"Home office Prison Service for 25 years."

"And what rank did you attain?"

"I was a Principal Officer for my last eleven years and was the Audit Manager, but was acting up to a Governor grade."

"Oh, so you know a lot about management?"

"Of people and security yes, I'd like to think so especially as I was an auditor on behalf of the Home Office."

"You had nothing to do with customer services?"

"No."

"Well, you might be wasted here as a security officer, you should apply for a higher position, within the company." and with that, he moved off with his entourage to meet another group of staff.

But as Heathrow owns all the retail outlet units and the outlets pay a lot of money to Heathrow for the privilege of having their goods on sale. Heathrow Security gets a percentage of the profits these outlets make therefore passenger's spending money is an important part of the operational function. The more time passengers are in the departure lounge then correspondingly, the more money they will spend and the more profit for Heathrow and the bigger our annual bonus would be. So, keeping the passengers happy and getting them through the security scanning process is an important part of the security operation. But it should never be to the detriment of our basic function of providing security.

Coming from a Security background, I found it obtuse to think I would be employed as a Security officer, only to be more concerned with providing customer service, which is what the company seemed to want.

Another strange side to the management's attitude towards their staff was on time keeping. As we worked in small teams if a member of staff was late or didn't bother to turn up for work, it played havoc with the RA's being able to organise the staff into effective teams. There wasn't a pool of spare staff, so they would have to 'rob Peter to pay Paul', close down one area of the operation to cover the missing member of staff. This wasn't tolerated, but your ethnicity again controlled the disciplinary action, or so I thought.

I remember on officer who'd disappeared during his shift saying to me the next day when I'd asked him,

"How do you get away with just vanishing half way through your shift?"

"Well Bruv, it's like this, we're mates, me and the RA's innit."

T5 never appeared to overcome its flawed implemented management structure as STL's and TDM's job descriptions and responsibilities used to change regularly. Although the company promoted officers to STL, I do not recall one STL ever becoming a TDM. It was a sad reflection that higher management didn't appreciate the skills needed for their managers to obtain the delicate balance between security and customer care.

When you consider an STL's title was Service Team Leader, not Customer Care Leader, you'd imagine that 'team leader' meant leader of the staff they were responsible for. Especially given that all STL's had groups of officers, their Teams, (these STL's and teams were often changed too). They had to write regular reports of your progress and ability. You'd believe that as you were a security officer, then their role would be one of team leader of security officers and not leaders of customer care teams.

There was never time put aside for officers, STL's and TDM's getting together and talking about the issues from the 'shop floor'. Although, towards the end of my time there this started to happen. But again, when you are a 21:00 (and expecting your normal shoot of 20:30) finish, and are called into a meeting at 20:00 with other staff who are finishing later than you and a TDM who was on duty until 23:00, who do you think would keep the meeting going the longest?

Many members of the security team would have made great TDM's, and in fact, several of my colleagues who became STL's were amongst the best employed at Terminal 5.

Thankfully, I never applied for an STL's or a TDM's position. I could see the real issues came from the higher management structure and filtered down to the lower managers positions, and I wanted no part in it.

My message to senior management is this: stop focusing on delivering the impossible, listen to your staff, and concentrate more on the thousands of security officers and other airside departments that ultimately drive Heathrow. Without them, the airport would cease to exist.

----

2 BREAKFAST WITH THE DIRECTOR

"Report to the Barcelona suite at 1430." I was told, by the RA (Resource Allocator).

What the hell for, I thought to myself. But hey, if it takes me off the concourse for a while, I'm happy.

On the landside of the Terminal building was where you'd find the administration staff, and offices. And each conference room was named after a city that British Airways flew into. The Barcelona suite was one of the bigger conference rooms, so I was curious as to why I was going there.

I'd only been working at T5 for a few months and was working in a team which comprised only me, when the usual working teams were of six people. I often got sent on individual jobs and collaborated with many other teams; I thought this was right for me because I got to meet many of my new colleagues quickly and also saw how different teams worked together or didn't work together in some cases.

"What do I do until 14:30?"

"Just hang around in the tea room, but don't be late at the suite, you're on the breakfast with the director meeting today."

The what? Breakfast with the director at 14:30 in the bloody afternoon, you're having some sort of laugh I thought to myself, but he wasn't!

There were several other officers in the tea room, and as a newbie, I didn't know most of them, so I asked, "Are any of you detailed to the Barcelona suite?"

"Yes." said one lad.

"Thank goodness, I thought I was the only one, by the way my names Tony."

"Yea, seen you around and thought you were a newbie, how long you worked here?"

And with that I had made a new acquaintance.

At the designated time along with several other colleagues, we started to assemble on the landside office area and made our way to the Barcelona suite. It was a big room with a long table in the middle and chairs gathered all around. The new Director of Operations arrived along with another gentleman. The new Director was around thirty'ish, somewhat attractive, and dressed very smartly; her hair was immaculate. She was obviously intellectual to get a job as Director of Operations, in the field of aviation; she had to be extremely knowledgeable about the running of a modern-day airport. She introduced herself and asked us to introduce ourselves to her and each other in a short sentence.

"Eric Little, I've worked here since T5 opened." said one.

"Tracy Pullman worked at Heathrow for twenty years T1 then T2, came here just before it opened."

"My names John Smith, worked here fifteen years...blah blah blah." We went around the room in the usual 'creeping death' system until my turn, "Tony Levy, only started here the same day as yourself and previously worked for HM Prison service for twenty-five years."

And so, we went around the assembled group of around twenty people.

The Director then gave us her vision for T5 and its importance to the whole operation of Heathrow Airport. She spoke of her priorities and aims and how she wanted to achieve them. All good management stuff. I'd been party to this thing many times while working in the prison service.

She spoke about the purpose of this meeting is to get together with as many members of staff as possible in a quieter environment away from the pressures of the concourse and introduce her to us and find out what we thought.

I thought at the time, "You know what, if you got off your arse and walked out of your office away from all your 'yes mam' subordinates, and came down to the operational area you could meet a whole lot more staff. You'd also witness most of the issues you want us to talk about. More than in this environment. It's a lot more intimidating for staff than if you were on the concourse, and could see the issues for yourself. Perhaps this is all about ticking boxes rather than gaining the truth, but I kept my thoughts to myself.

She asked us what improvements management could implement to ensure our jobs could be more comfortable. There was a lot of talk about the chairs that the x-ray reader sat on. About their state, some of them desperately needed repair, which was true. I'd often sat in a chair that wouldn't adjust up so my seating position, it was too low and uncomfortable. You might ask what difference a chair makes, anyway. If you're sitting down at a computer X-ray screen for twenty minutes and you're either too low or too high, your neck aches and your vision can be impaired, multiply that by twenty times a day and you soon develop bad posture injuries. But not only that you have to reach the console in order you can use the enhancement facilities on the machine to enable you to examine any item you find that doesn't seem right. Being comfortable can mean the difference between spotting an unauthorised item and missing it altogether with possibly disastrous results.

So, an important discussion point and one that the Director promised would be resolved immediately, and she made notes to that effect. During the remainder of my time at T5, this seat issue was never resolved, and I remember on one occasion I refused to sit at a machine causing the whole security screening lane to be stopped. There was a huge furore over my actions as stopping a security lane was not allowed. However, I stood my ground, and by some miracle, a good working chair was found, and replacing the broken one I continued to do my job, but remember a colleague saying to me.

"Fucking hell Tony, you've marked your card with management now, you wait and see. But bloody hell, good on you for having the guts to stop the machine."

"Yeah, well I've already been off sick with a bad neck and shoulder, I cannot afford to have more time off by sitting on these bloody broken chairs any longer." I never did hear of anybody else taking up a similar stance, but that was up to them.

Somebody else mentioned to the director about the timing of our breaks and how it was ridiculous to come on duty at 12:30 and sent on an immediate break until 13:15, then go over five hours before your main break. She seemed sympathetic to this but pointed out that the RA's had a difficult job balancing everybody's break times and maximising the efficiency of the operational requirements at any given time.

Great Management speak, I thought to myself, but it just highlighted that the shift patterns we operated were the real issue. If our shifts rotas were correct, then all these factors would be taken into consideration before they were implemented. It was something we had to be efficient at in the Prison Service but obviously not in outside industry.

The meeting continued. I remember looking at the clock and thinking, 'How can we talk about efficiency yet the Director of Operations is sitting here with twenty staff. So, who is covering our jobs right now? Efficiency, I don't think they know the meaning of it'.

"What do we think about communication?" asked the new director of operations.

Many of the staff sitting around the table looked at each other, and there were a few suggestions that things could be better. I thought, nobody was forthcoming, and as the 'new boy on the block' I thought I would let others lead.

But it wasn't happening so I said, addressing the Director of Operations, "I'm Tony Levy, only been working here the same time as yourself. However, not since I first stepped into T5 has one STL taken the trouble to introduce themselves. I don't know the name of my STL, have never met them or spoken to them, that I'm aware of. That's how bad the communication is, and although you introduced yourself to us, the person sitting next to you, who is he? He hasn't bothered to introduce himself to us."

Oops, me and my big mouth. There was a stunned silence, before the Director, looking gob smacked, apologised and then introduced the man sitting next to her. He was looking a little sheepish, but hey she asked in the first place.

"I'm sorry about that, and you are quite right, this is..." she pointed to the man and introduced him. I've forgotten who he was as I don't think I ever saw him again during my time at T5.

But I had set the ball rolling, and several people now chimed in with their thoughts on the lack of communication between managers and staff.

I had gotten into my stride now as communication was always a big issue in the prison service and one I had always had plenty to say about.

At an appropriate point, I said, "In fact, over the Easter period our CEO of Heathrow, Colin Mathews, came around the terminal and introduced himself to all the staff on duty, shaking us all by the hand and thanking us for our efforts over the busy Easter period.

When he came to me, I said, "Thank you, Mr Mathews, it's a pleasure to meet you too, but it's a shame I haven't been introduced to my own STL after working here for six months. I don't even know her name, yet she's standing over there watching us."

Now, you could have heard a pin drop. Then everybody talked at the same time. The Director called order, and then one by one everybody sitting around the table had a story to tell about the poor or lack of communication between the officers working on the concourse and their immediate managers and their Senior Managers. OMG, I thought, what the hell sort of organisation have I joined here. And I used to think the prison service was bad with communication but not a patch on how bad it was at this place.

The meeting continued but to be honest, I was losing interest in it. Then after some time, the Director closed the meeting thanking us all for our honesty and promising that the issues raised, which were similar to other meetings she'd held, would be addressed over the coming weeks and months. With that, we were dismissed, and the meeting was over.

As we walked back to the staff search area to go back into the security area and back to our duties, one of my new colleagues who was of Indian culture came up to me.

"Hey 'bruv' (I was to get used to this form of greeting from many colleagues here), you got balls speaking up like that to the Director, if you keep that 'jive' (talk) up your gonna become a legend here." With that, he walked off to join another officer of similar ethnicity.

With that my 'Breakfast with the Director' was over and I was never invited to one of these meetings again and to be honest we didn't even get breakfast. A cup of tea or coffee and some digestive biscuits was all that was offered! 'Oh well I'll be going on another break again soon' I thought.

Strange to think that after all the expense of removing large groups of staff from the busy concourse to find out what they felt about managers. The person who called the meetings was replaced herself within a short period, as were several other Terminal Directors during my time at Heathrow.

----

3 MANAGEMENT'S ATTITUDE TO STAFF

There had always been a perceived amount of friction and distrust between management and staff, and although the same could be said in most industries the amount of distrust here was frightening. But I failed to understand why there was so much friction between some officers and STL's, STL's and STL's STL's and their managers, managers and managers, and managers and senior managers. I remember once when in the prison service I'd said at a meeting of Governors and managers that morale was like shit; it rolls downhill. Never was this truer than at Heathrow T5. You could cut the amount of distrust with a knife, and this also seemed to follow along ethnic lines.

Some staff was often late on duty and no perceivable disciplinary action was seen to be taken against them yet others, and on one occasion including me, was marked down late, and this was recorded on my personal file.

My sin, I was on the staff bus that took us from our staff car park to the terminal building; the bus was involved in a traffic accident, and all traffic in and out of the staff car park was halted. There were many members of staff on the bus ranging from BA ground crew to the Retail outlet shop assistants, and the bus was holding around forty members of staff. I telephoned Manpower and reported what had happened along with several of my colleagues, and thought nothing of it, after all, it wasn't practical to get off the bus and walk the few miles to our terminal building otherwise many of us would have done that. But eventually the accident was sorted out, we all had a good laugh including the TDM who had been on the bus. I thought no more of the incident as we managed to report for work just in time for our start of duty, so all was well, a light-hearted incident to start our day off.

Several weeks later I was looking through my staff report when I noticed I'd a day that was marked down with one minute late recorded on it. I checked that date, and it was the day of the car park bus incident.

I went to the 'Manpower' office located landside of the terminal along with all the administration offices, and unfortunately helpful 'Dicky' was the only person there.

"Hi. I was looking through my staff record and noticed that there's one day I was marked down late can you tell me why?" I asked.

"Well, it's because you were late I suppose."

"What, one minute, I've been marked down as one minute late?"

"If you're late, you're late Tony."

"No."

"That was the day about forty of us including a TDM were stuck on the staff bus due to an accident. So, how were we supposed to get here on time? Although I seem to recall we did all get here on time and the TDM said he would speak to you and the RA's and explain not to mark us down late if we were late anyway, as he'd witnessed what happened"

"I don't know about that."

"Do you know who ticked me in on that day?"

"No."

"Guess what Dicky? I do, and it was you."

"I can't remember."

"Strange that, because I do and I'll tell you something else when I waited at the desk to tick in with you in the RA's office, you answered a phone call from a member of staff, and I stood there waiting for you to finish the call before I could tick in. So, if I was late it was your fault."

"I don't remember."

"I'll tell you what; I'll give you until my first break to remove this stupid one-minute late mark on my record. If you don't sort it out, I will report you to the TDM who was on the bus that day. You see, I have a superb memory obviously unlike you. So, you'd better remember very quickly."

and with that, I walked away from him. Great, I thought, we get grief from the passengers, and we also get grief from our management, what a great way to set examples for your staff.

Dicky was renowned for his inflexibility and his poor verbal communication skills with the staff. I had several unhelpful dealings with him over the years. I remember another occasion when I took over four hours to get to work. I had to travel on the notorious M25 to get to work each day, and on this occasion, there was a serious accident which caused the motorway to be closed for me and many others stuck on it.

The M25, for you non-UK residents is probably the most notorious road within the UK. Chris Rea, the UK singer and song writer, is purported to have written his hit song 'Road to Hell' while suck in a traffic jam on the M25 back in 1989, although this is subject to some conjecture. The Road to Hell was an apt name for this circular ring road motorway around London. I spent many hours travelling to and from work on this nightmare road. It was my only way to get there from where I lived, and it seemed always to be busy, and accident ridden, no matter what time of the day you travelled on it.

I was on this road on a typically wet and raining late morning early afternoon in winter, when after only five or so minutes the four lanes came to its usual grinding halt. Once on it, there is no way to get off except at the next junction, which everybody else would be trying to do the same and therefore all roads from then on would be grid locked. Being conscientious, and also using my hands-free phone system I telephoned our 'Manpower' and explained that although there was still nearly two hours before my shift start time, it looked likely that the problem on the M25 was going to be severe.

This had happened on several occasions when I'd travelled through rain, snow, fog and witnessed bad accidents and terrible driving. Luckily, so far, I'd never been late, and that was even during the London Olympics games with all the extra traffic, but then I allowed over two hours to make the thirty-eight-mile journey from my home to work.

"Hi, it's Tony Levy, I'm stuck on the M25, and we've been stopped for some time. I thought I would give you a warning that although I have about two hours to make it into work on time, it's looking worrying."

"Ok," says Betty one of the Manpower team, "just take care, don't take any risks and keep us informed."

"Thanks, I will."

The traffic moved slowly onwards and so far, it had taken me 30 minutes to move half a mile. Shit, at this rate I'd never get to work in time for my shift, I thought to myself. I noticed that no traffic was coming from the other direction, which was a sure-fire indication of an accident somewhere up ahead causing mayhem on both carriageways. This was not looking good. I turned my car radio to the local traffic information station only to be told that there was a serious accident on the M25 resulting in the closure of both carriageways. Well, thanks for telling me what I already knew; this was about as much help as a chocolate soldier in the middle of the Sahara Desert.

I thought I'd better give an update as I had now been stuck on the M25 for over an hour and a half

"Hi, it's Tony again, just an update, I've moved about a mile and am still four miles from the next junction so cannot get off this damn road."

"Ok'." says 'Dicky' our most helpful person in the Manpower office.

"We've heard about the accident on the M25. There are many passengers complaining about being stuck there and are going to miss their flights. The afternoon duty TDM is stuck somewhere on there too, so don't worry Tony but I have to warn you that if you are later than an hour from the start of your shift, we will turn you around and send you home and mark you down as absent."

What! What are you talking about, you insensitive prick, I felt like saying. Did he think I'm on this damn road for fun? Known as helpful 'Dicky' because of his lack of compassion and helpfulness I could have done without his attitude.

"Do you know how stressful this is, being stuck here, you compassionate prick?"

"Tony, don't talk like that, I'm just telling you how it is."

"What with the Afternoon TDM being stuck on here too? You gonna mark him late and send him home?"

"Don't be ridiculous."

"You started it, look I'll get to work when I can, but if I am late, it means I've been on this damn motorway for over 3 hours. If you think you're gonna turn me around and send me home for another three-hour stint on the M25, you've got another think coming."

"I'm just telling you how it is."

"And I'm just telling you how it will be if you do that." and I turned the hands-free phone off. Bloody unhelpful idiot, I thought to myself.

It took me over four hours to get to work, and because so many other members of staff including the PM, and TDM were also late, nobody got marked down. It was yet another example of how senior members of the staff treated and respected their staff.

The M25 was responsible for many stressful passengers taking out their frustration on security staff during the screening process, and security staff doing the opposite.

I remember a TDM discussion with a group of staff. It was one early evening when heavy snow had been forecast to fall, and there were warnings out of severe disruption to our flights and expected road traffic disruption. This TDM was saying smugly. "There's no excuse for being late due to the incumbent weather situation."

"Really?" I said, "What, even though I live in a village that's isolated from main roads, and the slightest amount of snow renders the village cut off from the rest of the area."

"It's your fault for living there."

"And of course, you live just around the corner and in walking distance from here?"

"Not quite but pretty damn near, yes."

"So you've no problem getting to work?"

"Of course not, and nor should you. It was your choice to live where you do."

"Yes, and the company accepted that when I joined. So, you should have some understanding and compassion as to how I get here every day on time despite the distance I travel, and that occasionally there might be exceptional circumstances."

"No, I don't accept that. If you're late it's your fault, not the weathers."

"Oh right, so that is why British Airways have already cancelled half their flights for tomorrow along with all the other airlines using Heathrow. It's all their own fault, and not the six inches of snow that our company is responsible for clearing off the runways, and won't be able to do."

What an idiot, I thought to myself, why do these managers come out with this rubbish? Don't they ever think before engaging their brains? Mind you, this TDM was an ex-cruise director who used to work for one of the big ship companies, so maybe he'd made those comments for entertainment purposes only. But it was yet another example of how management treated their staff, with compassion and understanding... Not!

The STL's role was a conundrum to me. Service Team Leader or STL, what a title, what did it mean? And why did they call the roles Team Leader then give them no management responsibilities? It was beyond my comprehension. They could write on your staff report yet could not discipline staff when it was proven that a misdemeanour had occurred, and especially if the person committing it was a 'mate' or 'Bruv'.

I recall one particular STL informing me that their job was customer service based. Then why the hell were they called Service Team Leaders then? Why did they have to do the same training as us Security Officers and pass the same screen reading National exam? What service were they leaders of, and what team? If it wasn't a security officer's team, it's a complete misnomer, and it explains why the STL role was given no managerial powers. It also explains why nobody seemed to understand their role, either they were leaders of teams of security officers or their role was one of customer service managers. Which is strange because Heathrow security does not have customers but has passengers, so I failed and still fail to understand what their function was, and I suspect so did many of them working those roles?

---

4 SECURITY? OR FLOW RATES?

Technical bits first: The level of airport charges that Heathrow levies each year is in accordance with the CAA's (Civil Aviation Authority) pricing formula. The formula set by the CAA determines the level Heathrow cannot exceed in charging its airline on a per passenger basis (passenger only), which is also referred to as the "maximum allowable yield". The maximum allowable yield is set following a period of formal consultation with the Heathrow airline community.

Heathrow Airport is subject to the Airport Charges Regulation 2011, which was transposed into UK law from a European Directive for its member states. This regulation aims to ensure a common framework for regulating airport charges, which includes consultation and transparency of information when setting airport charges. Airport charges are levied on a per passenger basis. The total revenue from airport charges is then recovered from Heathrow's structure of airport fees.

The structure of airport charges has been subject to formal consultation with the Heathrow airline community and has resulted in the total airport charges revenue being recovered through three categories; Landing Charges, Departing Passenger Charges and Aircraft Parking Charges. The three categories (excluding ANS) represent 21%, 75% and 4% of the total airport charges revenue respectively.

Right! That's as clear as mud, but what it means is that the regulating authorities set a charge to Heathrow Airport for every passenger it processes through its five terminals. As Heathrow owns everything within its boundaries, except the passengers who are customers of the airlines that fly into the airport, the airlines charge their customers for the services they provide within the confines of the Airport. Fuel, aircraft docking and parking, retail outlets, passenger car parks and so on, it's a huge complicated business plan and way above my pay grade or my comprehension, hence senior managers and above earning mega bucks and is well deserved for the job they carry out.

Ok, so we got that, Heathrow charges everybody for using Heathrow, but to make using the airport more attractive, the agreements Heathrow makes with its customers (the airlines) depends on how efficiently we deal with their customers.

Passengers come to the airport to use the airlines and the internal facilities provided. However, Heathrow also makes a financial deal with the airlines as to how quickly we can process their passengers through the security screening system. Depending on the time this process takes failure to keep to the agreed levels can result in heavy fines paid back to the airlines.

At Terminal Five which is exclusively BA and its partners Iberia the agreement is in place with the airlines that we will process their passengers within a particular timescale. Simply put, this process is called 'Flow rates'. The quicker the flow rate, the more passengers we can get into the departure lounges and the more money they will spend in the retail outlet stores. Terminal Five aims to process thirty-five passengers per security lane every fifteen minutes the process is quicker in summer when travellers are not carrying coats.

Airport staff usually receive an annual bonus which is dependent on the annual profits made by the retail outlet facilities within the airport. Nice! In the four years I was there I never received a bonus of less than £600, multiply that by all the staff that worked at Heathrow, and you can see just how much money is spent within the airport itself by you the travelling public, so please keep spending for my colleagues' sake.

If we fail to maintain the flow rates, then there's a huge fine to pay back to the airlines. There's an inbuilt safety feature, and that is that each terminal has a flow rate fail safe. Built into the agreement are a certain amount of breaches of the flow rate allowed each month.

It means that towards the end of the month when the breaches are beginning to get close to their maximums, management panic breaks out, and more pressure is put on the security staff to make sure we do not breach our timing structures.

Phew, have you stayed with me on this one? Even I'm surprised I knew all this stuff, but I have to say flow rates, breaches, bonuses meant diddly squat all I cared about was doing my job and making sure that no unauthorised items entered the departure lounge of any terminal I was working on.

I cared about doing my job so that my colleagues in other parts of the security equipment would have less stress placed upon them if passengers did not comply with the requirements being asked of them. However, when we were close to the breaches of our flow rates, management didn't care how long the queues of passengers were in waiting to get through the security arches. Nor did they care how many passengers would wait to have their hand luggage searched, as long as we did not breach our flow rate agreements.

Management didn't seem to see it in the same way as I did. Then again, I was employed as a security officer and not an airport manager, there was also the conundrum of balancing security with flow rates, and the pressure was always prevalent.

Basically, you join the queue at security, and we have x amount of time to get you from the back of the queue to the loading position for you to touch one of the grey trays. That's the point the timing stops. So how to speed up this process was always what senior management strived for, irrespective of the security staff's possible problems it caused, do I sound cynical?

This brings me around to the following chapter where I write about changing the working environment 'to enhance and improve the passenger experience'. The whole idea of changing any working systems has nothing to do with striving to 'continually improve the Passenger experience' but has everything to do with saving money and ensuring we comply with the strict timing guidelines we have for processing passengers without incurring failure fines.

No different to any other industries in our modern commercial world, so why make the pretence, why not just say the truth? I will never understand this modern business world, thank goodness.

----

5 TWO INTO ONE MORE EFFICIENT?

"Ok, we're realigning our security operations to enhance our passengers experience of our security operation. Living up to our new corporative motto of 'making every journey better' and also improving your working conditions making it conducive to a more ergonomic operational efficiency."

"What! What the hell does that mean in English?"

"We're making the operation more efficient."

"Oh, that's better, but how are you going to achieve that then?"

"By making two existing archways into one."

"And using the four officers on each archway?"

"No, only two."

"How's that more efficient then?"

"Oh Tony, you really don't understand the operational logistic of passenger flows do you?"

"Obviously not, but math's I'm good at, and two into one does not mean more efficient."

"It makes the whole operation more efficient; you really don't understand."

"Hang on more efficient? You mean save more money as there will be less equipment to maintain. But that means two security lanes would now have only one archway for the passengers to flow through, with only two officers on the archway. Surely this means that although at present we have two security lanes and two archways with two members of staff on each archway, now we would have the same two lanes but with only one archway and only two members of staff available for searching passengers. That's more efficient? And that's really going to make the passengers 'every journey better'?'"

Somebody, please explain that, how can it be quicker to reduce the amount of security archway machines, and instead of four officers working two WTMD machines we will now have two officers working one machines. At the same time, we will have to process the same volume of passengers moving through the archway, which previously had two archways. No, sorry, even a two-year-old can see that two into one cannot be as quick as four into two. Doubling the number of passengers and halving the number of archways and staff to run them. No, sorry, that just doesn't add up.

But it means a total saving of the amount of staff needed on each machine, even when you can put more security lanes into the system by the reduction of the size of the available space at each archway. Oh, now I am beginning to understand, it's not more efficient, but it's more cost effective. Now I'm getting it; I've been here before. Let's save money and claim we're more efficiently using our resources but really all we're doing is saving money. But that means we're now putting more strain on our staff as they will have to do more searching at the archway. Oh, sod them, staff you can replace, particularly if you get rid of the old gits and replace them with new younger staff on lower starting salaries. Oh, yes, been here done it and still got the t-shirt.

And that is the bottom line. Heathrow won't be speeding up the process nor will we be employing more staff. We're just going to make the staff we've got work harder, get more abuse and more pressure from the managers to speed up the process. Also, more pressure from the travelling public, as their queues will be longer and more stressful for them too. It leaves us to face the irate passengers who'll miss their flights due to the staff taking longer to process the doubled volume of passengers through the archway, yep its win win for management and well who cares about the staff or the passengers, anyway.

Oh, hang on, I've spotted the flaw in the idea. If the queues are longer, then we might end up with more breaches and therefore more fines from the airlines. No, that's not gonna work. It's back to the drawing board.

Hey, I've got an even better idea, if we copy some system I read about from that American airport, we can change the lanes so that there are four bays for passengers to load their hand luggage into on each side of the archway. That will mean eight passengers at all times waiting to go through the archway. We can then let the loader just control the flow of the trays along the conveyor belt, don't bother with the loading techniques it takes too long, but it will look like everything is working quicker. Better still, if we don't need real loaders, we can replace them with cheaper Purple Jax and save even more money. Don't forget the timing process finishes as soon as the timed passenger places their hand luggage onto the tray. So, we get this new position to place the trays on the machine and then the passenger just puts their stuff into the tray and timing stops, fewer breaches because we have more loading positions.

So, let's get this right, we remove one WTMD archway and reduce two staff, and have a slower movement through, but then we increase the amount of loading position from one to four and increase the timed flow of passenger from joining the queues to placing their items into a tray. That genius, pure brilliance! Who ever thought of this, give them a few quid bonus, let's say £200,000, that should do it.

Our shareholders will be thrilled by the amount of money we've saved. And the chaos on the security lanes will only be minimal, and that will be because the staff won't want to make the changes. So, we can sack a few at the same time as an example and get new cheaper officers trained up.

You know some passengers might complain, oh yes but to whom? There's only the security staff to take the flak so what's new there? Yes, brilliant, I think I deserve a bonus too. Let's ask for £500.000 that should do it, call it an efficiency bonus. Whoopee doobie do, I'm in the money!

After extensive on the job training and after both the North and South concourses were converted into the new two for one WTMD archways, with more archways put into the system resulting in the chaos the security officers predicted. In fact, in the south concourse, they had to build two extra lanes in a separate area to make sure the business and fast track passenger got through the system quicker. It was evident that the removal of the WTMD, and enforcing the two for one archway, caused massive delays for the Fast track passenger and resulted in many of them complaining.

Followed by the now complete refit of the security lanes, we could now load four passengers on each side of one archway at a time, resulting in eight passengers at a time joining the already waiting passengers to come through the WTMD. It came into force, and it was chaos. The loader was so busy pushing buttons to control the flow of the trays down the new lanes and could not carry out any real loading requirements, which resulted in more passengers leaving more unauthorised items in their hand luggage. This led to more bags being 'pulled' off for security searches and more conflict at the searching position. And more conflict at the WTMD archways due to the volume of passengers all waiting to come through at the same time. All in all, it made for a wonderfully tense atmosphere for most of the working day. The stress was fast becoming intolerable for many staff.

It appeared to be all about money. They'd removed one area of potential fines for not meeting their targets of passenger flows to an area that was not measured, therefore, doing nothing to make the process quicker just making sure the timing of the passenger flow was easier to meet. Brilliant management don't you think?

We had somebody from the original design team come to the terminal to sell us the idea of the new loading system along with the two into one archway. Although the archways had been in place for some time and we'd become used to working them, what a lot of staff did, they told me, was they slowed down their searches, so they didn't have to search any more passengers than they had previously. I'm not convinced that in reality happened, but why ruin a good story.

"You mean to tell me that with the new archway system of only one archway for two officers and then the loader having to load four passengers per side and both sides filtering into the one archway, that's quicker than having two separate archways?" I asked him.

"Yes, but with the volume of traffic you have through here I'm not sure the system can cope with it."

"What, we implemented these changes without an assessment of all the facts?" I said incredulously.

"Well, no, it was worked out on a very sophisticated computer."

"What was worked out, our flow rate or our profit margins?"

"You're just cynical."

"Yes, but you need cynicism to bring it down to its lowest common denominator and in this instance its money, you have to admit that."

"No, my team was brought in to make the screening process more efficient."

At this point, the concourse was at a standstill. It was evident no lane was coping with the volume of traffic. Not only did we have big queues at the loading position, but we also had big queues waiting to go through the WTMD archways and then huge queues for passenger's bags to be searched, so I said, "So, what you see here is more efficient is it, are you blind?"

"I have to admit that this amount of traffic is exceptional."

"This is not traffic; this is travelling passengers waiting to get through your more efficient system, please don't insult my intelligence."

"This system just cannot cope with this amount of traffic." he said again but quietly.

"You know as most of us do, that all you've done is move the bottleneck from where we were subject to being fined for breaches, to the other areas where we could not be fined. And it's irrespective of how the staff have to put up with more insults from passengers, and passengers having to put up with longer waiting in other areas, where the company doesn't get fined for poor performance. That's all you have achieved."

"Everything we do is to improve our customer's experience."

"Well, for a start they're not our customers they are British Airways customers. We supply a service called security to ensure the safety of BA's customers on their flights and safety for all those that work in this terminal. For us, they're just passengers not customers."

"Well, we still strive to improve their experience."

"What, by making them wait in three different queues so they can still get irate, but this time at three separate areas of the entire process? But hey, you put your laptop in the tray within the timescale you're allocated, so at least we're happy. Stuff you though, you're only customers. That's looking after and improving their experience."

"I think I need to move on to chat with some other staff."

"I think you'd better get on one of these lanes and work it yourself and then come back and talk to the staff, don't you?"

With that, he walked off leaving a few staff and me staring at his fast disappearing back. We never saw him on the concourse again, I wonder why?"

----

6 TSS TRANSIT TRAIN

I was with my first team, and as we came back from a break, the RA said to us, "You lot go down to the transit train its broken down again somewhere between T5A and T5B. Report to Mason Wright, the TDM, and there should be an STL with him." Mason was a tall black, and very handsome man that many of the girls fantasised about (well so the girls told me) and the STL (can't remember his name) I'd never met.

Great, I thought, a few hours away from the madness of the South concourse; anything has to be better than that.

The TSS transit train ran from Terminal Five to 5B and onto 5C. There was also another rail link already built in anticipation of another satellite mini terminal for a proposed 5D.

The seven of us, three female officers and four male officers, set off to the platforms of 5A Transit train. There were two platforms North and South, and passengers leaving this area were directed into the middle of the two train lines. Passengers arriving from flights into either of the two satellites of 5B and 5A arrived on either side of the centre platform, to keep the 'clean' passengers separated from the arriving 'dirty' passengers.

On our arrival, the platforms were packed with waiting passengers, and the trains were not running. The problem was how to get them from here to either of their departure terminals of 5B and 5C and also get the passengers that were disembarking from their arriving planes back to the customs area and the baggage hall, without the two groups meeting. Remember that passengers who had gone through the security screening process were 'clean', and those arriving were 'dirty', and the two could not mix otherwise there would be a massive security breach and chaos would ensue. Not that, to the untrained eye, it didn't look that way at present.

"I can't see either the TDM or the STL."

"Naw, I think we should walk down the wheelchair route towards 5B, they must be down that end." I said. We set off along the long tunnel underneath the transit system used by the electric wheelchair trolleys and eventually we came upon both the STL and the TDM.

"Hi, we're the team sent to assist."

Nothing came back; the two managers continued to walk towards 5B ignoring us. In fact, I thought they were oblivious to us being there. We looked at each other and just followed behind them.

We arrived underneath the 5B station, and the TDM turned to us and said, "Ok, you lot, three off you go with him (pointing to the STL), and the rest follow me." The three men decided that as they all came from the same area of London and travelled to work together and I think they came from the same ethnic background, they would stick together, so off they went with the STL, I remained with the three girls, lucky me!

There are two separate walkways down in these tunnels. And I thought to myself; this looks an obvious answer to the problem, clean passengers use one side of the walkway and dirty passengers the other, seemed an easy solution to me. We followed the TDM; the girls obviously thought he was good looking because I heard them say to each other and giggle, "Nice bum." and "He's tall." Oh well, they certainly weren't talking about me, the bum maybe but I was not tall.

"He's good looking though."

"Didn't notice a wedding ring, I thought he was married?"

As we followed him, we crossed over from one walkway to the other one and then headed back the way we'd come towards the main terminal building. He stopped at some point and turned around to talk to us, hooray I thought he knows we are here.

"I want one of you to stand back there where the escalators are."

I volunteered and said, "You mean where the broken escalators are?"

"What do you mean broken?"

"There's a sign there informing passengers that the escalators are not working."

"How do you know?"

"As we walked around I notice things; it's inbuilt from my previous job."

"What was that?"

"Prison Officer and then Manager."

"What, like in prison?"

"Yup, twenty-five years of prisons."

"Oh, you're the officer I've heard other managers talking about."

"Blimey, what would they talk about me for?" I wondered.

"You're a bit of a know all. You think you can manage better than them."

"Well, if you're refereeing to some of the STL's and the examples of poor management I've seen, well then yes, I probably am and could manage better than them. I was also the Audit Manager for my last five years in the service, so I learnt a lot about how to assess performance." Blow my own trumpet, well why not?

"How do you mean? Give us an example?"

"Ok, take today, for instance. We're told to report to you and the STL. We found you down here; we said we were your team, neither of you introduced yourselves or even acknowledged we were here. Neither of you told us what the plan is to resolve the issue with the TSS train, yet you expect us to know what we're doing and what you want." And I continued

"I don't call that good management, do you?" Oops, I might have gone too far, but by now I'd had enough of just walking around with no idea what we were supposed to be doing.

He went red, you could tell even with his dark complexion.

"Well, anyway, you stay at the middle area by the stairs and the escalators, and when the passengers walk towards you from the main terminal, you direct them either up the stairs and the lifts into 5B, or point the ones that need 5C in the correct direction. Don't let them go through these gates here to the other side or up to the platform ok?"

"Yes, sure. I take it that this side will be for the clean passengers and the other for the dirty passengers?"

"Obviously."

"Just wanted to check as so far we've no idea what your contingency plans are."

"Contingency plans?"

"You do have them I assume?"

"Of course, although it's got nothing to do with you. You're just a basic officer; only managers need to know."

"Not when we have to carry out those plans. Funnily enough, I've never heard of anybody here taking part in any contingency planning or even fire drills."

I thought to myself, well if you had contingency plans in place why has it taken you so long to put them into operation? As soon as the transit train broke down, the plans should have swung into action, after all the train breaking down had become a regular event. What a mickcy mouse company this was.

"We do all that at management level for your information."

"Great, good to know, so reassuring."

"Ok, you happy now?"

"What about a high vis (High visibility) jacket?"

"What do you want with one of them?" he said, getting a little agitated.

"If, as I assume, I am to be a focal point for guiding passengers to where they need to go then surely, I need to be seen, and a high vis jacket would be advisable, don't you think?"

"No, just wave your hand around."

"How about giving me a radio then?"

"What the hell do you want a radio for?"

"Dah! Communications, emergency contact with a manager, should there be an emergency down here."

"What sort of emergency?" Was I thick or was he really this stupid?"

"Some of our passengers, in case you hadn't noticed, might be older or not able to walk these distances. And they might need some medical attention, some of our passengers have medical conditions, and we are asking them to walk a long way. Suppose there was a fire?"

"If you get an emergency, just hit the fire alarm bells."

"What if I get an irate and violent passenger? I need a radio; how will I know when we have resolved the transit issue? I need to understand what I should do?"

"If you get a violent passenger just use your obvious skills from your experience in the prison service, now just get on with it."

"Sure, but I want you to know I am disgusted that you are not even supplying me with any communication device, given we are in an emergency situation. I have to register my dissatisfaction with this situation, and will not take any responsibility if things go wrong." Wow, now I've put him in a difficult place as I've said this in front of witnesses. I felt strongly about how amateurish this situation was.

He looked daggers at me

"Ok, but to be honest, this whole thing's a farce. I hope you learn some lessons from how you managed this situation." and I turned around and walked back to the stairs and lift area that he'd indicated.

What a terrible way to run an emergency. And yes, maybe I was a bit arrogant but come on we deal with 50,000 passengers a day, and in an emergency, we should be able to deal with it in a professional manner. If we had proper contingency plans and competent managers in place, this situation would have been easy to organise.

I stood in my new area of responsibility as the TDM, and the three girls walked off back to the main train station leaving me in complete silence and alone.

Ten minutes later I heard a noise, and there were a lot of passengers walking towards me, with a Security officer in the lead, he was wearing a high Vis jacket and was carrying two radios.

"Tony the TDM said you would need these," he handed me a jacket and radio.

"Thanks, he told me I didn't need them."

"Must have changed his mind, or come to his senses."

"What do you mean by that?"

"He's not great at handling emergencies like this; you'd think he'd be used to it by now. I mean this bloody train breaks down regularly."

With that, my colleague walked off with passengers toward 5C. I stayed on my post for around an hour when the throng of travellers reduced to a trickle. Another STL approached me from the direction of T5C; she was one of my favourites. She was Spanish and knew I had a home over there, and we'd often chatted about Spain.

"Tony, what are you doing still here?"

"Waiting to be told to return or given new instructions."

"The emergency finished ages ago, didn't you hear the radio?"

"I've heard nothing on this radio since it was given to me."

"Let's have a look." and she took it off me and then said "The bloody thing's got a dead battery! Who gave you this?"

"Well, an officer brought it and said it was from the TDM."

"Not Mason again! That man never checks the radios are working, including his, that's why we can never raise him on it."

Said it all really, didn't it?

----

7 NEXT TIME YOU CAN GET STUFFED

My colleagues and I had come back from a late break to be told, "Just mingle with the team on lane fifteen."

This was standard practice, as often due to the lateness of our main meal breaks, by the time we'd come back, all the security lanes required in the overall plan of the terminal were open, and there was no work for us to do. So, we were sent to mingle. To me who was used to the prison service's way of detailing staff to avoid wastage, this seemed a daft way to use your resources, but as I wasn't management, I accepted that this was another example of the poor use of staff and bad planning.

I always thought our shift patterns didn't optimise the use of the staff, in deploying them most efficiently, but was told, "Oh well, this is T5 what do you expect?" And it seemed to be the way. On most late evenings as the airport had fewer flights departing there appeared to be an abundance of staff left with nothing to do but mingle until we were all sent home. On other evenings the few staff left would be overwhelmed by the amount of passengers needing to be processed. Like I said, daft, and a total misuse of staff resources, and poor planning.

Mingling meant that most of the staff just stood around the equipment allowing the team that was already working there to continue. And they, the mingling staff, just stood around chatting. I liked to join in and would help my colleagues out by assisting bag searching or loading as we could not interfere with the existing team's rotation around the equipment. Or, if the security lane got busy, I would be an extra person at the walk-through metal detector helping with conducting body searches, just to speed up the process. However, many of the staff, when told to mingle either disappeared to the restroom to watch the TV or disappeared altogether. I never found out where some of these people went, but it annoyed the hell out of me. After all, we were all paid to work there, yet some of the staff waltzed around without a care in the world avoiding doing any work and getting away with it because their mates were either STL's or managers. Nepotism and favouritism were rife yet had become an accepted part of T5's operation. This nepotism and favouritism seemed to be run on ethnic background lines, I was amazed at what happened here, and it was common knowledge, but nobody was prepared to do anything about it.

I remember complaining to an STL about this behaviour and was told it would be investigated. The next thing this STL (who I thought was one of the good solid, reliable managers) was gone, removed from the job, and this seemed to be the pattern of how T5 was organised.

One particular Security Officer had been reported to several STL's regarding his sexist, racist, and belligerent behaviour, yet this officer was never disciplined or reprimanded. Several young Asian girls who were fantastic security officers left because of his conduct towards them. As far as I know, he still works at T5.

I write this not as a 'dig' at anybody but as a reflection on how management viewed their staff and their contribution to the efficiency of running the terminal. I do not question how they administer the day to day running of the airport, but I write this to show my perspective of what I witnessed each day I went to work, and how I perceived I was being treated by some of the staff at T5. As I didn't live locally, go out drinking locally, or play football with some of the STL's locally; I had a different perspective on life than they did. I lived 38 miles away in a lovely quiet village, was happily married, and loved leaving work and getting home to my wife; I would never be part of the 'mates' scene.

But I think during my four years of working there we had at least four different Terminal Directors who were brought in to 'sort' the terminal out and all failed. There were so many changes of Duty Managers and their roles within the terminal; I lost count of them. Since its opening all that went on inside the running of T5 had become 'custom and practice', and no amount of managerial changes would alter this until the fundamental issues guiding the running of the terminal were addressed.

But I digress; there were six of us mingling on Lane Fifteen when a mass of passengers arrived from the International Transfers area. It could often happen during the evenings if several long-haul flights had been delayed, and then all arrived around the same time, then rushed to get their connecting flights.

The way the terminal worked (I know it's changed now and thankfully so) is that part of the north concourse was divided up into International Transfers and Direct Domestic/International flights. For efficiency these two types of passenger were kept separate, meaning that if one area became busy, even if the other area was quiet, you could not mix the two kinds of passenger. The responsibility for the control of this was given to the 'Clio' role with the direction of the Duty TDM, via observation from the many cameras that they would monitor in the control room as mentioned earlier in this book.

Lane fifteen was now packed, and the queue was becoming long. It was a worrying development for the STL's and Duty manager as believe it or not; we only had a certain time to process passengers from the time they joined the queue until they reached the loading position at the start of the screening process. If we failed to make this time deadline, it was called a 'breach', and we were only allowed a certain amount of breaches each month. Failure had huge repercussions as the terminals contract with both British Airway and the DfT would result in huge financial implications, yes, we would get fined for our inefficiency, if we didn't process passenger within a certain timescale, (and we were checked many times a day to ensure we didn't 'breach'), hence the argument of efficiency versus safety. Seems crazy but you have to remember that the UK is one of the only countries in the world where the security of our airports is in the hands of the private sector and not the public sector.

I turned to my team and said "We're not going to get any sort of shoot tonight at this rate. We're all standing here doing nothing how about we open up the machine opposite, and we can get this queue down and be able to get off earlier, what do you guys think?

Rami said, "One of us will have to approach the STL about that. Opening another lane is off their 'plan' at present, and you know what they're like about following the plan."

The plan was how senior management devised how many security lanes were required to be open to maximise the efficiency of the whole operation regarding the number of passengers coming through security to the amount of available staff. It never seemed that efficient given the number of times many security staff were told to mingle.

"Yes, that's true but do any of you object to us doing that, to speed it all up?"

"No," said Rami, but you'd better approach the STL because I'm not going to suggest that and get my head bitten off."

"Ok I'm happy to do that, I'm used to getting my head bitten off I am a married man you know." I said, laughing.

"Yeah, go for it." said Stan and everybody else nodded in approval.

"Ok, I'll suggest lane fourteen and that way we can share the archway and get the passengers that need searching through quicker, and still keep the flow running. At the rate it's going now, we're gonna breach very soon."

I walked up and down the concourse and couldn't locate an STL. It wasn't unusual, as I used to say to my teammates, "When the going gets tough the STL's get going." And usually in the other direction. I saw a TDM, so I approached him and said "Look at the queues building up on lane fifteen and thirteen, we're going to breech. My team are standing around on lane fifteen mingling, shall we open lane fourteen and we can get this queue down and shouldn't breach?"

"Good idea, but you'll need to get an STL to sort that out." he said.

"I would, but I've walked up and down this concourse several times and cannot locate one. There should be at least three here, so what do you want to do?"

He looked all around and seemed hesitant to decide but the queues were getting longer, and he had nowhere to escape to and avoid making a decision. He eventually made up his mind and said, "Ok, you open that lane, and I'll inform the STL."

I returned to my team and told them we could open the lane, but I couldn't find an STL, so I approached the TDM.

"Bloody hell you did that? I would never have approached that TDM, well done Tony." said Bubbles.

We took our places on the machine and indicated to the 'Clio' that this lane was now open. Looking surprised, the 'Clio' directed the overflowing passengers into our security lane, and we went to work.

Due to the increase in operational lanes, we got the queues down quickly. And as I was sitting at the screen readers' position, I heard the thundering footsteps of an easily recognisable night STL approaching me. He stopped beside me and looking down on me he said, "Thanks, Tone. You probably saved the company several thousand pounds by your action. The TDM wants to know your name, and the others told me it was you who approached him with the suggestion. I was tied-up down the other end of the concourse, but gawd knows where the other STL's disappeared too, so well done to you."

"Thanks, but I only did it so we would get a good shoot from you." I said trying to add some humour.

"Well, we'll see what we can do." he said and stomped off.

A little while later, with the security lane still open but no passengers, he approached me again saying, "Tone the Terminal Manager wants to thank you for saving the company several thousands of pounds by your quick action. However, she said in future will you please go through the correct channels rather than approach the TDM direct. Oh, and I got a bollocking over it, for not seeing what was going on here."

"Well, she should have been in the control room watching on the cameras to see what was happening. So why didn't she do something about it? She has a radio she could have radioed to you, even if you were busy. What was she doing? Having a crafty cup of coffee?" and I added "Next time you can tell her from me to get stuffed and she can sort out her own crap.

I was livid. I'd just used my initiative and saved the company thousands of pounds for not incurring a breach fine, and she can only say that. Next time she can get stuffed.

I received no recognition for the action my team, and I took that night. Good management example yet again, but at least we got a shoot, and the passengers got through the screening lanes much quicker, so I was happy at that, and I hope so were they even though they didn't know what went on behind the scenes.

Several days later I spoke to one of the female STL's who I thought was reliable and one of the better ones. "Did you hear about the other night when we opened an extra lane off plan to avoid a breach?"

"Was that on the North Concourse?"

"Yup."

"Was that you who approached the TDM? Yes, we were briefed on the issue."

"Yes, it was my team and me; I approached the TDM as I couldn't find an STL at the time."

"We heard about that incident, well done to you, Tony."

"Do you know I received no recognition for my actions?"

"Well, no you wouldn't have done because the Duty Manager wasn't watching the cameras at the time. It all happened, and she got a bollocking from higher management for her neglect."

"So I get no recognition for saving the company thousands of pounds by my action?"

"Basically yes, but we all know what you did."

"Well, next time she and the company can get stuffed."

----

8 MANAGEMENT REALLY CARE?

10 December 2012, I awoke to find my neck had gone into a spasm and I could hardly move my head. Great start to my Wedding Anniversary.

To make it worse, my wife has got a doctor's appointment as she has a 'floater' in her eye, (Floaters are small pieces of debris that some people see floating in their eyes vitreous humour, which is a clear jelly-like substance that fills the space in the middle of the eyeball, and affects your field of vision). Some anniversary this would be?

To make matters even worse, her doctor booked an appointment for her later in the day to attend an emergency eye clinic in Dunstable Bedfordshire, our nearest A&E hospital. Great, she cannot see, and I'm in agony every time I move my head. Driving her to the hospital in the afternoon should be interesting. But we managed it.

But what had caused my neck problem? Was it the muscle I had pulled days earlier? Or was it the stress of the continuing battle with the Airport Human Resources department due to the overpayment of salary issue that had been going on for several months? I had with little success been trying to correct their error of overpaying me (yes, I know I shouldn't be so honest). This had been going on for several months, and I might as well have been hitting my head against a brick wall. I was getting stressed about it as the amount of overpayment was building up, and although I made sure I had the money to return the error, I was only prepared to return it at the same rate as they had overpaid me. Very fair I thought, but that was before I dealt with T5's HR department.

Off to the doctors I went, who gave me the bad news that I could not work for at least three weeks as I'd torn the muscle from my neck to my shoulder. Three weeks off!!!! Damn that takes in the whole of Christmas and New Year, good for some but not when we're on double time (I know I'm mercenary). I was also in a lot of pain and wouldn't be able to drive until I could move my head, this was a problem, and on our anniversary too, brilliant timing.

Also taking this amount of time off sick would have repercussions on my overall personal sick record as you will read later in this book. And it was ultimately a factor in my leaving the job three years later.

But how did these two factors come together?

I need to go back weeks and months to explain both issues coming together on our Wedding anniversary. So, let's go back!

Security requirements had changed (so what was new, these requirements often changed due to the world security climate), but because of our failure to comply with the DfT's requirement for the random security screening of passenger hand luggage, we had to change our ways of searching passenger hand luggage. As a consequence of this failure we now had to search virtually every passengers hand luggage once they'd come through the security screening lane. Previously it was about one in four bags that had to be randomly searched even if there was nothing suspicious spotted by the screen reader. All this has now changed and an automatic system is in place for the random searching of passenger's hand luggage, this is controlled by a computer-based DfT program, so we had no control over it.

Searching more passenger bags equals more stress, the stress of the build-up of travellers getting very impatient when finding out their hand luggage must be searched, even though they knew there was no reason for it to be done. Stress as the waiting time for passengers builds up, and some panic about missing their flights. And stress as we are approaching one of the busiest times of year for passenger numbers travelling through the airport. We also had the problem that British Airways do not always control the size and the weight of their passenger's hand luggage, so physically it could be an issue.

In our twenty-minute rotation on the bag search area, you could expect to search around four bags. Now, we were continually searching bags, sometimes overrunning the twenty-minute time slot as you cannot stop a bag search and hand over to somebody else once started, while you rotate around the equipment. But this now means until you finish your search no other member of your team can move around the screening equipment. And the screen reading cannot overrun their slot (again under DfT rules). Therefore, the whole security line stops. Multiply this by twenty to thirty screening positions, and you have a lot of pressure building up for every member of the team. You also have STL's now screaming at everybody to keep the machines running.

Your usual logic of not lifting heavy bags due to the pressure goes out of the window. Multiply this by several times a day and muscular injuries are inevitable, and sure enough, I picked up a large bag to swing it around to the search table (we now have trolleys to avoid this problem) and I felt a twang in my shoulder. But you cannot just stop your search or go off sick as you'll be stopped pay for that day. So, I bravely soldiered on, doing search after search, straining the already damaged muscle. By the end of the day I was in agony but due to the way our shift-pay worked and the company's sickness policy worked I just carried on. Damaging the already injured area until on the 10 December 2012 I awoke to find my neck locked and I could not move my head. Luckily, it was a day I'd already booked as annual leave so my wife and I could celebrate our wedding anniversary, some celebration it turned out to be!

Although in considerable pain, and finding it difficult to move my neck, as it was our anniversary, and we had so far had a rotten day, we decided despite her eye problem and my neck problem we would go out that evening for a nice meal in a local pub which we did.

We found a nice corner table near the roaring log fire and ordered our meal. My mobile phone rang, it was the HR department at T5. 'Blimey' I thought 'what the hell do they want ringing me at this time of the evening. And somebody's working this late, wow it must be important.'

It was the HR manager, who informed me they had now got to the bottom of the overpayment of salary, 'That's rich,' I thought, as I was now talking to the person who had caused the problem in the first place.

"Anyway Anthony, we've worked out how the administration problem happened so we can correct what went wrong on the payroll, and we'll be taking the money from you in this month's salary ok?"

Ok! Ok! No, it bloody well isn't ok. What a cheek, take all the money out in one go at Christmas! She's having a laugh, and she has disturbed my Anniversary meal to give me this news, very bloody compassionate I must say.

Let me go back again, but this time back six months to when I first checked my salary pay slip and realised that I'd received the wrong rate of pay. This was difficult because not only did we all get paid at different hourly rates and many of my fellow security officers worked lots of overtime, but we were all, depending on when we started working for the company, on different pay scales. I took several weeks to find a colleague was on the same basic pay and same hourly rate as me to confirm I'd been paid the wrong amount.

I contacted HR and informed them of the error, and they said they would confirm a mistake had been made and correct it at the next payroll run.

The next month I was again paid at the incorrect rate. I once again informed HR, who said the error would be corrected next month. It wasn't!

I tried to contact the head of HR but she was not in that week, so I telephoned our Glasgow Administration department who were responsible for our pay, to resolve the issue before it became a real problem as the amount overpaid was building up.

I spoke to a helpful woman who after checking all the records informed me that my basic pay scale had been changed when I moved from the late shifts to the early shifts. I informed her I had not done so and am still working the late shifts, to which she replied that she'd received a memo from T5 HR department that along with several other colleagues I'd changed my working shifts to earlies and therefore my pay rate had changed.

I once again explained that this was an error and asked if I could be informed who actually sent the notification to Glasgow. She advised that it was the very person I'd already been dealing with at Heathrow to resolve this issue.

Great, I thought, she isn't in this week so what do I do? The helpful woman at Glasgow said she'd need to receive a memo from my HR department informing Glasgow of the error and then they could correct the mistake. She would make a note on file that I'd contacted them to inform of the error. I asked at what rate would I need to return the overpayments? And after some negotiation, she agreed that I would repay the amount at the same rate as it had been overpaid. I confirmed that this would be on month by month basis and she agreed.

At least I could now get this problem sorted out once and for all and get on with concentrating on my work, rather than having this stress going on in the background. And I thought the prison service was inefficient, how wrong I was.

After several trips to the HR department, which I had to do during my precious break times, and this was wasting my breaks from working on the concourse, as they were intended for you to relax and allow the stress levels to relax. I managed to find a day when the HR Manager was at work, and it was convenient for me to chat with her.

I explained that I'd contacted HR in Glasgow, and they'd informed me of the error. They'd discovered that the e-mail they'd received gave them the wrong information about my change of shift rota and that they would need a follow-up e-mail to confirm the error. She said in a very aggressive manner.

"Well, who the hell sent the wrong information to them in the first place?"

"Actually, you did."

"It wasn't me." she said showing her annoyance.

"Look, I don't care who it was I just want to get it resolved."

"I'll sort it out, don't worry." she said in an offhand manner.

"Don't worry; I've had to give up several of my breaks to come and sort this out. And this is the fourth time I've come to you to sort it out. I hope you can sort it out this time as I'm getting fed up. Maybe I should have kept quiet and just continued to rip the company off instead of being honest and conscientious." I was getting annoyed with the attitude being shown by her.

"If you'd kept the money, and we found out, we would have sacked you for being dishonest." she said threateningly.

This wasn't going well. Her attitude stank, I'd come across this behaviour with management previously and had been amazed at how unprofessional they were here. I spent many years in HM Prison service as an audit manager and used to complain how unprofessional we were, yet I'd come to Heathrow and found private industries professionalism very poor and not in the same league as the prison service.

Nepotism, which I often complained about in the service was rife here. A friend looking after friends getting preferential treatment was ignored here, racism was ignored here, even though it was denied vehemently. Heathrow would not have survived the investigations of this behaviour that the prison service regularly undertook and passed.

I knew what the 'score' was, so I looked at my watch. "I have to get back to work. I'm asking you to please sort out this problem before the amount I owe gets out of hand. Thank you." and I walked away as she dismissively waived a hand at me.

The next month and still the issue was not resolved. I contacted HR again during one of my breaks, and as I approached the manager's desk, she looked at me and looked back at her computer.

"What?"

"My money's still wrong, so I thought I'd better inform you."

"Do you think that's all I have to worry about?"

"No! But I thought I should inform you as I didn't want to be accused of dishonesty. Obviously, I'm wasting my time. I'll just send an email to the terminal manager to resolve this problem if it's too much trouble for you."

And I walked away having decided that my break and a cup of tea were more important than dealing with this inconsiderate and unprofessional individual. Was all Heathrow T5 management like her? I was beginning to think so.

Once again, the following month my money was still incorrect. I sent HR an e-mail, and I copied in the Terminal Manager, I couldn't be bothered to speak face to face with this individual anymore. How she kept her job, I would never know although there were plenty of rumours around on the concourse about how, this sort of thing was also rife at T5.

And so back to this final month, and again my money was still incorrect. This time when I went to see her in the HR department, she was talking to the Duty Terminal Manager. Instead of being polite and waiting, I interrupted her and said across the Terminal Manager "My money's still wrong, it's now six months, are you going to sort this out before Christmas or do I keep the extra money as a Christmas present?" I continued before either stopped me, "I've done all I can to inform you of the problem you've created. And I'm now at the position when I've done all I can to correct your error. As you've failed to do so, I would be legally correct in keeping the overpayment without paying you back. However, I don't want to do this (although as the amount was now considerable, I was tempted). This is your last chance to correct your mistake, and I will pay the amount back at the same monthly rate as you overpaid me. I'm sorry to interrupt you and the Terminal Manager, but I have to get back to work now, making sure our passengers are safe. I trust you'll sort this out now, thanks." and I walked away.

There might be repercussions, but I didn't care, I'd had enough of her attitude and complete lack of consideration to both the company and me. She had done this with her failure to correct the error she'd made although she had denied it. I don't know how she sent an email then denied it, even though there was proof of her duplicity (strong word I know but that was how I felt).

So, we are sitting in the pub on our wedding anniversary it's around 1930, and we're having a lovely meal despite both my wife and my health issues. My mobile phone rings, it was the HR department at T5,

'Blimey' I thought 'What the hell do they want ringing me at this time of the evening? And somebody working this late, wow it must be important.'

"Hello." I say.

"Anthony, it's Elaine HR Manager."

"Yes, I know who you are, how can I help you."

She informed me she had now got to the bottom of the overpayment of salary, 'That's rich' I thought 'as I was talking to the person who had caused the problem in the first place.'

"Anyway," she said "we've worked out how the administration problem happened so we can correct what went wrong on the payroll. We will take the money from you in this month's salary ok?"

"No, it's not ok. I had already agreed with Glasgow that the money would be recovered at the same monthly rate as it had been taken. I also informed you of that at our last meeting when the Duty Terminal Manager was present, so no I'm not prepared to pay the money back in one go."

"I don't think you're fair." she said.

"Fair! If I wanted to, I would keep all the money as you've failed over a period of six months despite me finding out what went wrong and informing you every month of what needed to be done. You failed to correct it, and now at Christmas, you want to take over £1200 pounds off me, no way."

"Well, Anthony you owe us the money, so you have to pay it back."

"I'll tell you what Elaine if you take all the amount off me in one go I will take you personally to court and claim that you are being vindictive and have ignored the fact that you caused the problem in the first place." I continued "Now, if you'll excuse me, this is my wedding anniversary, and I'm with my wife having a nice meal, and you're not going to spoil it. So, as it's my rest day tomorrow I will telephone you, and we'll continue this conversation. I have to warn you that you will not take out all the money in one go otherwise I will take action. I have already agreed with Glasgow how to repay the overpayment, so it's nothing to do with you now, is it? If you want to go down this avenue, then I'll take legal action and pay you back at £1 per month, so it's up to you. Thanks for calling and sorting out your mistake, bye." and I put the phone down.

I was livid, this person had caused the problem in the first place by her sending of the incorrect information via the e-mail and had then ignored every attempt I'd made to get her to rectify her error. And then she'd ignored that I'd already agreed how to repay the overpayment. I could have offered to pay it back at a £1 per month if I had so wished. Then she telephones me on my annual leave day in the evening and gives me this information. What a way to treat your staff?

I telephoned her the next day as I had to report I was now on long term sick. She was all sweetness and light.

"Ok Anthony, I've sorted out the overpayment and starting from this month's salary payroll will collect the same amount per month as was over paid to you, is that ok?"

"Yes, of course." I replied, thinking well I'd already told you that but if you need to big yourself up, then be my guest, I was just glad to resolve this issue. But I said, "Please send me the confirmation in writing, thank you."

"I will, but if you're now going to be sick for a long period, this might reflect on your HR attendance record, and you could breach a trigger point for monitoring staff sickness."

"Well, thank you for informing me of this. I'll mention this to my Doctors next time I see them. I'm sure that my health will be taken into consideration of how it could interfere with my so far exemplary sick record."

This would be my first period of sickness since starting at Heathrow back in February 2011, but not my last nor was it to be my last dealings with HR and the compassionate way they dealt with their staff.

----

9 I WORK AT B&Q

"Oi you lot don't let me catch you using mobile phones while on the concourse!" shouted an STL at my team and me, as we walked off for a short break from the security screening machines. I'd had a few run-ins with this STL previously and had lost all respect for him, as I'd seen him favour certain ethnic officers and passengers above other staff and passengers. In my previous life as a prison officer, I would have reported his behaviour as being possibly racist. However, at Heathrow, those sorts of complaints were not supported. And I wasn't going to continue to be spoken to by some of the STL's in the way this one usually expressed himself to us. It was unprofessional and downright rude. How can a supervisor expect to get any respect when they talk to staff in the way some of them did? Thank goodness, I never took the job as an STL, as I would hate to be associated with some of them.

I stopped and went back to the STL, "Why did you say that to my team and me?" I asked.

"Because too many of you are ignoring the rules and using your phones while on the concourse." he said.

"Oh, you mean like those four officers over there, and the one over there on the back of the machine. Oops, silly me this rule doesn't count if you are from certain ethnic backgrounds, here does it?" I said defiantly.

"What do you mean?"

"You know very well what I mean. And I've seen you using yours on here too."

"That's different I use mine for work reasons." he said.

"Oh yeah, like in security issues and ending the conversation with darling." I said and continued "Personally, I don't give a shit what you do with your mobile phone, but don't keep digging my team out for you to try and use your authority, especially after what I have witnessed in my time here. You think we all come from a Tesco's warehouse, or labouring jobs and are all as thick as two short planks. Some of us had extremely important and sophisticated jobs, and many of us have more qualifications than you've had hot dinners, so don't talk like I'm a piece of shit, because I will not stand for it from you."

Wow, I'd lost my temper with him, but it had been coming for some time. This STL had never introduced himself; this was not unusual behaviour from the STL ranks as in my experience. I'd worked at Terminal 5 for nearly six months, and not one STL had introduced themselves and that including the one who was responsible for my team and me. What a terrible way for managers of staff to operate and alien to any of my previous training in the public sector.

In fact, over the Easter period the then CEO of Heathrow, Colin Mathews, came around the terminal introducing himself to all the staff on duty, shaking us all by the hand and thanking us for our efforts over the busy Easter period. When he came to me I had actually said to him, "Thank you, Mr Mathews, it's a pleasure to meet you. It's a shame that I've been introduced to you yet worked here six months, and don't even know the name of my own STL who's standing over there watching us, as they couldn't be bothered to introduce themselves."

The team I was working with were gob smacked, as I think Mr Mathews was but hey tell it like it is, that's me.

Back to my story: Several days earlier I was out on patrol with a female colleague who was new to the job, and this was her first patrol detail. We were to cover a particular patrol in which you have a mobile computerised hand-held machine (patrol track) that gives you a route you have to follow and areas you have to check. And to ensure you carry it out, you have to link the machine to a control point at the area you are routed to. Sounds complicated, but it was simple. I loved the patrol detail; it gave you the excuse to walk albeit around a designated area of the terminal, walking at the pace you wanted with no STL's interfering with you or passengers you have to process. I used to describe it to new staff as a gentle stroll taking in your surroundings from a security perspective, although one particular designated route meant you had to check out every public toilet around the Terminal, or as I called this one 'bog patrol'. But despite this, I loved the patrol details as did many of the staff.

During this patrol, we were over in T5B, a satellite terminal from the main T5. You got there on the little transit train along with all the general passengers whose aircraft were leaving from T5B. It wasn't as busy as the main T5 terminal nonetheless it could be very busy from time to time. We were following our designated 'patrol track' route, when we came across a security access door that should have been locked, you could only gain access via a swipe machine and your identity card, but it was actually open. Inspecting the door, I realised that due to this door being unlocked a passenger, or any member of staff could gain access to the actual apron area where all the aeroplanes were located and subsequently any other part of the airfield. This was a real and potential dangerous breach of security.

I radioed my immediate superior, my said STL. Now talk about sloping shoulders, here is what happened: Using my call sign and his I called him, "Alpha one to control are you receiving?"

"Yes Tony, what's up?" Now it's a total taboo of radio procedures to use real names, but hey this is Heathrow!

"Am at point xxx in T5B on a security patrol and have found a security door in the unlocked position over."

"Well lock it, you can use your keys."

Did he think I was a complete dimwit? Bloody hell twenty-seven years in the prison service I think I'd have been able to use my initiative to work this one out and use my keys, before calling an STL.

"Negative, the door's stuck in the unlocked position, and needs an engineer to fix it, over."

"Well, bloody well contact engineering and let them know the problem I'm on another job at present."

"So, how do I let engineering know? Over."

"Bloody hell, ring them."

"How do I ring them over?"

"What the F.... is your problem? Use a telephone."

"Believe it or not I know I need to use a telephone, but there's no phone near this door over."

"Well, use your mobile phone. I'm busy."

"Negative. As we're not allowed to use our mobile phones while on the concourse, I don't have a phone with me, over." I did, but mine was on pay as you go and I wasn't going to waste my money on company work.

"Bloody hell! Try radioing them."

"Again, I've tried that already. I wouldn't be wasting your valuable time otherwise, would I? Over." I said, getting angry and fed up with this STL.

"Wait there and keep the door secure I'm coming over."

"Affirmative. I will make a note on my patrol track machine, over." although I said the patrols were a stroll, there was a designated time to complete each one, and you had to account for any deviation to the times.

"Bloody hell, you're on patrol." said my STL. Now, who's being clever, I'm sure I'd told him I was on patrol. Otherwise, why would I have been in T5B checking security doors?

"Affirmative. Can you radio the staff detail team and get somebody over here to 'man' the door? And then we can continue or patrol over."

"Tony, can't you radio them? I'm very busy."

"I'll radio them but not sure if they would take any notice of me. Don't you think it would be better coming from an STL? Over."

"Ok," he said, "but try. I'll be over as soon as possible."

"Ok, out."

And so, halting our patrol we both waited. I radioed the detail office who told me to inform the duty STL as they needed his authority to send a member of staff to guard the unlocked door. However, who was the duty STL, yup you've guessed it, the same STL who I was dealing with already.

"Alpha one to control, are you receiving over?"

"Tony, what now?"

"Alpha one, the detail office said I had to get you to give them permission to send an officer over here to cover the unlocked door, over."

"Tony, I'll be there in a minute just wait there." where the hell he thought I'd be going is anybody's guess. So, we waited. I explained to my colleague what was happening and why we had to wait. She asked why we could not continue the patrol and I said that we only had one radio and each patrol needed two persons to cover it for safety and security reasons. But I added that the STL should not be too long now. I then asked her "How do you like working at B&Q?"

"B&Q? I've never worked at B&Q."

I told her my story, "I once told a Terminal Director during an open meeting when he asked me about my job; I love working at B&Q."

"B&Q? You work at Heathrow, why do you say B&Q?"

"Well, it's because anything you need done you have to do it yourself, hence B&Q."

"Ha ha, I see what you mean, but you really said that to a TDM?"

"Yes, I sure did."

"Bloody hell, I bet you're popular with management?"

"Well, needless to say, he didn't find my comments funny."

"I bet."

"However, throughout my time working here, nothing's changed, and it's true if you need something done you will have to do it yourself. Hence I tell everybody I work at B&Q."

"Tony, I'll remember that I really will."

She found this hilarious, but over the next few months, she too realised why I did indeed call Heathrow working at B&Q.

After an hour or more, my STL appeared along with a new STL, who was being shown the 'ropes'. It was evident that my STL had been informing the new STL of how stupid the staff were and how he was such a brilliant STL and how to treat the staff. In other words, trying to be the 'big man'. He would have lasted two minutes with his attitude in the prison service, but this was Heathrow.

I inform him of the problem, and he got his keys out and tried to lock the door, although you can see it had come away from it upper hinges, and he says to the new STL, "I'll show you how to report a fault to engineering. As none of this lot knows how to do it, properly." and he inclined his head to my colleague and I as he said it. I was livid; I'd forgotten more about security than he'd ever known and he thought he was going to talk to me like this in front of a new STL and my new colleague.

"That'll be great...I never knew how to report a fault properly, so it will be a real pleasure to watch and hear a professional like you show us mere mortals how it's done." I said in my best sarcastic voice.

At this point, his mobile phone rang, and as it did so, he walked away from the three of us. So we stood there making small chat.

Eventually, he came back, and I said to him, "Perhaps you could now contact engineering and report this fault and get another officer over here so we can resume our patrol?"

"That was a work call, very important." he said with a smirk on his face.

"Of course, but I'm sure I don't know anybody called 'yes dear'. I might be a lot older than you, but my ears work bloody well, so don't come that old crap with me. I don't care who you are, please don't insult my intelligence."

I could tell he was annoyed and embarrassed but to be honest, I was also embarrassed by his unprofessionalism in front of new staff.

He got his mobile phone out again and first telephoned engineering giving them the details of the fault, and then he telephoned the detail office and told them to send somebody over immediately, to cover the door until the engineers arrived.

"Right, it's all sorted. You two, (referring to myself and my colleague) will have to wait here until an officer comes to cover the door, then you can resume your patrol."

He went to walk off with the other STL, and then as an afterthought and maybe to reassert his authority he said over his shoulder, "And don't let me catch you using your mobile phones on the concourse."

What a dick head he was.

We waited a further thirty minutes before an officer of the same ethnicity as my STL sauntered over carrying a chair, a cup of coffee, his radio and a book, he sat down on the chair. "Ok, I'm your relief. The STL said you can carry on patrolling now." and he got out his mobile phone and played some game on it.

How could you have any respect for the STL's, after the way some of them spoke to you and showed obvious favouritism to their ethnic groups? I'd spent 25 years in the Prison Service ensuring everybody was treated as equals and that institutional racism would not be tolerated and in fact was a disciplinary offence, only to come to Heathrow and find it rife throughout the whole management structure. A lesson in the real world of commerce!

----

10 BEGINNING OF THE END

I had a foot problem (Plantar Fasciitis) this started in April 2014. It was to lead to my resigning from the job. But how did this happen? What caused my foot problem? Was it avoidable? To explain, I have to be a little self-indulgent and explain what happened over the past two years with my health. You never know it might give you as a passenger a better understanding of the pressures we security officers have to endure and still be professional in achieving our function of providing security for you all.

In December 2012, the DfT ruled that throughout the four terminals (Terminal Two had not yet re-opened) Heathrow was not compliant with the amount of searching of passengers bags it was carrying out. A new procedure was put in place which led to many more passenger bags being rejected for search; in fact, almost every bag was now to be rejected for searching so we could become compliant in the DfT's requirements, and for us to keep our contract to operate as an airport. It left both the staff and passengers very frustrated. You, as passengers, because you were forced into being delayed at the security screening area while your hand luggage was being searched for no real reason save to comply with the DFT's quota system. And us, as officers, as it led to many more bag searches, and some of your hand luggage can only best be described as very heavy.

British Airways were not great at following their hand luggage weight restrictions. Hence some hand luggage bags being too heavy for some of the staff to even lift. So, we were given permission to get the passengers to move their luggage from the rejected belt onto the searching table for us to search their bags. Ridiculous, I know, but nobody wants to upset British Airways and lose their exclusive business.

During this period, I picked up a particularly heavy bag, and as I did so, I felt a twinge in my neck and right shoulder. Due to the pressure put upon us by both our supervisors and the passengers, I carried on working, now during a twenty-minute session of bag searching, we'd search one or two bags. With the new procedures in place we were continually searching bags for the full twenty minutes, we were at this position in our rotation around the security equipment. You may recall earlier I explained that there was a strict laid down rotation of staff moving around the security equipment, twenty minutes screen reading, twenty minutes at the front of the system bag loading, twenty minutes searching passengers on the walk-through metal detector (archway) and then twenty minutes searching. Therefore, during a long session between our allowed breaks, which could sometimes last over four hours, yes, no real consideration for the health of their staff, you could start work at 12:15, be sent on the first of your two breaks at 12:30, return to work at 13:00 and then work until 1930 before getting your next break. Or you might be sent on a second break with two hours of returning from your first and then work from then until your shift finished, again over four hours which is a hell of a lot of bag searching, screen reading, loading, and archway searching to have to go through. And an enormous strain on the fittest of staff let alone an old git like me in his sixties and not as fit as I once was.

So, you can image, and I expect no sympathy, that at the end of the day you can be physically exhausted but come back the next day and do it all again. December's a very busy month, and we would process between 40,000 to 60,000 passengers a day in terminal five alone, so physical and tiring.

Over the next few days, my shoulder and neck pain worsened until on the 10 December, which was my wedding anniversary, my neck and shoulder locked and I couldn't move my head. It resulted in me having to take time off work and going sick on a doctor's note for the next few weeks until I could return to work.

This started the Heathrow process for monitoring staff sick. Although it has to be said on occasions, some staff were able not to be included in this process, whether by accident or by being 'mates' with the supervisors and sometimes it seemed it was dependant on your ethnicity.

On my return to work I had to see the Occupational Health Advisor (OH), they advised me not to lift heavy bags but get the passenger to move their bag from the rejected area to the search table. This was fine, but I think it was missing the point that no passengers should be allowed to bring in hand luggage that was over the British Airways weight restrictions, in the first place. Management never seemed to address this issue with BA, who after all were the people that allowed the overweight bags to come into the airport restricted zone. Musculoskeletal (MSD) injuries were common at Heathrow, although it has to be said some of the staffs MSD's had to be questionable.

There was a lot of staff sickness that in the past had gone unchecked and now the Terminal was and rightly starting to crack down on staff who took regular days off sick for no apparent reasons. Like all monitoring systems, this one seemed to prejudice genuine staff issues and sickness rather than root out the 'shirkers'.

I had an exemplary sick record during my twenty-five years working in the prison service, but now whether it was due to my age, or the environment and condition I was working in, it seemed every time somebody in the terminal sneezed I got a cold. Later, during the same winter, I developed a really bad cold.

I don't know if you'd realised this, but it can be very difficult to be able to search a person, or their hand luggage, or look at an x-ray screen and not be distracted by bouts of sneezing, or a running nose as you try to search. The severity of my cold meant that it was not in the best interests of the passengers to have this sneezing, runny-nosed, germ ridden security officer spreading his germs all over them and their possessions. I thought it wise to take a few days off until the symptoms eased.

I went through the correct reporting procedure; we reported our sick to an independent sick reporting company who informed our own STL's and Personal (HR) department about our sick, and we had to report fit for duty to the same company who then reported this all back to the relevant departments at Heathrow. Amazing cost efficiency, or what?

I'd breached the amount of penalty points I could accrue during a twelve-month period and was called for a hearing. This was conducted not by a manager but by a fellow officer who was seconded to the HR department. I took along my union representative to the meeting, but it turned out it wouldn't have mattered what I said. The result was a forgone conclusion, and the person I was meeting was not a trained HR member of staff and was, therefore, following her only script in coming to her decision. The result was irrespective of any mitigating circumstances; I was placed on a level 1 warning, any more sickness over the next twelve months would result in moving to level two, and level three could cause an employment review where you could face instant dismissal.

Having managed staff while in HMP where we had a similar procedure, I wasn't worried. My original shoulder and neck injury was caused at work. And long-term sick caused by work related injuries (over ten days) was not supposed to count towards the 'penalty points' system, as I never took days off unless I was genuinely sick, I didn't think I had anything to worry about.

The formal written warning of my level one breach took weeks to arrive, and when it did, it was written in what I can only explain as poor English and reflected none of the mitigating circumstances. It didn't take into consideration any recommendation the OH nurse had mentioned, and it didn't even reflect any comments we'd spoken about at the meeting. The letters started 'Dear Anthony, Further to our meeting of earlier today' yet it was dated some considerable time after our meeting and was signed by a member of staff who I'd never met and didn't even know. My union said the letter was a joke, and they'd sort it out, but this never happened.

However, one day before the twelve-month period ran out, I was taken ill on my way to work, and although I arrived at work, an RA saw how bad I looked and told me to just go into the restroom and take it easy for a while.

I sat in the new restroom down in the Immigration Hall as it was the quietest, but felt terrible. I thought I was having some sort of stroke or heart attack. One of my female colleagues (sorry I have forgotten your name, but you know I'm crap at names) asked if I was ok, I think I said no I feel unwell and couldn't see out of my right eye.

She must have thought I looked very unwell as she called an STL and one appeared shortly afterwards. He also thought I looked so bad he called an ambulance.

Airport ambulances were trained medics who rode around Heathrow on bicycles with all their medical equipment, these medics did a fantastic job throughout Heathrow, and I think many passengers and staff owe their lives to these wonderful caring people.

The medic came and connected me up to all sorts of monitoring equipment, took my pulse connected me to a blood pressure machine, and slowly I felt better. I believed I was having a heart attack or a stroke and had gone blind in both eyes with a kaleidoscope effect in my eyes. The medic thought I did not have any serious health attack; it was more likely to be a migraine episode brought on by stress. He recommended I should go home as soon as I felt well enough, and go to either the local A&E department or my doctor. I explained that I lived thirty-eight miles away, and he suggested I rested for a few hours, and if I felt well enough, I should then leave the airport but if not, I was to call him back, and he would arrange for an ambulance to take me to the nearest A&E department.

Migraine! I had suffered a few severe headaches recently but had put it down to the inadequate lighting on the concourse. It had become a real concern to everybody working in T5 as the ceiling lights had been designed so high in the roof that conventional methods of changing failing lights were not possible.

When the vast £4.5billion terminal five was constructed, its designers seemed to have overlooked one fundamental problem: how to safely change 120,000 light bulbs when they are up to 120ft above the ground. Since opening in 2008, not a single bulb had been replaced on its large single-span roof. In some areas, up to sixty percent of the lights had blown, making the concourse increasingly gloomy. There were increasing incidents of staff complaining about migraine headaches, and passengers complaining about dim lighting during the winter months. Having tried cherry-pickers and hydraulic boom lifts to replace the ceiling lights, to which none were deemed to be practical or safe enough, a team of specialist wire walkers were given the job of preventing the lights going out completely. And the lights were replaced over several nights.

I realised that the kaleidoscope effect in my eyes was a symptom of a migraine, so I took the medics advice and reported back to the RA, who was very sympathetic. Thank you so much 'Pat', she suggested I waited in the restroom until I felt well enough to go home. I telephoned my wife and explained what had happened, and she made me an appointment with my doctor for later that day. Once I felt well enough and thinking nothing of the consequences of going home from work, I informed the RA that I was going home and had a doctor's appointment for later that evening. This decision was to cause me even more of a headache than the actual migraine attack I had suffered.

Several weeks later I had heavy cold and flu like symptoms, as did many of my colleagues at the same time. You can imagine one person has a cold and in a place like T5 with the number of passengers travelling around these sorts of symptoms spread. Many of us would continue to work through these recurring episodes, but on this occasion, I felt so bad I could not drive my car hence three days off from work.

Some months later I received a retrospective letter informing me I'd now breached the level two of the staff sickness monitoring system and had to attend a further meeting.

I approached my union about this latest meeting; they informed me that management had again gone against their code of conduct and that the Union would represent me at the meeting and ensure all was corrected. They also said the day I was sent home from work with the migraine attack had taken place one day before the original sickness warning had 'run out'.

"Yes! But I was sent home by a medic; surely the company cannot use that as a day's sickness when I only went home on the advice of a medical expert, what am I supposed to do?"

"I know Tony, it's crazy, and usually this wouldn't happen, so I don't know why they are digging you out over this. They are also calling you up for a meeting several months after the three days sickness you had, they can only do this within a certain timescale, and this is way outside those parameters, so I don't know what they're playing at."

Once again, we go off to a meeting with yet another colleague who was seconded to the HR department (why they couldn't provide HR trained staff to deal with HR issues was beyond me). And once again it didn't matter what either my union rep or I said. The decision had already been made that I was now to go on an official level two warning, and if I had any further sick days during a twelve-month period, I would be subject to a level three hearing and an employment review with the possible consequences of immediate dismissal.

I remember saying at the time, "You realise that as you haven't complied with your procedures you're now risking me taking you to an employment tribunal for constructive dismissal, don't you?"

"We've followed all the correct procedures, so we've no worries on that score." she said.

My union rep said, "Well actually 'Sharon', you should be worried because Tony is quite correct. The one day he was sent home does not count against his sickness record, and therefore he was not still within the original twelve months warning. He accepts that he should be placed on the initial twelve months warning but not this level."

"We don't see it that way, the one-day sick stays on his record."

"But for what reason?" I said, "It states in your procedures booklet that this is not the case. In fact, even my first sickness should not be on my staff record as it was caused by a direct result of an injury at work, and therefore isn't supposed to be classed as sick for the recording system."

"Where did you get that from?"

"Does it matter?"

"Yes."

"If you must know I got it off the Intranet, you know our internal information link on the computer in the restroom."

"You shouldn't have access to that area."

"Why not? All officers should have access to how the company record information about them. Have you ever heard of the 'Freedom of Information' Act?"

"But that information should not be available."

"Listen, it doesn't matter whether I have access or not I have the information, and you've failed to follow your own laid down and agreed on procedures. If you want to go ahead with your action, then just do it, I'm getting pretty fed up with the way you conduct HR matters, it's a case of look after your mates and sod the rest of us."

"Tony, I think you're wrong on that one, but I know what you mean. I'm sure Sharon doesn't operate that way."

"Maybe not Sharon, and I apologise for any inference that you do. But I will not detract that statement as I know it goes on with other members of the office staff on this floor. If you're both honest with yourselves you know it does too." and I continued, "So, issue your warning in writing, and I will take it to a tribunal if push comes to shove. I've been to tribunals before in my previous job, both to get staff dismissed and to save their jobs, so I have no fear of going to one. But what you are doing is a joke."

I walked back to my union rep's office.

"Tony, just let them do what they want, and we have a real shot at taking them to a tribunal and making them look stupid."

"I agree but to be honest I left the 'service' (prison service) as I'd had enough of all the internal politics, I don't want to get involved in all that crap again."

"No, it won't come to that. They will see from the transcript of the meeting they are in the wrong and are not following their procedures in this case."

No official letter ever came with the transcript of the meeting, so I assumed that they'd realised their error and were hoping the situation would just go away.

However, when I was diagnosed with Plantar Fasciitis' and had to have two weeks of completely resting my foot and then came back to work to be placed on light duties, I realised that I'd reached the end of my working career.

My body was telling me I couldn't handle the physicality of the work anymore, or so I felt. And I'd had enough of all the insults from passengers, the arguments with them, the lack of management support, the internal squabbling, the constant changes in procedures, the drive for efficiency and monetary saving. And above all the unfair way the company were ignoring their procedures and giving out sickness warnings to some staff and not others, I thought here we go again just like the prison service.

Everything I'd ever stood for, all my principles I'd fought for were fast going out of me. My desire to continue to stand up and fight against what I believed were unfair practices, prejudice, and just plain corruption at work had worn me out. I couldn't get any enthusiasm for continuing with it all, I wanted to get out of here and leave it all behind, and I wanted to get back to our home in Spain and our vision of El Dorado.

You know when you've come to an end, and I felt I'd reached this point. I'd had enough, and this was the beginning of the end for me working at Heathrow.

----

11 PLANTAR FASCILITIS THE FINAL STRAW

I'd started to get a severe pain at the bottom of my right heel, so much so I was in agony especially if I had to get out of bed during the night and place my foot on the floor. Some mornings, rather than suffer the initial pain I'd crawl out of bed and gradually stand up, which seemed to help me cope with the pain of standing. I was struggling at work and in pain all the time. I thought it was my shoes. I always wore my shoes down on the outside of the heel as my usual gait was to walk on the outside of my feet, from my running marathon days I knew I was a supinator. Supination (or under-pronation) is the insufficient inward roll of the foot after landing. This places extra stress on the foot and can result in iliotibial band syndrome of the knee, Achilles tendinitis, or plantar fasciitis.

My doctor had told me I need to ensure I wore shoes that had a good solid heel. As we could order shoes through our staff uniform annual allowance, I ordered these better-supported shoes. I was due for my annual uniform order anyway, so it was convenient to get the shoes that would help. The uniform order was never processed due (I found out afterwards) to the relevant Manager never signing my form to allow for these shoes to be ordered from the manufacturer.

For some weeks I continued to struggle on at work but always in pain. On one occasion an STL (who was an ex-policeman, we'd always got on well with each other) came up and said, "Tony, you look like you're in pain and not your usual self, is everything ok?"

"No, I'm in agony. I'm suffering from plantar fasciitis it's known as 'policeman heel'."

"Ouch, I know how painful that can be. I had a few colleagues who suffered from that, but I think you'd better go on light duties for the rest of the day and rest that foot."

"Yes, I agree. I have two days off after this so I can rest it at home."

With that, I was put onto light duties for the remainder of the working day. After two days rest the problem was getting no better, so I made a doctor's appointment and off I went.

"You need complete rest for up to two weeks for that foot."

"I can't take that amount of time off."

"You will have to, that heel's very inflamed, and working by standing on concrete floors will just exacerbate the condition."

"But I can't justify going sick when I don't feel ill."

"That foot will not get any better without rest, with or without the work shoes you are waiting on." I'd explained about the footwear issue with my uniform to my doctor. "As I said all you will do is exacerbate the problem and it will take longer to recover."

"What sort of timescale am I looking at?"

"Two weeks with your foot elevated, and it could still take up to eighteen months to ease the severity of the pain, and it could always come back. You're working on concrete floors with hardly any friction mats, is that correct?"

"Yes, the union keep on at management, and they have put some matting down in certain areas but anywhere behind the security machines is still just concrete floors."

"Well, there you go. Your choice, but my recommendation is to take two weeks complete rest and then we can assess how it's going. I'll write a letter to your company requesting you wear your shoes if they cannot supply the correct footwear, and maybe light duties for a while. It can be a long recovery period without the correct footwear and support."

"What do you think has caused this problem?"

"The primary cause of this issue is concrete floors and being on your feet for many hours each day. This problem is known as 'policemen's heel' especially the old-fashioned beat police, who are on their feet for the whole of their shift."

"But I worked in the prison service for twenty-five years and never had this problem."

"Yes, but for the last ten to fifteen years you were more office bound, so you weren't on your feet all day."

"Well, that's true."

"Does the airport have impact matting everywhere you work?"

"Well no, they do in some places, but it's very worn down. I know the union have been arguing about getting more ever since I worked there."

"There you go then, I cannot categorically say that not having the correct matting is a direct reason for your problem, but I'm willing to say to your company that it's a contributory factor as is the wrong shoes you were initially given with your uniform."

"Ok." I said, "I'm happy to go along with that, at least if this problem is caused by work-related issues, which it seems it is. It means they cannot use this against me as a sickness, and under their own rules being as it's work related it means it doesn't count on my penalty points score for being sick. I'll take your advice and go sick and rest my foot. Thank you, Doctor."

I took the, as it turned out to be, fateful two weeks off from work, as my doctor had recommended.

Upon my return, I still had no idea when the footwear was to be delivered and had now asked three different STL's to investigate on my behalf. Eventually one of the STL's found out that the procurement manager had not even processed the order. Once it was, I got a delivery of the footwear within two weeks. The damage, however, had already been done to my foot. I'm convinced had the footwear arrived shortly after I ordered it I would not have needed to take time off, so I hold the company partly responsible for me having to go sick.

I was allowed on production of the letter from my doctor, to wear my footwear, as long as they were black to conform to our uniform. I did this, although I found it strange as many other officers wore whatever they liked on their feet. I asked one of my colleagues, "Pranav, how come you can wear those on your feet?" I pointed to his jazzy trainers.

"Easy mate, it's a 'Bruv' thing innit." he said. Oh well here we go again I thought, one rule for one and one for everybody else.

I also had to return to work but on light duties after a recommendation from my doctor and the companies' occupational health assessor. I hated light duties because of some of the people I had to work with but accepted that it was necessary. I never enjoyed my time on light duties, and it was yet another straw towards breaking the camel's back and my final decision to resign.

I purchased a pair of black trainers that had special inserts built into the soles for people who supinated. They cost over £120, and I also bought special inserts to go in all my shoes and probably spent in the region of £300 to £400 on them. To be honest, the pain was so severe at times I would have paid double this amount if it would help alleviate the problem.

Gradually, my foot issue eased, and I requested to return to normal duties, which I was allowed. However, sometime after this, I was issued with yet another medical review hearing, this time to be held by a TDM. The TDM in question was a lovely lady from Poland and we'd always gotten on well on the concourse. I always thought she was fair and honest with the staff, so I wasn't too worried by this news. I believed that as soon as I presented my case, she would see the injustices that had happened and use her position to rectify the initial decisions. But how wrong was I?

Again, along with my union rep, we went to the meeting which was once again an obvious foregone conclusion. Although the TDM expressed sympathy with my condition, she would not accept that the delay in the supply of my footwear was a contributing and indeed a mitigating circumstance for leniency. No, she was recommending an employment review, with the possible outcome of instant dismissal.

"But what about the fact that the second level breach was incorrect? The day Tony was sent home does not count and therefore the second level warning should not have been issued." said my rep.

"I understand that and have some sympathy but cannot revoke that decision."

"But that is prejudicial to the whole procedure."

She was not listening.

"Ok, but what about the company taking responsibility for their failure to supply the required footwear." I asked.

"The company cannot be held responsible for that. It was a genuine mistake."

"Genuine mistake? That lazy manager was renowned for not sending off uniform orders because he thought he was saving the company money, you know that very well."

"I cannot comment on that decision."

"Can you explain why this present sickness is being counted towards my overall sick record? The policy clearly states long-term sick does not count towards your overall sick record."

"That's only for absences caused by work-related issues, or females who are pregnant."

"Well, this is a work-related illness. The missing shoes and not enough impact mats for the staff working areas is clear indication that my foot problem directly results from these two issues."

"We have impact matting, where it needs to be."

"Does Health and Safety agree with that?"

"We are in discussions with them over this issue."

"You're not, the talks broke down as you well know." said my rep.

"This is an area I cannot discuss." said the TDM.

"Ok," I said, we're not getting anywhere here. You know the company's in the wrong yet you're being intransigent. Your mind was made up before you entered this meeting. HR must have told you, like the other meetings I had, what the outcome was before you even heard the full story. This is just a kangaroo court, and I hope you're satisfied that you're party to it." and I continued, "Do whatever you have to do, and I will see you in court. This is constructive dismissal, and I will instruct the union to take the case on board. This company doesn't deserve good, conscientious workers hence the state the terminal is in."

"Tony, I have some sympathy with you, and I know your work record is exemplary, but my hands are tied on this matter."

"Well, thank you for being honest with me at last. But I mean what I say, I'm happy to go to court. But I'm sure the company can well do without the bad publicity this will cause." and then added as an afterthought, "Still, at least you have given me a full chapter for my new book all about what happens here at Heathrow."

"You're writing a book?"

"Yes, it's his second book, the first was about his twenty-five years working in the prison service, and he pulled no punches on that one. I know because I too used to work for HM Prison service before here and believe me the book was true." said my rep.

"Yes, but don't worry I will not mention you by name."

"I think this meeting is over. I will write to you with a summary of the events here." and with that, we were both dismissed.

As I walked back from the meeting towards the union office with my rep, I said "You know what I've had enough of all this crap here. Management are out to make an example, and they've picked me as I'm an easy target. If they had picked on an ethnic member of staff, they would have had a Race Relations issue to deal with, so they have used me, the white member of staff as I'm the easy target. I'm not sure I want all this. I might just resign and go back to live in Spain."

"No mate, don't do that, they'll get away with it yet again. Do that and you make it easy for them? I reckon we have a good case for constructive dismissal. I'll contact the NEC and get some advice, but don't do anything rash just yet ok?"

"Ok." I said, but I'd had enough of it now.

The official letter from our meeting arrived two days later than the actual agreed timescale. Once again management had failed to comply with their own laid down procedures. Which in effect gave my case much more credence. If management couldn't keep to their procedures how then could they impose those same procedures on their staff, it was beyond me.

But I'd come to the end of my wanting to fight the case. The letter did not refer to mitigating circumstances; it did not refer the shoe issue or the impact matting issues. It made no reference to the unjust way I'd been previously dealt with; it was as if all those points we'd spoken about never happened. It was just curt, and stated that I had breached the next level and it recommended the employment review.

I took a copy of the letter to the union, "This is great." my rep said, "They haven't even bothered to mention anything we spoke about."

"I know, it's just all one sided. They're out to get me."

"It seems that way, but the review doesn't necessarily mean they will dismiss you. I think they are looking to have an example of how they will treat too much sickness but still working here as a warning to others. After all, they cannot get rid of you on your work ability; you're back to regular duties. Your staff record has so many commendations from both STL's and passengers they would look stupid to get rid of you."

"I don't feel that way and to be honest I'm thinking of just resigning."

"No, don't do that Tony. I spoke to the NEC, and they believe that depending on the result of the review there is a good chance of a constructive dismissal case against Heathrow. They would take that case themselves, you know the union here wouldn't be involved, but the National Union executive of Unite would take the case."

"I'm not sure, to be honest, I want to retire back to the sun in Spain. We only came back for two years, and now it's nearly five."

"Look, you're going on holiday for three weeks, have a good think about it and when you come back come and have another chat with us and we'll take it from there, ok?"

"Yeah, sure." I said, but deep down my mind had been made up.

I'd spent twenty-five years in the service fighting and arguing for staff and prisoners to be treated with respect. Here I was after a further five years back in the same situation seeing the same injustices as before, and for what, to be the one yet again who was sticking his head above the parapet just to get it shot at by big business. No, give me the life of sun, sea, cheap red wine, and relaxation, that's all I wanted now.

Plantar Fasciitis hadn't just been a pain in my foot, but it had become the biggest pain in my neck I'd ever suffered. My mind was made up, but how to leave without having to work my notice, that was my thought as I went off on a three-week holiday back to Spain and my home there.

----

12 GONE IN 60 SECONDS NO! 30 SECONDS ACTUALLY

My wife and I had gone on our three weeks holiday to our home in Spain for the last week in February and first two weeks in March 2015. I'd come off my restricted duties and was allowed under doctors' orders to wear my footwear if they were black to fit in with our uniforms. It did seem a bit strange that I had to get permission when so many other members of security staff seem to wear their own choice of footwear, without needing permission. But the shoes were helping my condition, and I was so relieved to get off working restricted duties. Some staff looked for any excuse to get on restricted duties, one officer in particular used to brag about it. How this individual got away with for so long, I wouldn't like to speculate. However, I've already spoken about him in a previous chapter, but ethnicity played a big part of your working life at Heathrow.

Here I am, it's the 30 March 2015, and I'm sitting waiting for an employment review. What the hell has one of these got to do with working at an airport you might ask? Well, in my case due to the ongoing problem with my right heel, which resulted in me having time off work sick, along with some other health issues over the past two years, my sickness level has reached a critical stage. According to the managements unprecedented interpretations of their procedures for managing staff's illness, here at Heathrow. I covered all this in the previous chapter, but suffice to say they had breached their regulations and protocols throughout their dealings with my case.

According to their latest interpretation of the rules, I've breached the highest level (not uncommon here there are many staff that suffer musculoskeletal injuries due to the nature of the work) and I have now been called to an employment review, where I can be ultimately sacked on the spot. Given I want to go anyway, and have been hanging on and trying to manage my heel problem whilst awaiting a voluntary redundancy package that the company have been dangling like a carrot in front of us all for the past 18 months, it seems ironic that I'd had enough of the carrot and was just about to hand my notice in. Now, due to this employment review, I might either be sacked, which could be interesting given that the company have breached all their procedures and protocols while managing my sickness over the past two years. And they could well end up in an employment tribunal should they sack me, or I could be placed on a final warning, which would be tantamount to constructive dismissal.

I have decided as I want to return to my life living in Spain, and I was going to hand my notice in anyway, why not be cheeky and go for it and ask them if I were to resign immediately would they still pay me in lieu of notice? Cheeky I know, but should they sack me then it could have the same outcome but with the company being dragged through the courts of law, having to face a long drawn out employment tribunal which they might well lose and receive a lot of bad publicity. So maybe my offer might not be so bad, given the current economic climate and Heathrow's application to build the third runway. Bad publicity and several local politicians who objected to a third runaway and public opposition from the London Mayor, I don't think Heathrow would want a long drawn out public employment tribunal.

I'm with my union representative, "Tony, we can take management to the cleaners over this. Not only have they breached their code of managing staff sickness by not following the agreed formula, but they have not even given you the correct paperwork."

"I know, I looked at all their laid down procedures, and had I been younger I would go ahead with the meeting and then take them to an employment tribunal for constructive dismissal. I think we would win the case, but to be honest, I just want to leave the place and get back to my life in Spain."

"Really?"

"Yes, I was holding on for this redundancy package, but they seem to have misled everybody over this in covering up for getting rid of staff from T2 while they pull it down and rebuild. So being honest I just want to leave."

"Well, if they sack you which seems the way they want to go, we would be very confident of winning an employment tribunal, and you'd probably get what they would have given you had they made you redundant. They might have done you a favour, in the long run, by doing all these procedures wrong."

"To be honest, I don't want to go down that line, don't want the stress and don't need it living back in Spain."

"But you wouldn't." he said, "As a member of the union, as long as you keep paying your union fees we would take the case up. You probably wouldn't even need to leave Spain for a tribunal hearing, which I and the NEC think you have a great chance of winning."

"I don't think so." I said. "I'll tell you what, ask the airport manager if I'm willing to volunteer to resign today and leave Heathrow immediately as long as they pay me a month's salary in lieu of notice, I'll go today. That's what I want."

"Are you sure? I think you could end up with about eight grand out of this if it went to a tribunal. Even if you handed your notice in today, we would still have a case for constructive dismissal at a tribunal."

"To be honest, I've had enough. Enough of the stress, the crap management, the nepotism, the downright racism, and just the day-to-day crap of some of the lazy members of staff who get away with murder, at the expense of the conscientious staff. They take the piss. Not to mention the lack of support from management when dealing with the ever-increasing abuse we're getting from passengers. I've just had enough, honestly. I'm beginning to think we're not paid enough to take the abuse we're having day in and day out. I'm worn out by it all, and my health is suffering."

"Well, if that's how you feel, what do you want me to do at the meeting?"

"Make an offer to the Terminal manager along the lines of me leaving today but with a month's money in lieu of notice before the meeting and lay it on about an employment tribunal and the associated bad publicity for Heathrow."

"Ok, I'll telephone him and see what he says."

To which he did, although I didn't hear all the phone conversation the gist of it was, that my representative pointed out all the management breaches of the laid down procedures to the Terminal manager along with the potential outcomes to these breaches and the prospect of a tribunal whether I was sacked today or not. He must have laid it on pretty good because he put the phone down and turned to me.

"Ok Tony, he's agreed immediately, but we have to go through the formalities of the meeting with the new head of personal and the terminal manager. Are you ok with that?"

"Well, that only took him thirty seconds. Even Nicolas Cage got sixty seconds to get rid of all his cars in the film, and this lot took only thirty seconds to get rid of me. They must be glad to see me go."

"I don't think that's the case, but the Terminal manager knows they have fucked up big style and you could take them to the cleaners, hence his quick answer."

However, I readily agreed, but I still thought they'd decided very quickly. They must have either wanted to get rid of me, or they knew just how much they'd messed up the whole procedure and would be made to look ridiculous if it had gone to a tribunal. Win win for me and win win for the company.

So, we go along to the hearing, me, my representative the TM (Terminal Manager), Head of HR (as they were now called), the manager who had brought the proceedings against me, and a secretary to take the minutes.

The TM starts by saying, "Tony and I have come to an agreement he will leave the employment of Heathrow T5 with immediate effect but will receive a month's salary in lieu of notice."

The latest Head of HR, (Personnel) an attractive young Asian girl said, "No, we cannot do it in this way. We have to go through the formal procedures to comply with our laid down employment policy."

"As much of your laid down employment policy has been abused by some of your colleagues, and I'd be looking at taking a case of constructive dismissal to an ET (employment tribunal), the TM and I have agreed rather than cause any adverse and unwanted bad publicity for Heathrow Airport I'd leave today. I'd hand in my notice and receive a month's salary in lieu of notice. But if you would prefer a court case as a worst-case scenario or an employment tribunal at best, which if you look at what your predecessor has done with managing my sickness record, you'd stand to lose. Worse still, the publicity would not be good for Heathrow, so it's up to you. But as the TM and I've agreed then what's your problem?"

The TM then said he wished to have a private chat with the Head of HR and they both left the meeting.

The reporting manager spoke to me.

"Tony, is this what you want?"

"Yes, I've had a belly full of Heathrow and the crap that's been thrown at me. In any other industry, I would have a good case for claiming racial prejudice against me by management over this sickness. Especially when some of the other staff have had similar sickness and haven't even had a warning issued about it. Now, why do you think that is?"

"Well, if that's what you want, ok. I hope there are no hard feelings towards me."

"Of course not. It's not your fault you've inherited a bad system that's being abused by senior management. You're just the one in the firing-line. You've never mistreated me, and it's not your fault you're only ever told part of the full story, so no hard feelings at all.

The TM and Head of Personal came back into the room, and the Head of HR asked me, "Are you certain this is what you want?"

"Of course, Heathrow comes out of this ok, and I get what I want. That is to leave after the way I've been treated so unfairly, so yes."

"You will have to write a letter of resignation then."

To which, I produce one out of the folder I'd been carrying with me "Had this all prepared." but what I didn't tell her was that I'd already written my notice. That was before this hearing had been called, so all I did was change the date at the top of my letter of resignation.

And that was that. I'd resigned with a month's salary in lieu of working my notice, with immediate effect.

Why did I do it this way? Simple, I would have had no compunction about dragging Heathrow's reputation through the gutter, as they'd treated me appallingly over the four years I worked there. But it would not have been fair to all the conscientious, hardworking, dedicated staff, who wanted to work there and do the best job they could for the company and the passengers. I also felt that Heathrow needed their third runway and it would be a good decision for the country if they did. So, I didn't want to harm their prospects with the bad publicity that my case might well have generated.

I had to wait outside while the paperwork was drawn up, and as I waited my TDM walked up to me (he was an ex-armed policeman whom I had the greatest respect for). He was one of the real genuine members of management who I'd always respected and gotten on well with. He was also the days Terminal Duty Manager, so he had to deal with my leaving with immediate effect.

"Tony, you got what you wanted, and I'm pleased for you. You leave immediately but do you want to go back airside and say goodbye to your team I'll find out where they are working and let you know."

"Thanks, I appreciate that I'd like to say my goodbyes to them."

"Ok, let's get the paperwork completed, and then you can go say your goodbyes and then give me all your security stuff, keys, passes, etc. and go home whenever you want. Have you told your wife?"

"Just telephoned her and gave her the good news, thanks." I said.

"Right, I'll get the official letter then you can go."

With that, he disappeared into an office, and I waited in waiting area.

After a while he came back and said "Tony, can I ask you to come back here tomorrow around 5 pm and we can do all the handing over of keys, passes, car park passes and uniform."

"Sure, but what's the problem?"

"Well, if you leave today, the 30 March, it means you've not completed the full year, and therefore your airport bonus will be deducted from your final salary. I told the TM that that was not fair on you and he agreed so we need you to sign all the paperwork from tomorrow and you will get your bonus."

"The sneaky bastards," I said, "no wonder they agreed quickly. My bonus is around £900. Of course, I'll come back tomorrow; thanks, I appreciate you doing that."

"I don't think we've been entirely fair with you and I know you're the sort of person that if you think there's an injustice, you cannot accept it and will fight tooth and nail to rectify the injustice irrespective of what it would do to you. I wasn't prepared for them to shaft you at the end. You never let me down, and you always did your job one hundred percent, so I didn't think it was right." he said.

"Thanks again, I'd never have disrespected you, and you've always been fair to me so I appreciate you making sure I would not get ripped off at the end. You're right; I would take anybody on if I thought something wasn't right."

He laughed and said, "I know you're the sort of person if you felt you had been treated unfairly you would go all the way to prove it and I don't think Heathrow would have wanted the bad publicity you'd have given them."

"You're right there, but hey at least this will be a chapter in my next book."

"You can still say your goodbyes and go home now if you want."

"Yes, of course. Thanks again."

From going into the meeting to coming to this point, it had taken thirty minutes not bad after over four years of working at T5.

Off I went, back for the last time, airside through staff search area, into the detail office to ask if they knew where my team were. They told me they would be on a break in a few minutes. I went down to the restroom I knew they'd use, had my last cup of tea out of the vending machine and waited to say my goodbyes to them.

They appeared sometime later, and I explained what had happened, they seemed stunned, but all appear to understand my need to leave Heathrow one of them I really cannot remember who but think it might have been 'Rami' said, "You have not been yourself since coming back from your holiday in Spain."

"No! You know what did it, the final straw that broke the camel's back?" I asked.

"Go on what?" they all said.

"It was my first day back at work. I was on my first archway (WTMD), and the first male indicated he had to be searched, so I went through the usual spiel, and he started to get aggressive with me and called me a 'fucking idiot'. I said to him, "Do you know what, I've just come back from a three-week holiday in my home in Spain, and the first person I have to search back here is you, and you have the audacity to swear at me. I don't get paid enough to take this crap anymore so shut your gob and let me do my job." I need to pack this job in, I thought. Because the next person who talks to me like that, I might not be able to keep my temper under control and I might lump them, and the job just isn't worth that. So, I knew I had to go asap, sorry guys".

We chatted a little more about what my plans were, and we said our goodbyes, and that was that. I left the terminal, got the bus to the staff car park, got in my car, joined the rush hours traffic on the M25 and got home around 6 pm.

I went back the next day to sign all the paperwork and hand over my passes and uniform. My TDM wished me success in my new life back in Spain, we shook hands, and that was the end of my working career, at long last.

"If ever you're in my part of Spain come and look me up and we'll have a beer or something."

"Thanks, Tony, you never know I might just pitch up at your casa one day and take you up on that offer."

"Well, you'd be most welcome. And once again, thanks for everything especially at the end, it really was appreciated.

My apologies to Nicolas Cage and his film 'Gone in 60 seconds' but I took around 30 minutes, to officially complete my final time at Heathrow. I believe that once I'd pitched my offer to the Terminal

Manager, he decided in only 30 seconds. So, I think I beat Nicolas Cage's time after all.

----

13 BACK TO SPAIN

On Sunday 12 May 2015, my wife and I set off to Portsmouth to get the car ferry for the two-day journey to Bilbao Spain, and to the start of our new life of El Dorado.

The two-day ferry trip around the Bay of Biscay passed without incident. We ate in the restaurants and milled about the ship just whiling away the time. We had a few glasses of Vino Tinto and thankfully on the Tuesday morning we docked in the port of Bilbao Spain.

We had our cool box full of goodies and a flask filled with fresh tea. And with a full tank of petrol, we waited patiently in the queue to disembark the ship and start the long drive to our home in the South.

We arrived at the port of Bilbao at around 7 am. After the lengthy process of disembarkation, we slowly moved along and out of the bowels of the ship to join our fellow passenger vehicles waiting in the queue to go through customs and passport control. We crawled forward and with a cursory look into our car and a quick look at our passports we were waived through, and we joined the road out of the Port of Bilbao.

With our reliable Tom Tom satellite navigation system plugged into the car (whatever happened to reading maps?), we followed the instruction given to us by the strict voice of the system. Although we missed the first exit onto the motorway to lead us towards Madrid, the female voice of the 'Sat Nav' soon got us onto the correct road. Driving through Bilbao in the rush hour traffic was interesting, to say the least. But eventually, we joined the Motorway heading towards Madrid.

The roads through Spain are not like the crowded ones of the UK and are no comparison to my daily journey on the 'road to hell', London's orbital motorway, the M25.

The north of Spain around Bilbao is an amazing contradiction to the dry flatter sunnier Costas. Incredible scenery surrounded our journey, with high pine clad mountains surrounded in the early morning mist. It was gradually giving way to the sun's heat breaking through and burning the damp mist off to reveal wonderful green valleys. We could have been travelling through Switzerland or Austria such was the scenery. With wonderful log cabins set into the cliffs, it was a fantastic peaceful scene. This area of Spain is so different to the coastal regions, and we vowed we would come to this part of Spain for a break from the August heat of the Costas at some stage.

On into the heart of Spain and the scenery flattens out as the heat rises. Traffic was light and other than the flat landscape dotted with sparse farm houses (Finca's as they are called in Spain), the journey becomes mundane. As we got nearer to Madrid, the roads get busier; we saw more buildings, wider roads, fast motorways, then onto the outskirts of Madrid heading towards the airport. Vast wide multi lane motorways, nothing traffic wise to compare to the M25 back in England, but even so, many more lorries that don't seem to have speed restrictions on them. It seems those GB stickers on my back bumper are a target for other road users to intimidate me but to no avail. My Tom-tom informs me of every turn and change of Motorway I need and we are soon past Madrid and back onto smaller, quieter roads, with no traffic and the scenery become blander and dried up looking fields. On these roads you can see all around you for miles.

Traffic was so light you could take in the magnificent vistas and enjoy the views. Great idea this cruise control on our car, it made the drive so much easier.

After a few comfort stops and a refuelling stop, the landscape again changes. We come across the countless orange and lemon groves, with mandarins and tangerines growing alongside limes and almond trees in abundance and small vineyards. We knew we were approaching home, and then we made it to our village and finally, home. The drive took us

around nine and half hours without ever having to go above the speed limit; it was comfortable and almost pleasant.

So here we are, back 'Home' to live our dreams in our own El Dorado!

Or is it? Well, that would be a whole different book to write, wouldn't it?

EPILOGUE

IMAGINE

'Imagine there's no countries it isn't hard to do, nothing to kill or die for and no religion too Imagine all the people living life in peace'

Fantastic lyrics to this classic song, but oh how so true those words written all those years ago are so poignant in today's modern world.

So, my story has come a full circle. I'm back to my life in 'El Dorado' in a much better financial position than when we first tried to retire, and this time it will work.

I hope you enjoyed my book and I hope you saw yourselves on some of the pages or at least recognised the behaviour of people I have written about.

I make no excuse for mentioning nepotism, mates, Bruvs or racism during this book. I'm saying these things with the experience of carrying out Audits of such behavioural activities within the prison service and using that experience in viewing what I saw at Heathrow. Others would dispute what I say. However, I remember one officer from an ethnic background telling me one day it was all right to be given preferential treatment by fellow ethnic STL's, as they were all mates. When I pointed out that this behaviour could be deemed racially prejudice he looked at me like I was speaking another language and said you could not be racist from one ethnic person to another from the same cast. I pointed out he might see it in that way, however, if he got preferential treatment over somebody from a different ethnicity then that was indeed racial prejudice. He did not understand this concept. I remember him saying that 'only white people can be racist to non-white people, and non-whites could not be prejudice against white people.' I was gob smacked but, to be honest, this was the general opinion of many of the ethnic groups working within Heathrow and particularly from the majority who came from Indian backgrounds. So, I reiterate that I make no excuse for referring to this attitude throughout the book.

I worked at Heathrow on the concourses for over four years. I have many more stories I could tell you about the weird and wonderful way we all approach and behave at airport security. So, if David Walliams or Mat Lucas ever want to write another series of 'Come Fly With Me', I have all the material they would ever need to make a great comedy series.

I sincerely hope I've caused no offence to anybody. But in this modern world of air travel and all the dangers that go with it, maybe next time you are travelling through an airport or going to work at one, you might just think a little more carefully as to how you go about your business and how you talk to people, whether a passenger or a member of staff carrying out a thankless task.

I remember some security expert on television talking about terrorism, and he said we (the people working within any security service) have to be lucky every day, the terrorist only needs to be lucky once.

I'd much rather have lived in a world where security officers at airports, train stations, ferry stations, or busses, trains, underground stations and trains, were unnecessary. However, that is not the way of the world so the security industry is a necessary evil for us all to tolerate to ensure we can live the life of relative safety and hope that our children and grandchildren get the same opportunities to go about their legal business in safety in the future.

Let's hope, for our children and our children's children's sake we can achieve some form of peace throughout the world before we destroy ourselves.

I'm now starting the last chapter of my life, and I hope and pray I leave this world in a better, safer place than when I arrived. World events seem to shatter this dream on a remorseless monotonous regularity.

We, the quiet population of the world from whatever ethnic and religious backgrounds we come from, need to stand up with one voice and demand, that those that want to deny us the opportunity to live in a peaceful world should go away and leave us all in peaceful coexistence.

I hope you've enjoyed my book and have a better understanding of the workings of security at all airports in the effort to ensure you can go about your life and business in a safe environment as we can provide in today's world.

John Lennon got it right when he wrote the lyrics to Imagine, "You may say I'm a dreamer, but I'm not the only one. I hope someday you'll join us. And the world will live as one."

The End, or is it?

PS

"An eye for an eye will only make the whole world blind."

Mahatma Gandhi

P.S As I wrote much of this book the terrible atrocities at Brussels Zaventem airport had just taken place (22 March 2016). Once again throwing our world into chaos and disarray over how we can overcome these terrorists, and once again showing how our soft underbelly at public places is now increasingly becoming targets for these aggressors.

Whether we like it or not, we are now entering an even more critical phase in our quest for world peace and safety. And we all, and I include everybody in the world, have to expect and tolerate more security and more security checking at all our main public places, including of course airports.

Airport Security has always concentrated on making the airside the safe place. Yet Brussels once again proved that terrorists would look for the easy target or soft target as the press call them. I'm afraid that unless we address this blind spot in airport security, this area will always be vulnerable. But will the public accept being searched when entering an airport's public area, or a train station concourse, or a bus station or football stadium etc.? I think not.

Unless we can accept that being searched is part of maintaining our individual security, then these terrorist's will always have a soft target to take on. Security screening has to change in response to the latest terrorist's events, but us the public have to accept this and encompass it whether grudgingly, or not.

We all, as members of the human race have a role to play in keeping our public places safe, that unattended bag you have just ignored may contain a device, or it may be just be an innocent mistake, but unless it's reported who knows. That person acting strangely, are they just getting nervous about flying or is it something more sinister, who knows. But please don't ignore their behaviour if it seems suspicious.

We owe it to ourselves, our children, our neighbours, and everybody to be as vigilant as the security that we hope governments are putting into place. We are the biggest weapon in stopping these attacks and as we are also the targets; it seems prudent to me that we don't ignore that bag or that package or that strange behaviour but report them to the nearest authorities, please.

Often at the airport, the behaviour of our fellow passengers or members of the public in the landside areas can give signs they may not be what they seem. We must report what we see to the authorities. Many times, when walking around the terminal on the landside area's I experienced left packages that I would investigate (thankfully finding nothing of suspicious nature), but often reporting strange occurrences to the police. You never know that one time you see something and report it might be the time you save hundreds of lives. So, let's all be vigilant.

Please be patient with us and have an understanding of us too. And please accept that we're not searching you and your possessions for fun, it's for your safety and for your life!

ABOUT THE AUTHOR

When author Tony Levy received his devastating cancer diagnosis, far from crumbling, he decided to write his second book, El Dorado? No! Heathrow. With his admirable background as a Prison Guard, followed by an even more challenging position in Airport Security, he was able to manifest an instinctive response to threats, and it was this that helped him turn a bad scenario into positive action.

The British born author creates a literary storm with insider revelations, yet he modestly regards it as his job to expose only the truth to his ever-increasing audience of readers.

Tony, who can tell many a tale about celebrity showdowns now resides in Spain with the love of his life, wife Jacinta. Although living it up in the sun, his distinctive style continues to grip readers around the world, who are held captive by his shocking revelations. And once again, he doesn't disappoint as he tells all about life inside Britain's busiest airport, from flight statistics to embarrassing passenger stories, you will one minute reel in surprise, and the next rock with laughter.

Printed in Great Britain
by Amazon